WITCH HUNTS IN THE WESTERN WORLD

Persecution and Punishment from the Inquisition through the Salem Trials

Brian A. Pavlac

GREENWOOD PRESS
Westport, Connecticut • London

Library of Congress Cataloging-in-Publication Data

Pavlac, Brian Alexander, 1956–
    Witch hunts in the western world : persecution and punishment from
the inquisition through the Salem trials / Brian A. Pavlac.
        p. cm.
    Includes bibliographical references and index.
    ISBN 978-0-313-34873-0 (alk. paper)
    1. Witchcraft—History. I. Title.
    BF1566.P38   2009
    133.4′309—dc22   2008040910

British Library Cataloguing in Publication Data is available.

Library of Congress Catalog Card Number: 2008040910
ISBN: 978-0-313-34873-0

First published in 2009

Greenwood Press, 88 Post Road West, Westport, CT 06881
An imprint of Greenwood Publishing Group, Inc.
www.greenwood.com

Printed in the United States of America

The paper used in this book complies with the
Permanent Paper Standard issued by the National
Information Standards Organization (Z39.48-1984).

10 9 8 7 6 5 4 3 2 1

CONTENTS

PREFACE

The academic literature on witches and witchcraft has increased by leaps and bounds over the past few decades, as has popular writing about witchcraft. This book participates with the former to help illuminate errors and fantasies of the latter. Too many misconceptions still possess the popular imagination about witches. This book should contribute to efforts for sound research and reasoning regarding this magical subject.

As I began reading centuries-old treatises on witches, I kept groping for terminology to describe those who studied and hunted them. It seems to me they belong to a unique genre, although often related to or part of works of theology (the study of the Christian God) and demonology (the study of demons as if they were real). The clumsy term "witch theorists," seems too close semantically to historians who build theories to explain the witch hunts within the context of rationality. I have therefore coined the term "strixology," drawing on a Latin word for a witch. Strixologists write about the problem of witches, whether they were real and their magic could actually change the natural world. During the time of the witch hunts, these writers were usually trying to explain the witches' origins, character, and powers and how they could and must be fought. Increasingly as the hunts went on, strixology refuted the reality of witches, contributing to the decline of the hunts. Today, this genre would include the many writers whose instructional manuals on the occult and Wicca crowd bookstore shelves. If the topic of writing is witches, it is strixological.

This text should provide a satisfactory overview of all the most important aspects of the witch hunts. Much more can be read, with fascination. No book today can be written without the help of hundreds of scholars who have labored and published the readings and sources used to research this book.

I do not cite these many scholars in order to make the text more accessible to general readers. The Selected Bibliography at the end offers useful and accessible treatments in English for those who want to dig deeper into the hunts. The bibliographies in those books provide connections to still more resources. In this book, I also offer a few quotes in English from primary sources, which present the best means to interact with the past. The footnotes to those quotes reference modern, published, or Internet collections of primary sources. All quotes from the Bible in this book are from the King James Version from England in 1611, because of its well-beloved language and its origins at the time of the witch hunts.

ACKNOWLEDGMENTS

I thank several people: colleagues Cris Scarboro and Jean O'Brien who read versions of the manuscript; the editors at Greenwood Press who suggested, adopted, and helped edit the book, especially Carrie Lett; the librarians of Corgan Library, especially Tom Ruddy and Judy Tierney who provided me with more books than I could wish for; and John Pollack of the University of Pennsylvania. Last of all, I dedicate this work to those three magical women in my life, who most certainly are not witches. I thank my daughters Margaret and Helen for their ongoing tolerance, patience, and suggestions. Helen helped with the illustrations, in particular. To my supportive spouse, Elizabeth S. Lott, whose careful reading and corrections were invaluable, I offer my unbounded appreciation and love.

CHRONOLOGY

900	*Canon Episcopi* makes its first appearance in a law code.
1140	Gratian's *Decretum* further establishes the *Canon Episcopi*.
1022	Heretics burned at Orléans, France.
1120	Heretics burned at Soissons, France, as observed by Guibert of Nogent.
1176	Heretics executed at Rheims, France.
1098–1291	Crusades take place in the Holy Land.
13th Century	Rise of the heresy of *apostolic poverty* and heretical groups of Waldensians and Albigensians/Cathars leads to founding of the Franciscans and Dominicans and to the Inqusition.
1231	Pope Gregory IX's *Excommunicamus et anathematisamus* excommunicates heretics and turns them over to secular governments for execution.
1225–1274	Thomas Aquinas founds scholasticism with works such as *Summa Theologiæ*.
1233	Inquisitor Conrad von Marburg is assassinated.
1258	Pope Alexander IV's *Quod super nonullis* allows inquisitors to hunt witches as heretics.
1309–1377	The popes reside in Avignon under the influence of the French king, rather than in Rome, soon called the Babylonian Captivity.

1323	Bernard Gui publishes his inquisitor's manual, *Practica inquisitionis haereticae pravitatis.*
1307–1309	King Philip IV of France puts the Knights Templars on trial for heresy.
1316–1334	Pope John XXII issues the bull *Super illius specula* to encourage hunting heretical witches and accuses people at court of sorcery.
1318–1325	Jacques Fournier, the future Pope Benedict XII, conducts an inquisition in Montaillou, France.
1324	Lady Alice Kyteler tried for witchcraft in Ireland.
1337–1453	France and England fight the Hundred Years War.
1347–1359	The first wave of the Black Death kills millions in Europe, aided by a climatic change called a "mini-ice age" that lasts until about 1700.
1350–1650	The Commercial Revolution develops capitalism in Europe.
1375	The mistress of King Edward III of England, Alice Perrers, is accused of witchcraft.
1376	Nicolau Eymeric writes his inquisitor's manual, *Directorium inquisitorum.*
1378–1417	The Great Schism creates first two, then three popes who claim to lead Christendom.
1391	Hunt in Paris executes "La Cordière" and Macette de Ruilly.
1395	Judge Peter of Bern hunts witches, including Stedelen, in the Simmenthal.
1398	University of Paris under Jean Gerson condemns magical activities.
1400–1600	The Renaissance revives learning of Greco-Roman culture and spurs Europe into the early modern period.
1400–1455	Alonso Tostado writes both skeptically and credulously about witches.
1405	Trial of Louis, Duke of Orléans for attempting to kill King Charles VI (d. 1422) with magic.
1410	Martin of Arles writes his *Tractatus de superstitionibus contra malefica seu sortilegia.*
1411	Witch hunts kill many in Pskov, Russia.

1421	Witch hunts take place in the Dauphiné province in France.
1427–1428	Bernadino of Siena involved in trials of Finicella in Rome and Matteuccia Francesco in Todi.
1428	Duke Albrecht of Bavaria tries and drowns his daughter-in-law, Agnes Bernauer.
1431–1439	Council of Basel fails to achieve reform of the Church, but becomes the center of information about witches.
1431	Joan of Arc burned at the stake.
1432, 1441	Margery Jourdain and Eleanor Cobham accused of witchcraft.
1430s–1440s	Bernard of Como hunts witches in the Duchy of Savoy.
1435–1438	Johannes Nider writes his collection, *Formicarius*.
1437	*Errores Gazariorum* is published.
1437	Claude Tholosan writes his *Ut magorum et maleficiorum errores*.
1440	Martin Le Franc writes his *Champion des dames*.
1440	Baron Gilles de Rais executed for witchcraft in France.
1450	Beginning of European explorations of Asia and Africa.
1450	Printing press invented in the Holy Roman Empire.
1456–1479	Vlad the Impaler, the later model for Dracula, rules off and on in Transylvania.
1459–1452	Witches hunted in Arras by Jacques du Boys.
1458	Nicolas Jacquier writes his *Flagellum haereticorum fascinariorum*.
1467	Alphonsus da Spina writes his *Fortalium Fidei*.
1470	Giordano or Jordanes da Bergamo writes *Quaestio de strigis*.
1474–1516	King Ferdinand of Aragon and Queen Isabella of Castille create the kingdom of Spain.
1478–1834	The Spanish Inquisition hunts heretics and, to a lesser extent, witches.
1483	Jane Shore admits doing witchcraft in England.
1485	Henry Krämer (Institoris) conducts failed witch trials in Innsbruck.
1486	Henry Krämer (Institoris) writes *Malleus Maleficarum*, the most infamous witch-hunting manual.

1489	Maria "la Medica" executed for witchcraft in Brescia, Italy.
1489	Ulrich Molitor writes his *De Lamiis et Phitonicis Mulieribus* for authorities in Innsbruck.
1492–1503	Pope Alexander VI Borgia tries to expand witch-hunting outside the Papal States.
1492	Discovery by Europeans of the Americas.
1494	France invades the Italian peninsula, leading to more than three centuries of political divisions there.
1507	Johann Geiler von Kaysersberg writes *Die Emeis.*
1510	Cornelius Agrippa von Nettesheim publishes *De Occulta philosophia.*
1510	Bernard Ratengo hunts in Como, Italy.
1513–1523	King Christian II allows witch-hunting, supported by Bishop Peter Palladius of Sealand.
1515	Andreas Alciati calls witch-hunting a "new holocaust."
1517	Martin Luther starts the Protestant Reformation and Lutheranism, while also encouraging hunting of witches.
1523	Bartolomeo Spina writes *Questio de strigibus.*
1523	Gianfrancesco Pico della Mirandella writes his *Strix, sive de ludificatione daemonum.*
1526	Hunts in Navarre lead the Spanish Inquisition to take on authority over witch-hunting.
1528–1559	English Reformation establishes Anglicanism as the Church of England and separates from papal authority.
1529	Martín de Castañega publishes *Tratado muy sotil y bien fundado.*
1532	Caroline Code/*Carolina* in the Holy Roman Empire regulates witch-hunting.
1534	Paulus Grillandus writes *Tractatus de hereticis et sortilegiis.*
1534–1549	Pope Paul III issues the bull, *Licet ab initio,* and establishes the Holy Office [of the Inquisition], which endures until 1965.
1536	John Calvin in France establishes Reformed Churches in the Dutch Netherlands and Germany, Presbyterians in Scotland, Congregationalists in Wales, Huguenots in France, and Puritans in England.

1536	Queen Ann Boleyn executed for treason against her husband King Henry VIII of England.
1536, 1543	Archbishop Juan de Zumárraga hunts witches in Mexico.
1543–1687	The Scientific Revolution begins to establish new ways of examining the natural world.
1550	Tsar Ivan IV of Russia convenes Stoglov that supports hunting witches.
1550	Trial of Jochum Bos in the Netherlands.
1555	Olaus Magnus publishes *Historia de Gentibus Septentrionalibus*, which discusses witches in Scandinavia.
1555–1648	The Catholic or Counter-Reformation sees the Wars of Religion damage Europe.
1556	Pietro Pomponazzi publishes the skeptical *De naturalium effectuum causis sive de incantationibus*.
1562–1598	The French Wars of Religion between Protestants and Roman Catholics divide France and encourage witch-hunting.
1559, 1562	Witch hunts carried out in the Yucatan.
1563	Johann Weyer publishes the skeptical *De praestigiis daemonum*.
1563–1584	Archbishop Charles Borromeo of Milan hunts witches.
1564	Calvinist Lambert Daneau writes *Les Sorciers*.
1565–1566	Nicole Obry suffers possession in France, inspiring imitators.
1566	First witch hunt in Chelmsford, England, executes Elizabeth Francis and Agnes Waterhouse.
1568–1639	Tommaso Campanella gets in and out of trouble for his magical and heretical ideas.
1572	Thomas Erastus publishes his *Dialogues against Paracelsus* to refute Weyer.
1575–1650	Hunts in Friuli of the *benandanti* who believe they fly in dreams to fight witches.
1575	Hunt in Salzburg executes Eva Neidegger and Rupert Ramsauer.
1578	The Lutheran Jakob Bithner hunts witches in Roman Catholic Styria.
1580	Jean Bodin publishes his *De la démonomanie des sorciers*.

1581–1593	Hunts in Trier in the Holy Roman Empire kill Dr. Dietrich Flade and others.
1581–1648	The Dutch fight their war of independence from Spain.
1582	Second witch hunt in Chelmsford, England, kills Ursley Kemp and others.
1584	Reginald Scot publishes his skeptical *The Discoverie of Witchcraft*.
1587	Walburga Hausmännin executed in the Dillingen, Augsburg.
1588	Michel de Montaigne writes his skeptical *Des Boîteaux*.
1589	Third witch hunt in Chelmsford, England executes Joan Prentis and Joan Cunny.
1589	In Warboys, England, the Throckmorton family get "Mother" Samuel executed for witchcraft.
1590	The pastor's wife Anne Pedersdotter in Norway burned as a witch.
1592	King Philip II of Spain regulates witch-hunting through the Spanish Inquisition.
1595	Nicholas Rémy publishes his *Demonolatriae*.
1597	King James VI Stuart of Scotland publishes *Dæmonologie* in reaction to the North Berwick Witches of Gilly: Duncan, Agnes Sampson, and Dr. John Fian.
1597	Thomas Darling, the "Boy of Burton," gets Alice Goodridge executed for witchcraft, although he later confesses to fraud.
1599–1600	Martin Del Rio writes his *Disquisitiones magicarum Libri Sex*.
1599–1603	Samuel Harsnett publishes skeptical works about witchcraft, *A Discovery of the Fraudulent Practises of John Darrel …* and *A Declaration of Egregious Popish Impostures*.
1600	Pappenheimer family executed for witchcraft in Bavaria.
1602	Henri Boguet publishes his *Discours des sorciers*.
1602–1603	Mary Glover's possession in England leads Dr. Edward Jorden to publish his skeptical *A briefe discourse of a disease called the Suffocation of the Mother*.
1606	Anne Gunter in England proven a fraud.
1608	*Thesaurus exorcismorum* collects works on exorcism by Girolamo Menghi and Valerio Polidori.

1608–1611   Witch-hunting in the Basque regions around the Spanish and French borders.

1609   Possessions of the Ursuline nuns at Aix lead to the execution of Louis Gaufridi for witchcraft.

1611   Barbara Rüfin, Michael Dier, and Magdalena Weixler hunted as witches.

1612   King Christian IV of Denmark hunts witches in Køge.

1612   Hunts of the Lancashire witches of the Pendle Forest in England lead to deaths of Old Demdyke, Old Chattox, and others.

1613   Pierre de Lancre publishes *Tableau de l'inconstance des mauvais anges et demons.*

1618–1648   The Thirty Years War afflicts the Holy Roman Empire and Europe.

1609–1611   Elizabeth Báthory imprisoned for murdering women and children and then bathing in their blood.

1620   *Instructio* of the Roman Inquisition aims to limit witch-hunting, but is not sufficiently publicized.

1620   Possession of Elizabeth de Ranfaing leads to execution of Dr. Charles Poirot.

1626   Francesco Maria Guazzo publishes his *Compendium Maleficarum.*

1626   Herman Samson publishes his *Neun ausserlessne und wohlbegründete Hexen-Predigten.*

1625–1627   Paul Laymann and Adam Tanner publish their skeptical works about witchcraft.

1627–1634   Possessions on nuns in Loudun, France, lead to execution of Pastor Urban Grandier for witchcraft.

1623–1631   Witch hunts in prince-bishoprics Eichstätt, Würzburg, Cologne, and Mainz. The hunt in Bamberg kills persons of high status, such as John Junius, Ernest von Ehrenberg, and Dorothea Flöckin.

1628   The Count Palatine mandates Ursula Zoller to better care rather than execution for witchcraft.

1631   Friedrich Spee anonymously publishes his skeptical *Cautio Criminalis*, which would eventually gain wide readership and approval.

1633–1634	The boy Edmund Robinson fraudulently hunted Lancashire witches of the Pendle Forest in England, soon called Pendle Swindle.
1635	Benedict Carpzov publishes his *Practica Rerum Criminalium*, which would influence witch-hunting in central and eastern Europe.
1635	In Iceland, Sherrif Mágnus Björnsson has Jón Rögnvaldson executed for sorcery.
1637	Anne Hutchinson persecuted in Massachusetts.
1648–1680	Hunts carried out in Liechtenstein, leading to a change in dynasty.
1610–1643	King Louis XIII and his minister Cardinal Richelieu rule France.
1646	Trial of La Mercuria.
1644–1646	The "Witch-finder General" Matthew Hopkins hunts witches near Chelmsford, England.
1652	Joan Peterson, the Witch of Wapping.
1652–1663	Hunts in Finnmark, Norway, of Sami/Lapp and cunning-men.
1653–1656	In the city of Lemgo of the Holy Roman Empire, "Witches Mayor" Hermann Cothmann hunts witches.
1653	Anne Bodenham attacked as a witch because of her association with Dr. Lamb.
1654	Cyrano de Bergerac publishes his "Letter against Witches."
1656–1658	Bernhard Loeper's exorcisms encourage hunts in Paderborn in the Holy Roman Empire.
1657	A hunt in Lukh, Russia, goes after *klikushi*.
1658	Possessions of nuns in Auxonne and Louviers, France.
1658	René Besnard found guilty of witchcraft in French Canada.
1660–1662	The Great Scottish Witch Hunt brings confessions from Isabel Gowdie.
1661–1663	In Lindheim, friends of accused witches try to rescue them from the Witch's Tower.
1662	Sir Matthew Hale presides over trials in Bury St. Edmunds, England.
1662–1666	Elizabeth Seager and others tried for witchcraft in Hartford, Connecticut.

1662–1664	In Lowestoft, England, Amy Denny and Rose Cullender found guilty of witchcraft.
1665	Karin Persdotter executed for witchcraft in Finland.
1670	Major Thomas (or John) Weir and his sister confess to crimes of witchcraft and are executed.
1670	Lisbet and Ole Nypen executed in Norway.
1671–1672	Elizabeth Knapp suffers possession in Groton, Massachusetts.
1672–1678	Sir George "Bluidy" MacKenzie publishes *Pleadings in Remarkable Cases* and *Laws and Customs of Scotland in Matters Criminal*, which promote better legal procedures.
1673	The *Chambre Ardente* Affair scandalizes King Louis XIV.
1680	Authorities try to capture Zauber-Jackl in Salzburg and instead execute many vagrant children.
1687–1789	The Enlightenment promotes modern ideologies and skepticism.
1668–1675	Hunt beginning in Mora, Sweden, expands to Stockholm.
1689/1690	Joseph Glanvill's *Sadducismus Triumphatus,* including material by Henry More, is published.
1689–1692	Cotton Mather publishes *Memorable Providences Relating to Witchcraft and Possessions* and *The Wonders of the Invisible World.*
1691	Balthasar Bekker publishes his skeptical *De Betoverde Weereld.*
1692–1693	Witch hunt takes place in Salem, Massachusetts.
1699	Hunt carried out by Bishop Casimir Czartoriski of Cujavia and Pomerania.
1700	Ludovico Maria Sinistrari publishes his *De Demonialitate.*
1700s	Witch hunts carried out in the Piedmont.
1701	Christian Thomasius publishes his skeptical *Dissertatio de Crimine magiae.*
1702	Rev. John Hale publishes his skeptical *Modest Enquiry into the Nature of Witchcraft* in reaction to the Salem hunt.
1705–1706	Grace Sherwood ducked as witch in Virginia.
1712	Jane Wenham, the reputed Witch of Walkerne, is one of the last witches tried in England.

1718	Francis Hutchinson publishes his skeptical *An Historical Essay Concerning Witchcraft*.
1727	Janet Horne dies as the last witch executed in Scotland.
1728–1729	Witches are hunted in Szeged, Hungary.
1730	France of Marie-Catherine Cadière and Jean-Baptiste Girard caught in scandalous trials in Toulon, France.
1731	Tsar Anna of Russia restricts witch-hunting.
1736	English Parliament passes Witchcraft Law that ends witch-hunting.
1742–1745	Last executions for witchcraft in France.
1756–1766	Abiquiu Hunt carried out in Mexico.
1770	Tsar Catherine the Great of Russia ends witch-hunting.
1775	Anna Maria Schwägelin executed as the last witch in the Holy Roman Empire.
1782	In Switzerland, Anna Göldi is one of the last witches executed in Europe.
1789–1815	French Revolution and Napoleon.
1793	Prussians in occupied Posen hanged two witches, the last execution of witches in eastern Europe.
1818	Ana Barbero in Seville, Spain, is the last person tried for witchcraft in Europe.

CHAPTER 1

An Introduction to Witch-Hunting

THE PENDLE WITCHES

Four hundred years ago, in the Pendle Forest of Lancashire, England, justices of the peace were hunting witches. One hunt had arisen out of a rivalry between two families, each led by a matriarch. Eighty-year-old Elizabeth Southerns, called Old Demdike, led the Device family, which included her daughter, Elizabeth Device, and grandchildren Alice, James, and nine-year-old Jennet. The decrepit and nearly blind Anne Whittle, called Old Chattox, and her daughter Anne Redfearne were their bitter rivals. Old Demdike and Old Chattox and their relatives drew prestige from practicing folk magic, but only meager incomes. Local people came to these cunning women for healing, finding lost items, and telling fortunes. They scraped out a living on the margins of decent society, mutually implicated in petty crimes involving thefts, blackmail, and bribes to local officials.

A more serious crime hung in the forest air of 1612, that of witchcraft. The Devices blamed Old Chattox for bewitching Old Demdike's husband to death eleven years earlier. Some clergy also claimed that the women practiced their folk magic with the help of the author of all evil, Satan himself. They suggested that certain women formed a pact with the Devil and thereby gained monstrous powers of witchcraft, with which they harmed good Christians. Both religious and civil authorities feared this witchcraft enough to take legal action against alleged witches and render their just punishment: death by hanging.

A simple confrontation with a stranger triggered the hunt in Pendle Forest. On March 21, 1612, Alice Device allegedly cursed the traveling peddler John Law because he would not sell her pins. John Law then claimed to have fallen under a strange illness, after encountering a big black dog with a fierce countenance of fiery eyes and dreadful fangs. Law's family, who were not from the area, appealed to the local justice of the peace, Roger Nowell. After a brief investigation, Nowell arrested Alice, her mother Elizabeth, and Old Demdike, as well as Old Chattox and her daughter, Anne Redfearne, locking them all up in Lancaster Castle on April 4. On April 10, friends and relatives met at Old Demdike's home, called the Malkin Tower, and allegedly plotted to free the witches by blowing up Lancaster Castle. These efforts compounded the tragedy.

Two weeks later, after Old Demdike's children confessed to the conspiratorial meeting at Malkin Tower, the authorities rounded up more suspects. As questioning intensified into torture, the accused made accusations against one another. Old Demdike admitted that she had fallen under the spell of a mysterious devil named Tibb, whom she met in the forest. Tibb took the shape of a boy in a brown and black coat, or as a familiar or imp: an animal-shaped demon in the form of a black cat or a brown dog. At their second meeting, he placed a Devil's Mark on her, a spot under her left arm from which he sucked her blood. At their third meeting, she began to do *maleficia*, or harmful magic, for him. She then taught her daughter Elizabeth and grandchildren James and Alice (but not the youngest, Jennet). She also converted her neighbors. Old Chattox claimed that Old Demdike had brought the Devil to her in the form of a seducing man, who later sent to her imps called Fancie and Tibbe. Several murders were laid against the witches, as well as killing cows. Old Chattox and her daughter, Anne Redfearne, were said to have killed Robert Nutter, after Anne's refusal of his sexual advances and his subsequent promise to evict them. Other listed motives for murder were refusal of a meal as a bribe, not giving up a shirt promised to another, complaints about the use of a can of milk given as charity, and even revenge for being nagged or laughed at. The murders were supposedly accomplished by using the familiars, burning pictures, or breaking clay images.

In August, Sir Edward Bromley and Sir James Altham heard the evidence in a trial lasting a mere two days. Both men had experience judging cases of witchcraft. In another trial earlier that year in nearby Samlesbury, Judge Bromley had allowed all three of the accused to be acquitted. In that case, fourteen-year-old Grace Sowerbutts had blamed three women for tormenting her and bringing her to a sabbat, a gathering by night of witches where they danced and had intercourse with demons. Judge Bromley found Sowerbutts' testimony not credible, learning that a Roman Catholic priest had fed the girl lurid tales of bloodsucking witches who murdered babies. In a different trial held the previous month, however, he and his colleague, Judge Altham, sentenced Jennet Preston of York to death. Although Preston had been acquitted on a different charge of witchcraft earlier that year, in July the jury found her guilty of killing Thomas Lister by witchcraft. A deathbed accusation by the victim and the bleeding of his corpse when Preston had touched it convinced the jury. Evidence sent by the diligent Justice of the Peace Nowell attesting that Preston had been part of the Malkin Tower conspiracy linked the two cases.

Primed with all this information, Sir Edward needed little convincing of a dangerous conspiracy of witches. In the Pendle Forest case, he readily accepted both fantastic evidence and hearsay. Young Jennet Device's evidence against her own family seemed most convincing to the court. Nevertheless, five of the accused managed acquittal, including little Jennet. Old Demdike escaped execution by dying in jail first. Although Anne Redfearne was found innocent of the murder of Robert Nuttle, local people so insisted on her guilt that they convinced Judge Bromley she had killed Robert's father twenty years earlier. Bromley sentenced Margaret Pearson for the "crime" of having given a child some milk, which she had allegedly made with an imp in the form of a toad. Pearson had to stand four days in the stocks in four different towns with a sign on her forehead explaining her crimes, followed by one year in prison. The judges condemned a total of ten people to death, including many of the Device and Redfearne families. Officials hanged them quickly, just a day after their conviction, on August 20, 1612. The guilty climbed the ladder on the scaffold and had nooses put around their necks; the ladders were taken away, and they strangled as they twisted and turned.

A simple refusal to give a beggar pins escalated into imprisonment, torture, and death. Between 1400 and 1800, such a course of events remained a possibility throughout European countries and their colonial possessions. Tens of thousands of people in Europe and European colonies died as a result; millions of others suffered torture, arrest, interrogation, hate, guilt, or fear. This book describes the key facets of these witch hunts, from their origins in attitudes toward magic and religion since ancient times, through the medieval inquisition of heretics during their intense activity beginning after 1400, to their end through rational legal reforms by 1800.

THE PROBLEM OF WITCHES

Does magic work? Do witches exist?

How anyone answers these questions shapes their attitude toward the contents of this book. The world appears different depending on whether one believes, or does not believe, that witches and their spells cause real change. These issues of belief and reality lie at the heart of witch hunts, so much so that the most famous witch-hunting manual, *The Hammer of Witches*, also begins with similar questions.[1] The manual, of course, answers the questions in the affirmative.

This brief history relates how Western Civilization, once upon a time, not only believed in witches, but "hunted" them. The infamous European witch hunts happened because people believed that witches conspired to destroy Christian society. The fallen angel Lucifer, Satan, the Devil, allegedly empowered witches to cast spells and so harm people, animals, and property. This belief led authorities to arrest, prosecute, and punish reputed witches through the justice systems and political power.

Sadly, all this suffering sought to solve a problem that did not really exist. There was no Satanic conspiracy of witches. Of course, people throughout history have believed there were, and are, witches that could harm society. Likewise, certain people have even claimed to be witches. Yet no good evidence exists that witchcraft has ever harmed anyone or anything through magical means. Most historians, scientists, and theologians do not believe that witches or magic have any real transformative power. Witches' alleged abilities derive from imagination. Even the leaders of the Christian Church taught for many centuries that people claiming to be witches were deluding themselves. This teaching changed by 1400, beginning the witch hunts in western Europe. For most Christians it changed back again by 1800, helping to end such hunts.

THE HUNTS AS SOCIAL, POLITICAL, AND RELIGIOUS PHENOMENA

For the past thirty years many historians have written numerous books and articles to try to understand how witches came to be hunted after 1400 in Europe. To try to explain the hunts, historians suggest many theories that tie the facts, opinions, and myths together. Sometimes a certain theory comes to dominate professional or popular views of history. Not one of the many theories proposed over the last two centuries has succeeded in satisfactorily explaining the hunts (see Chapter 8). Whatever the theory, the ultimate reasons reside in human nature and the cultural conventions of an age. People naturally look for explanations about why things go wrong. Culture also suggests mental tracks or inclinations that make people assume certain causes behind both good and evil events. Humans see patterns in random objects—a devil face in the smoke cloud of the World Trade Center Twin Towers, the Virgin Mary in a shopping mall window, or Elvis in a potato. Sometimes, they see witches.

Two phenomena allowed the witch hunts to erupt when and where they did. First, a widespread belief in witches as an imminent public danger fabricated a justification, and more importantly, late-medieval and early-modern Christian intellectuals wove people's long-held superstitious fears about malevolent magic into the Christian worldview. Fearful clergy preached harsh punishment, rather than repentance and mercy, for the witch-criminals. Certainly, many people during the premodern age believed in a world soaked in magical qualities. Indeed, Christian society may have legitimately attacked, as it did at times, folk who worked herbal magic or played with conjuring and divining. Those practices could reasonably be determined to be sins within Christian doctrine. But hostility to such magic did not require torture and death to replace the usual treatment of sinful transgressions with penance and reconciliation.

Second, political leaders addressed this alleged danger of witches with lethal force. The political leaders, whether lay or clerical, were supposed to believe what many of their spiritual superiors preached about sinister sorcery. Political elites likewise responded to pressures from the lower classes to hunt witches, as more recent research has shown. People "from below" demanded that these dangerous witches be punished by those "above." Rather than either allowing mob justice of vandalism and lynching parties, or preventing such, political leaders themselves set the wheels of justice rolling to crush witches. It is difficult to say which was easier in any one situation, embracing or resisting the hunting of witches. Either way, the witch hunts flourished in the cooperation of Church and State. Church officials provided ideas and reasons, and state agents carried them out.

Fortunately for potential victims, not everyone accepted the reality of a satanic conspiracy of witches. Neither Christian institutions nor political organizations consistently applied enough effort to go after imagined witches at all times and in all places. If indeed the early modern popes and Protestant clergy had systematically taught that witches existed and were to be rooted out, then many more people would have suffered in hunts. And some regimes heeded those who warned about injustice, further rescuing potential witch-hunt victims. Because of these gaps, many areas of Europe never suffered witch-hunts at all, and most areas only experienced them for the briefest of years, not decades.

Nevertheless, too many chose to believe that witches were real and threatening and that the best way to fight them was arrest, torture, and execution. Did neighbors hesitate with Christian compassion before they denounced others to prison and near-certain punishment? Did inquisitor-priests feel uncertain as they twisted the thumbscrew? Did judges have reasonable doubt as they pronounced sentence for mutilation and burning? Some undoubtedly did, but many did not. What truly motivated the hunters in their minds and hearts? We can never fully know.

Walpurga Hausmännin

Take, as another example, the notorious case of Walpurga Hausmännin, an elderly woman who had practiced as a licensed midwife for nineteen years, but fell into poverty. Her case was part of wider hunts based in Dillingen, the residence of the Prince-Bishop Marquard von Berg (r. 1575–1591) of Augsburg. At the time of her trial, Walpurga had allegedly been a demon's lover for thirty-one years. The affair started when, early in her widowhood, she had arranged a tryst with a coworker and the "Evil One" showed up instead. He used the name "Federlin" (Little Feather) and thereafter fornicated with her often. He had her sign a pact with the Devil with her own blood, although he guided her hand since she could not write. They rode together on a pitchfork to sabbats, where she worshiped the "Great Devil" himself, a large man with a grey beard dressed like a prince. At these meetings she cursed holy objects (such as sacred Eucharistic Hosts she had stolen), fornicated, and feasted on roasts, suckling pigs, or dead babies, all without salt.

Walurga confessed to a wide range of crimes, the worst being forty-three murders, mostly of children she had helped to deliver. Her methods were quite varied, ranging from the plausible—pressing on their brain, to the highly unlikely—applying a poisonous salve, through the nearly impossible—sucking their blood, all the way to the ridiculous: she gave to the son of the local chancellor "a hobby-horse so that he might ride on it till he lost his senses. He died likewise."[2] Some dead babies she had later exhumed to eat or to use their body parts in making potions. Only baptized children were spared from her cannibalism, because of that blessed sacrament. She had also injured people with a salve, killed cattle, pigs, and geese, and raised hailstorms once or twice a year that damaged farms and fields. The prince-bishop's court confiscated her goods for his treasury. Then on September 20, 1587, officials bore her on a cart to the place of execution before crowds of men, women, and children. Along the way they stopped five times to rip at her arms and breasts with hot iron pincers. At the pyre, they cut off her right hand (symbolizing her broken trust as a licensed midwife) and then burned her, before throwing her ashes in the river.

The fear of witches such as Walpurga was shared by many in the territory of Augsburg. Some peasants thought the government moved too slowly and so suggested selling some of their land to pay for persecuting still more witches who caused hailstorms. Meanwhile, the credulous bishop heeded the accusations of a fourteen-year-old boy, despite the lad's reputation for troublemaking. A skeptical local magistrate tried to tell the prince-bishop that the boy was not to be taken seriously, but a hunt nevertheless killed more than two dozen women. A woman of higher status, the patrician Margaretha Kellerin, even fell victim. Prince-Bishop Marquard set up a special court in Schwabmünchen, partly because the town had its own hangman, Hans von Biberbach, to handle executions efficiently. Town officials pursued the hunt with little enthusiasm, however, only carrying on because of the pay and mandates of their ecclesiastical lord. Within a few years, a new prince-bishop hardly hunted witches at all.

DEFINITIONS OF MAGIC

Witchcraft is one portion of the larger subject of magic. Entering into the world of magical thinking is often difficult because of its secretive or occult nature. The word *occult* describes the hidden understanding of magical processes beyond our senses. Usually, only a few, select specialists were believed to be able or privileged enough to gain magical knowledge and power. The secretive nature of those who practiced occult arts naturally raised suspicions that occultists were up to no good. Occultists have often defended themselves by claiming that any form of magic can be defined either as good ("white") or evil ("black"), depending on its origins and purposes. Black magic derives from demons and causes harm, such as flooding homes and villages. The term *maleficia* (from the Latin "evil things made") describes such damaging magics. White magic, in contrast, draws on natural-connected supernatural forces and aims to help people, for example by bringing rain to nourish crops.

Practitioners of the occult also distinguish between "High Magic" and "Low Magic." High Magic, often called sorcery, requires deep learning and scholarship of arcane texts, formulas, and rituals in order to master formidable supernatural forces such as demons. Sorcerers (if male) or sorceresses (if female) need to study complicated formulas, rituals, or secret language. In contrast, Low Magic, which includes most witchcraft, is easy to learn or even innate to people alleged to have special abilities. With little training or literacy, simple magical practitioners, such as shamans or witch doctors, claim to tell fortunes, defend against hexes or magical curses, and cast or break love charms, as well as cause, diagnose, or cure disease. Likewise, cunning-folk allegedly have helped people gain good luck, heal illnesses, find lost items, and prevent hexes. These wise-men or wise-women helped with countermagic, preventing magical evil by burning or boiling the charm or image believed to cause the curse, saying special prayers, or using holy or magical items such as crosses or amulets. Cunning-folk might also communicate with fairies, sprites, leprechauns, or other supernatural spirits. In their need to reduce their fear of the unknown future, people sought out diviners, prognosticators, seers, scryers, or soothsayers.

Belief in more serious forms of magic helped feed the witch hunts. Witches joined in the night ride, a wild chase with faeries and spirits through the woods. Much feared was the magic with the dead, or necromancy. Witches were reputed to raise the dead as monsters (zombies, the walking dead, or vampires who drank blood). They provoked spirits to haunt their family, friends, or enemies. A common belief was that witchcraft allowed transvection, or magical travel through flight. Flying was important for witches to cover great distances quickly, either to gather with fellow witches or to work some sort of harm. Flying might have been in the form of a spirit or specter; in the physical body by itself, perhaps helped by a magical ointment, salve or unguent; or using some sort of device, like the classic broomstick. Flight might also result from metamorphosis, or a witch's ability to transform into an animal or monster. In the shape of a bird or bat or dog, a witch could cover great distances quickly. A witch might kill while shaped as a fearsome werewolf or hide as a mere mouse.

Loose terminology used by the historical sources complicates our understanding of these beliefs. People in the past did not always make fine distinctions between high or low, black or white magic. And the words they used—cunning-folk, witch, magician, wizard, sorcerer, just to cite English variants—were often used interchangeably, making it difficult to distinguish what was meant. Today's magicians are entertainers who specifically say they work tricks and illusions to produce apparent violations of the laws of nature. Wizards are usually characters from legend, fiction, and fantasy, such as the Merlin of the Arthurian stories or Harry Potter in that series of books. Still, a witch, whether male or female, has often been defined as a person who uses magic to harm neighbors and society at large.

THE WITCH IN GREECE AND ROME

Fear of witches in our own Western culture is rooted in the ancient world of Greece and Rome. European history really begins with the Roman Empire (509 BC–AD 476), the great conquering and organizing structure of ancient Europe. Roman domination amalgamated many diverse peoples, including Etruscans, Italians, Greeks, Carthaginians, Egyptians, Palestinians, Mesopotamians, Celts, and Germans, among many others. To hold on to their conquered subjects, the Romans tried to Romanize their new peoples, to make them more similar to Romans.

Roman Religions

A key factor in this integration was religion. The religion of the ancient Greeks and Romans is now called paganism, a word drawn from the rural dwellers of the empire. The term *paganism* today includes any of the polytheistic religions that existed in and near Europe. Polytheistic religions involve many deities, gods and goddesses and other divine figures, often connected to natural forces.

Polytheistic religions reflected the socioeconomic importance of farming. All civilizations, until recently, centered around agriculture. Many ancient gods and goddesses symbolized both natural forces of fertility and aspects of human nature. In Greek and Roman belief, Zeus/Jupiter was the god of storms, Aphrodite/Venus the goddess of love, Ares/Mars the god of war, and Athena/Minerva the goddess of wisdom. The ancient peoples worshiped such gods in public ceremonies involving processions, songs and prayers, and sacred meals. In these meals they poured libations of milk, wine, or blood, as offerings to share with the gods. As late as 216 BC, the Romans carried out human sacrifice. Even after this date, and for the next several centuries, Romans killed thousands of people and animals in the gladiatorial games dedicated to the gods. The priests and priestesses who managed the religious ceremonies were government officials who helped maintain the state's success by appeasing the gods. The Romans required that all their conquered peoples make sacrifices to these gods and to the god of the city of Rome itself. The Roman emperors also began declaring themselves divine, another of the many gods for all Romans to worship.

Many stories and mythologies of the Greeks and Romans, which still inform our culture, connect to magic and witchcraft. The divine figure most identified with magic was Artemis/Diana, twin sister of Apollo who ruled the sun. Artemis/Diana ruled the moon and embodied the phases of the moon. Likewise, believers changed the image of Diana herself, identifying her with Hecate. Her incarnation as Hecate bore three faces, representing the three divisions of the universe for the Greeks: the heavens, the earth, and the underworld (Hades). Diana or Hecate would often hunt at night, accompanied by nymphs and other magical creatures, or by the souls of the dead in the form of women. Followers of Hecate, especially in the region of Thessaly in northern Greece, gained a reputation as witches, infamous for their sexual appetite and for grave robbing (especially stealing the noses from corpses).

Another divine figure was Pan, who had a human upper torso and face, but whose lower body was that of a goat, with goat horns and billy-goat beard. Pan was mainly a fertility and nature god, often associated with satyrs. These wild men-creatures, also half-man, half-goat, were constantly sexually aroused and looking for an outlet for their passion. The satyrs most often pursued maenads, women dedicated to a goddess, who also participated in wild sexual ceremonies. Both Pan and satyrs would feed into later Christian imagery of the Devil. Overall, though, magic and witchcraft were only a minor aspect of Greek and Roman mythology and religion.

Roman Religious Options

The Romans allowed most people to keep whatever religions they had, as long as those beliefs did not prohibit them from carrying out the proper Roman civic-religion sacrifices. In general, the Romans were both tolerant and syncretistic, willing to adopt beliefs and practices from other religions. Whatever a person believed about the gods hardly mattered, as long as it did not disturb the public peace. As a result of Roman syncretism, a great religious diversity flourished.

Many Romans pursued other outlets for coping with the spiritual and supernatural. Philosophers encouraged more thoughtful and rationalistic methods of confronting life's ultimate questions. At the same time, secretive "mystery" cults involved emotionally powerful ceremonies (perhaps involving drugs and orgies) and the promise of salvation for their followers, usually based on a god who had died and been resurrected. Fertility goddess cults based on Magna Mater or the Great Mother, Demeter, Cybele, Ishtar, and Diana of Ephesus were popular. Mystical works attributed to the god Hermes Trismegistus (Thrice-Great) fascinated many with a scholarly inclination. These works comprised a large body, or corpus, allegedly written by the grandson of the gods Hermes and Æsclepius in the first century AD, although his followers claimed that they were much older. All these attitudes existed next to the Roman civic religion and public cults. Many of these religious beliefs and figures would resurface in later Western concepts about witchcraft and magic.

Roman Witch-Hunting

The Romans' sincere belief in the validity of properly pronounced predictions, however, made divination one area in which Roman leaders regularly punished illegal magic. Only officially recognized oracles, colleges of augurs, or the politically appointed system of pontiffs could use magic to divine the future. The government wanted to control information and so held exclusive rights regarding proclamation of the divine. Emperors were especially concerned about any prediction of their own deaths. Such knowledge could encourage revolt and destroy public order.

Thus, the main form of "hunting" against practitioners of magic in ancient Rome seems to have been against unauthorized diviners. The original founding laws of Rome, the Twelve Tables, prohibited cursing crops and property. Later interpretations expanded this prohibition into concerns about sorcery and incantations that could harm people. Only a few examples of persecutions against magic survive in historical accounts. In 33 BC, Agrippa, on behalf of Augustus Caesar, drove astrologers and sorcerers from Rome. Likewise, Nero banished some in AD 52. Only three emperors, Tiberius in AD 16, Vitellius in AD 69, and Valens ca. AD 370, are on record for executing diviners. A different assault on practitioners of magic took place, according to the historian Livy, in three waves between 180 and 150 BC. Roman magistrates tortured and executed several thousand persons in Italy for the crime of *veneficium*. That term technically means poisoning, yet the real issues seems to have been some sort of conspiracy connected to an outbreak of disease. These few incidents provide too little information to understand Roman attitudes toward witch-hunting.

While banned and discouraged, magic rarely drew the ire of the regime. Historians have increasingly noted how many in the empire used love charms, curse scrolls, or protective amulets. Books of spells may have been publicly burned, as by Augustus in 31 BC, but not the people who owned them. An orator could display his skills by arguing that witches be burned before even committing a crime, because "the law hates the capacity in itself to perform witchcraft."[3] Such rhetorical exercises, however, remained for entertainment and admiration, not legal precedent. According to law and rhetoric, magicians and witches should have been burned, but the Romans do not seem to have done so. Magic usually remained in the realm of personal fear and imagination, not at the attention of government officials.

STORIES OF ANCIENT WITCHES

Instead, witchcraft and harmful magic mostly remained cultural dramatizations that fed the imagination. Greeks and Romans told stories of the *strix*, a woman who turned into a screeching owl, killed babies in their cradles, made men impotent after having sex with them, and feasted on human flesh. Another kind of witch, the *lamia*, was a blood-sucking, flesh-eating person having risen from the dead. Yet *striges* and *lamiae* were merely figures of legend. No laws were passed against them; no people were arrested for committing crimes in the form of such imaginary monsters. Likewise, sorceresses, such as Circe and Calypso, were mere subjects of poetry. The most famous Roman story that features witches is the *Metamorphoses*, better known as *The Golden Ass*, by Lucius Apuleius. In this novel, a man is transformed into a donkey because he sought out the mysteries of witchcraft. His adventures include many tales of witches, some resembling *striges* and *lamiae*.

Ironically, Lucius Apuleius found himself accused of witchcraft. We know of his trial from his defense, called the *Apologia* ("Apology" or "Defense"), written around AD 157. Persons accused him of bewitching an older wealthy widow to fall in love with and marry him, a mere young philosopher. One of Apuleius' defenses was that no one who really believed in magical powers would accuse anyone, since "the man who exposes a magician, credited with such awful powers, to the danger of a capital sentence, how can escort or precaution or watchmen save him from unforeseen and inevitable disaster? Nothing can save him...."[4] This observation about the lack of magical retaliation always remains one of the weakest points in persecuting witches. We do not know how Apuleius' accusers circumvented it; few since have ever rationalized an answer either. Roman histories and legal records reveal few other prosecutions for magic.

ILLICIT RELIGIONS IN ROME

The Romans did, however, persecute a few religions that offended their usual tolerant and syncretistic attitudes. They labeled such false and dangerous religions as "superstitions." Our modern definition of superstition is "relatively harmless nonsense based on false magical thinking." For the Romans, however, superstition was a dangerous false belief that could undermine the divinely supported public order.

About the only foreign religion that the Romans decided was absolutely too evil to continue was that of the Celts, often called druidism after the name for its priests. Unfortunately for their side of the story, the Celts left no written records, and we can only view them through Roman eyes. The Romans charged crimes against the Celts to justify the elimination of druidism: secret meetings allegedly full of human sacrifice, cannibalism, and unnatural and incestuous sex orgies. Social groups often use such accusations to place the "others" beyond the boundaries of decent and accepted human behavior. Such characterizations assure the accusers of their own human decency, while justifying persecution of the enemy.

During the same time in which they libeled the druids, the Romans also defamed the Christians in a similar manner. At first, Romans found Christianity hard to understand. Christianity began with a Jew named Joshua benJoseph of Nazareth ("Jesus" in Latin) in Roman-occupied Palestine. In the writings that became the New Testament of the Christian Bible, Jesus called on people to embrace the kingdom of God; they should love God and their neighbor. He was critical of wealth and an advocate for the poor, defenseless, and marginalized.

Jesus died at the hands of the Romans. The Roman government crucified him for the crime of treason, alleging he had claimed to be the King of the Jews. But Jesus's followers reported that he had risen bodily from the dead, appeared to and preached to his disciples, and then ascended into heaven.

BASIC CHRISTIANITY

While empirical historians cannot assert the validity of any supernatural aspect of this man, his followers soon called him the Messiah (in Hebrew), the Christ (in Greek), the Anointed One (in English) who would save those who followed the Way. Over the next several hundred years, his followers, the Christians, slowly worked out more precisely what they believed and how their faith differed from that of mainstream Judaism. Jesus became understood as the incarnate son of God, born of the woman Mary. Christians argued further that Jesus the Son was part of a Trinity of God the Father, along with the Holy Spirit. Jesus's death by crucifixion and subsequent resurrection provided salvation, or life after death. Believers went to Heaven after death, to spend eternity with God, angels, and other saved souls. Their rituals involved worship regularly on Sunday, the Lord's Day (purposely avoiding the Jewish Sabbath), coming together with processions, songs and prayers, and a sacred meal, the Eucharist. In the Eucharist, they believed they did not so much offer their votive gifts to God, but God shared with them in a memorial of Christ's sacrifice. They developed these beliefs and their worship by building an organization, called the Church. Its leaders were bishops, assisted by priests and deacons, who supervised the forms of worship and the details of doctrine.

In the cosmopolitan intellectual environment of the Roman Empire, pagans and philosophers opposed the Christian world view. In reaction, philosophical argumentation became a key tool of Christian theologians. In those Christian doctrines, the supernatural may be more important than the natural. As the Christian apostle Paul wrote in Hebrews 11:1, "Now faith is the substance of things hoped for, the evidence of things not seen." Christians looked for miracles, where the divine world breaks into ours, defying the laws of nature or statistical probability. Water becomes wine; a man blind from birth suddenly sees.

Such miracles were common to many religions, observed the Romans. Although the Roman regime had tolerated the Jews, because their religion was older than Rome itself, these new Christians were suspect. Christians were reputed to conduct secret meetings full of human sacrifice, cannibalism, and unnatural sex orgies. As reported by one ancient author, they would have an "infant covered over with meal ... slain by the young pupil.... Thirstily—O horror!—they lick up its blood; eagerly they divide its limbs.... On a solemn day they assemble at the feast, with all their children, sisters, mothers, people of every sex and of every age. There, after much feasting ..., the connections of abominable lust involve them in the uncertainty of fate."[5] Worst of all, such Christians refused to show loyalty to the government because they would not make sacrifices to the true gods of Rome. Ironically, Romans called Christians atheists who hated mankind because of their indifference to the "true" gods, whose goodwill supported peace and prosperity at home and victory in war abroad.

ROMAN PERSECUTIONS

Thus the Romans persecuted the Christians. Unfortunately for paganism, the Romans never carried out these persecutions thoroughly enough. Where the Romans did seriously hunt Christians, they sometimes used the method of inquisition. This meant sending in investigators who asked citizens to report any criminal activity—in this case Christians worshipping and refusing to sacrifice to the sanctioned Roman gods. Roman law allowed slaves to be tortured for information. Once exposed, if Christians refused to recant, the Romans punished them with exile, enslavement in mines or as temple prostitutes, or the ultimate penalty of death, often in cruel ways. Crucifixion or slaughters in the arena, either by gladiators or wild animals, were popular entertainments. But when Christians were killed, often they became martyrs. The Christians slowly won converts and Christianity spread throughout urban centers of the Roman Empire.

At the beginning of the fourth century, the Emperor Constantine ended the persecutions and allowed religious toleration. Even more, he began to disestablish the pagan civic cult as the state-sponsored religious organization. Romans converted to Christianity in droves. As Christians became more numerous, they in turn began to persecute the pagans, destroy their temples and shrines, and murder their leaders. The pagan gods were demons, whose worship needed to end at any cost.

MAGIC AND WITCHCRAFT IN THE BIBLE

The role of demons soon helped differentiate the European witch hunts from other cultures' attitudes toward witches. Christianity developed a real concern about demons and "devils," the term used in the King James Bible. That religious text told how the ancient Hebrews considered the gods of their Middle Eastern neighbors, Baal, Ashtoreth, etc., to be demons. Many stories in the Hebrew scriptures, the Christian Old Testament, describe the triumph of God's prophets over pagan priests and their demons.

Jewish beliefs about witchcraft remained rather insignificant to their faith, although magic was a concern. One minor commandment was "Thou shalt not suffer a witch to live" (Exodus 22:18). In actual Hebrew, the word translated as "witch" was *mekasshepha*, which properly meant a poisoner who used supernatural means. This commandment did not stand out as particularly alarming, listed among so many other divine commands, such as paying restitution for stealing, paying the dowry of or marrying virgins one had seduced, and not charging interest. Several other commandments, though, label as an abomination such things as consulting mediums, wizards, or necromancers, using divination, or making a son or daughter perform the (today unclear) ritual of passing through fire. The Hebrew kings Saul and Manasseh did consult diviners, thereby provoking the anger of God. Several prophets, including Daniel, Jeremiah, and Malachi, likewise warned against magicians, soothsayers, and diviners.

During the rise of Christianity, magic and witchcraft played an insignificant role. Only two magical references occur in the New Testament. The three "Wise Men" or "kings" who visited the baby Jesus were actually magi, astrologers and diviners from the court of Persia. Later Simon "Magus" (the Magician) asked to purchase the miracle-making power of the Holy Spirit from the apostles. Although in the original story he is simply admonished, later legends have him struck down by divine lightning. Simon's name subsequently became the term for the sin of simony, trying to buy salvation or positions in the church hierarchy.

SATAN

The previously mentioned Satan soon came to dominate Christian views about magic and witchcraft. Satan means "opponent," "obstructer," or "adversary." As Jews translated their sacred writings into Greek, they used the word *diabolos*, which gives English the word "Devil." Later Christian tradition identified Satan with the tempting serpent in the Garden of Eden. Satan's first official appearance is in the book of Job. There Satan plays accuser, arguing to God that Job would abandon his faith if he suffered. Satan loses the friendly wager, after destroying Job's family, livestock, property, and health. Mainstream Jewish thought, however, hardly focused on Satan.

The Christians of the New Testament saw things differently. Demons appear in the Gospels, with names like "Legion" (because he united so many demons in one person) or Beelzebub, the Lord of the Flies. "The" Devil (with an upper case *D*) is Satan, whereas other devils (with lower case *d*'s) are his assistants in evil. Satan tempted Jesus in the wilderness with all the powers of the world; was behind demons possessing people; and entered into Judas Iscariot, who betrayed Jesus to the Jewish leaders. Satan tempted husbands and wives to commit adultery and featured prominently in the apocalypse described in the last book of the Christian Bible, Revelation.

Christian writers built on these comparatively minor actions in the Bible to transform Satan into a powerful figure, one who sought his own souls for Hell. He took on the additional name of Lucifer, "the lightbearer," linking verses from the Old and New Testaments. He became assisted by demons, many of whom were the false pagan gods and powerful spiritual beings. The image of Satan/the Devil/Lucifer were drawn from the ancient deity Pan, with horns, goatee, bare chest, and lower torso and legs in the form of a cloven-hooved goat. Other monstrous additions, such as red skin and long pointed tail were later variations, as were a large erect phallus or a second face on the buttocks.

DEMONIC MAGIC

Demonology became the "serious" study of these supernatural beings, either to understand their actions or to gain control of them. Demonologists began to list and categorize monsters mentioned in the Bible, such as Leviathan, Belial, and Behemoth. A debate arose among demonologists about whether demons could actually affect the physical world or only acted through illusion and deception. Their main role in Christian thought was to work with Satan as tempters and harmers of humanity. The temptation of St. Anthony, portrayed by artists over the centuries, allowed fantasy to run wild in renderings of demons tormenting the hermit.

One of the worst things demons did was to possess humans. Possessed people suffered fits, marked by bodily collapse or convulsing limbs, babbling in strange tongues and voices, spitting out strange and dangerous objects, and and/or a loss of senses. One impressive aspect of Jesus's ministry was his working of miracles to cure illness: he made the blind see, the lame walk; he cured lepers and brought the dead back to life. Another form of healing was his performance of exorcisms, or casting demons out from possessed persons. Christ and the apostles cast out devils without much complicated ceremony, as recorded in the New Testament. In the Gospels, these demonic possessions were real. Jesus's exorcisms showed his divine power as superior to that of Satan. Eventually, the Christian Church established an elaborate ritual of exorcism. An exorcist invokes the demon, says prayers to bind him, and exhorts him to leave in the name of Christ. The similarity of exorcism to conjuring worried Church authorities, who feared that some exorcists might actually be using sorcery in league with the demons.

In books eight through ten of his work *The City of God*, Bishop Augustine of Hippo (r. 396–430) commented on the issues of the Devil and magic. Augustine helped to define orthodox Christianity for the next few centuries. He cautioned Christians against offering to demons *latria*, worship due only to God. These beings of the air, between God and men, are a "race of deceitful and malicious spirits, who come into the souls of men and delude their senses, both in sleep and waking."[6] Thus Augustine reaffirmed the spiritual nature of demons, which deceive people with fantasies and falsehoods. In other works, Augustine condemned Gnostic heretics as committing sexual sins in their secret meetings, where they also murdered and cannibalized babies. The Roman accusations against the druids and Christians are here neatly repeated. Augustine's thoughts on these matters would largely define Christian thinking for centuries.

GERMAN MYTHS

Augustine wrote the *City of God* to define orthodox Christianity against Greco-Roman critics who claimed the pagan gods had withdrawn their protection from Rome. The late fourth and fifth centuries saw various German and Asiatic peoples rip the western half of the Roman Empire apart. Many believed it was more than coincidence that no sooner had the empire been converted to

Christianity than the barbarians succeeded as never before in 800 years. For a time many Germans were willing to make accommodations and live as allies or loyal peoples within the empire, but eventually they destroyed the Roman administration and bureaucracy in the western provinces and took them over for themselves. The kingdoms that the barbarian Germanic kings built up in western Europe were the ancestors of modern European states.

The dominant Germans brought with them their own religious concepts. Actually, many of the invading Germans were already Christians, although of a heretical Arian kind. A few German peoples, such as the Franks or Anglo-Saxons, invaded as pagans. Their gods shared parallels to those of ancient Rome. Odin was the god of wisdom; Freya, the goddess of fertility; Thor, of storms; and Tyr, of war. One goddess Holda, or Bertha, concerned herself with fertility and domesticity, a maternal nature goddess. She frequently led a wild hunt through woods and forests of the night, very much like the Greco-Roman Artemis/Diana/Hecate. These similarities would later lead to Germans using Greek and Roman names for their goddess' night ride.

The Germans who entered the borders of what had been the Roman Empire became converted to Catholic Christianity by the seventh century. Historians still debate how much this conversion, or later ones for the next few centuries, changed real beliefs. Intensity of faithfulness to Christianity, as to all religions, has varied widely according to time and place, even where one official faith is sanctioned by the political regime. Other forms of worship were absorbed. Christians borrowed from pagan holidays, such as turning the winter solstice into Christmas. Churches were built on the site of sacred groves; pagan fountains were renamed after Christian saints. Maypole dancing and yule-log burning sanctioned welcoming the fecundity of spring or holding off the chill of winter, although not the underlying paganism with which they began. Most historians doubt that such remnants of folk belief survived as manifestations of sincere pagan faith. Once Rome had become Christian, the new faith's cultural dominance went universally unchallenged for centuries. Christianity was no longer one option among many. Everyone was born and baptized into the faith.

THE MIDDLE AGES

As detailed in the next chapter, new challenges in the Middle Ages would draw on ancient magical traditions and combine them with new theology to lay the foundation for the witch hunts after 1400. The ancient Greco-Roman civilization passed away, but magical thinking certainly endured. As the Christian Church of the Middle Ages deepened its conversion of the conquerors of Rome and evangelized other pagan peoples, it absorbed and adapted their attitudes toward magic. God's miraculous wonders remained superior to any evil work of the Devil.

By the twelfth century, a growing economy, increased trade, larger urban population, and changing status of peasants brought on a new age. With new ideas came new dangers to the Church. Calls for *apostolic poverty* resulted in heresies of Waldensians and Cathars, who opposed the spiritual monopoly of the Church under its papal administration. Preaching by mendicant orders, but also crusade and the inquisition, mostly eliminated theological heresy altogether by the fourteenth century. The Cathars had largely been killed or converted. The Waldensians were confined to isolated pockets of territory, and the Hussites were limited to Bohemia.

Although heretics were no longer a serious danger to the established Christian order, a need for heretical enemies remained. Along the way, heretics had been labeled with fantastic, impossible crimes of human sacrifice, cannibalism, and unnatural sex orgies. Thus, inquisitors had already begun to link imaginary magical evils with actual theological heretics. By 1400, the magical threats stood on their own with a new heresy of witches, although the connection remained built on fantasy more than reality. The witch hunts required more than a lack of theological heretics, however. Theology, or rather its branch of demonology, shifted from believing that demons were mere spirits to scholastic arguments about their taking physical form. Political rulers only needed to act on their fear of witches to begin the hunts.

EUROPE AT THE BEGINNING OF THE WITCH HUNTS

By the end of the Middle Ages, three powerful realms, France, England, and the Holy Roman Empire, dominated Europe. The Holy Roman Empire was the largest in size and population, but increasingly the weakest among the three. Its territory covered today's nations of Germany, Austria, Liechtenstein, Switzerland, Luxembourg, the Netherlands, and the Czech Republic, as well as parts of Belgium, France, Denmark, Poland, and Italy. Since the mid-eleventh century, the Holy Roman Emperors had been weakened by changes in dynasty, conflicts with the popes, wars in Italy, and competition with the other German princes. After 1250, a group of seven electoral princes chose a new emperor after the death of each. Numerous princes, kings, dukes, prince-bishops, counts, margraves, imperial knights, and even free cities had become semi-independent by 1500, often free to ignore the weak elected emperor's commands. The Habsburg dynasty consistently managed to get their members elected emperors after the fifteenth century. Nonetheless, the Habsburgs remained most powerful in their home of Austria, rivaled by dynasties who ruled states such as Prussia, Bavaria, and Saxony.

Meanwhile, the kingdom of France had risen in strength at the Empire's expense. At the close of the Middle Ages, however, France and England were locked in a struggle for domination called the Hundred Years War (1337–1452). These two states had been direct rivals since Duke William of Normandy had invaded and conquered England in 1066. At the time of the Norman invasion, England had become unified as a state with a mixed population of Celts, Roman-Britons, and Anglo-Saxons.

During the Hundred Years War, English skill several times nearly defeated the French. Yet France would eventually be victorious, driving the English off the Continent. After losing to France, the English fought a brief civil war called the Wars of the Roses, out of which emerged the Tudor dynasty. The Tudors stabilized the state and largely completed English domination of neighboring Scotland, Wales, and Ireland. The unification of Scotland and England in 1603 created Great Britain. The British navy then proceeded to establish England as the world power. Meanwhile, France's absolute monarchy developed the mechanisms of modern bureaucratic government, becoming the most powerful state in Europe. In 1494, the French Valois dynasty illustrated its new-found power by invading the Italian peninsula, traditionally a region only interfered with by the imperial Germans.

The French invasion of Italy allowed them to share in its flourishing wealth and culture. During much of the Middle Ages, the wealthy cities of Italy had prospered, but had been fought over and ruled by German emperors and popes. The epidemic known as the Black Death, which killed a third of the population of Europe, at first made people think the end of the world had arrived. Instead, history went on. In Italy, wealth multiplied as Europe began to undergo the Commercial Revolution (1350–1650), based on capitalism. The simple idea of reinvesting profits, the essence of capitalism, helped Italian merchants and bankers grow in power and prestige. The rich spent some of that wealth on knowledge and culture.

THE RENAISSANCE

The result was the Renaissance, or a rebirth of interest in classical Greece and Rome that led to modern innovations. During the fifteenth and sixteenth centuries, intellectuals invented the term for themselves, seeing the thousand years of the Middle Ages as one long departure between the ancient Greeks and Romans and a new rebirth of Greco-Roman literature, art, and philosophy adopted by Renaissance elites. Meanwhile, the Renaissance fascination with Greece and Rome spread to other European realms, which experienced their own cultural blossoming. Helping in this effort was the invention of the printing press, which made books cheaper and more widely available than ever before in human history.

It is ironic that an age of openness to new learning coincided with the beginning of the worst of the witch hunts. The intellectual ferment in schools and universities revived ancient concepts of witches along with the other heritage of the classics. Drawing on ideas of Plato, some scholars sought the key to controlling magical powers through highly learned sorcery. They dabbled with magical tomes, experimented with alchemy, and toyed with conjuring demons. Others scoffed at these efforts or considered them sinful.

Another modern idea debated by Renaissance intellectuals was the *Querelle des Femmes* ("The Woman Question"). Some people suggested that women should try to justify their equality or equivalence with men. The misogyny of those who denied any fair comparison of women's mental or moral capacities with men's certainly fueled the focus on women as witches. The printing press spread those fears along with all the other ideas.

THE EUROPEAN EXPLORATIONS

Just as France was trying to establish its hegemony in Italy, Portugal and Spain used their position on the Atlantic coast to begin exploration of Africa, trying to reach the Indies, where wealth from spices lay. They established military trading posts in Africa and Asia. More significantly, they seized control of much of the newly discovered North and South America.

France and England soon followed the example of the Spanish and Portuguese and established their own colonies in the Americas and on the fringes of Africa and Asia. They often confronted the native civilizations in those places with hostility and ignorance. Surprisingly, the European colonizers did not significantly impose the witch-mindset part of Christianity in their new colonies, even though European colonizers could easily have identified indigenous religious systems with a diabolic attack on Christianity. While some Europeans considered native deities to be demons, the dominant tendency was to treat local faiths as superstitious falsehoods. Christian colonizers even treated native traditions of magic and witchcraft as powerless superstition rather than imminent disasters. Such beliefs needed to be eliminated, but not through hunting and executions. Thus, witch hunts remained largely confined to Europe; only a few witch hunts affected native peoples during the West's worldwide expansion.

The governments that began to conquer the world experimented with the centralizing tendencies of the early modern state. Central regimes had become more powerful and effective than ever before. Absolutism, or granting supreme power to the monarch, became the most popular style of governance in Europe. Parliamentarianism, or exercising authority through elected delegates, developed in a handful of others, such as Switzerland, the Netherlands, and Great Britain. Whether through one ruler or by many representatives, though, the central governments increasingly relied on appointed, educated bureaucrats to manage taxation, public works, law enforcement, diplomacy, and warfare efficiently. Governments benefited from the growing wealth created by capitalist economic growth, innovations in peaceful and martial technology, and people's desire for a stable society in a time of change.

A practical revolution in the legal system shifted laws from private justice to public order. The state took on responsibility for enforcing the law, exercising a monopoly on lethal violence. Crime did not hurt individuals so much as the "commonwealth" or the state itself. Therefore these regimes carried out witch-hunting, or not, as part of their official duties. Sometimes the central regime embraced hunting, perhaps to enforce its legitimacy or divide its enemies.

More often, higher courts tended to slow down, moderate, or lessen the harshness of hunts. Educated bureaucrats and legal scholars often saw the flaws with hunting more clearly than petty local magistrates. When local jealousies, rivalries, and fears provoked accusations and prosecutions, the modern centralized judiciaries might take a cooler, detached look at evidence, procedure, and consequences of hunting. Eventually, they would shut hunting down entirely.

THE REFORMATION

Serious religious divisions in Europe divided Christians just after the witch hunts had become established. The Catholic Church in western Europe had been administratively and spiritually dominated by the papacy in Rome for centuries. In 1517, Martin Luther in Germany instigated an antipapal revolt, beginning a new direction for Christianity called Protestantism. Jean Calvin's Calvinists and England's Anglicans soon joined Luther's Lutherans in the separation of their Christian churches from Roman papal authority. Smaller religious groups, often collectively called Anabaptists, also multiplied.

The Reformation's impact on witch-hunting has been much examined by scholars, considering the coincidence in timing. As religious conflict rose to the level of the so-called Wars of Religion from 1550 to 1660, so also the most vicious period of witch-hunting took place. The differences in religious belief, whether Roman Catholic against Protestant, or Protestant against Protestant, motivated states to fight wars against one another. During these decades, Roman Catholics, Lutherans, Calvinists, and Anglicans alike hunted witches. Surprisingly, they usually hunted their own faithful, not those of the other creeds. Only the tiny sects of Anabaptists seemed neither to believe in nor fear witchcraft. Perhaps Anabaptists felt no need to blame witches, because every other kind of Christian persecuted them.

Persecutions of witches within Christian denominations could be explained by a need to police the faithful. Zealots went after any deviation from the official line of their particular belief, whether it was in the sacraments, idolatry, personal morality, or witchcraft. Reformers legitimately worried that magical practices deviated from the proper, and miraculous, religious doctrine. To make a pact with the Devil violated the First Commandment to have no other gods. Luther, Calvin, and many popes declared witches to be a real danger. This heightened sensitivity to sin certainly touched off some hunting. Demonic theology, mutual suspicion, and inquisitorial procedures further prolonged the hunts encouraged by religious leaders in different states.

MODERN STATES

By the middle of the seventeenth century, though, Europeans had begun to stop using religious differences as a motivation for war. The cultural monopoly of one organized Christian Church was irrevocably broken. That opened an opportunity for new ways of thinking about the natural and supernatural. Just as Europeans had accepted the political division of Christendom, they then began to tolerate religious and intellectual diversity. The Treaty of Westphalia, which ended the worst of the religious wars, the Thirty Years War (1618–1648), established a fragile system of balance of power under which Europe would operate for the next few centuries.

In this balance of power, each state considered itself sovereign and independent. Between the larger Great Powers such as England, France, and Austria, lay smaller buffer states, such as the Dutch Netherlands, the Spanish Netherlands (Belgium), and Switzerland. Italy remained occupied and divided until the nineteenth century. Spain and Portugal clung to their empires, but their Great Power status withered away. As the era of religious wars vanished by 1660, the witch hunts went into a long, slow decline, until they had completely disappeared by 1800. Worries about sin-neutral criminality (theft, murder, etc.) outweighed crimes connected with the sins of religious moralists. Authorities looked to charge women with infanticide, not witchcraft.

The northern and eastern fringes of Europe, though, took up hunting as it declined in western Europe. The states there gradually became more integrated into the political, economic and cultural circles of Europe. Russia, Prussia and Austria, and the Muslim Ottoman Empire divided up the diverse peoples of Eastern Europe among them. The kingdom of Poland-Lithuania had for a few centuries been the largest state in Europe, but Prussia, Austria, and Russia carved up Poland among themselves in the last decade of the eighteenth century. The rise of Russia after 1600 made it one of the Great Powers of Europe, especially after it defeated Sweden in the early 1700s. Russia became the leading state with a majority of Eastern Orthodox believers after the rise of the Ottoman Empire had conquered most Greek Orthodox. In the north, Sweden had briefly surpassed its neighbors Denmark and Norway, almost achieving Great Power status as a result of its victories and conquest during the Thirty Years War.

The cultural concepts of dangerous witches promoted by intellectuals in western Europe reached into eastern Europe and flowed in with a process called westernization. Northern and eastern European rulers adapted what worked for the Great Powers of western and central Europe. The fringe states absorbed and reworked innovations such as stronger legal systems, administrative bureaucracies, and capitalistic economic practices. So, regimes in northern and eastern Europe took up, in a limited way, witch-hunting ideas and practices. Only the Ottoman Empire withdrew more and more into seclusion from Western ideas.

THE SCIENTIFIC REVOLUTION

As religious wars subsided, a new method of science rose to compete with religion in its explanatory power about the universe. An interest in science began as intellectuals forged new techniques for examining the natural world.

The Scientific Method meant that natural phenomena could be explained through repeated experimentation and observation. Scientists could then dissect the causes of natural events with more accuracy than ever before in history. Hence scientists explained that a hailstorm resulted from a clash of a warm mass of air with a cold one rather than being provoked by an angry deity, a generous God, or a malevolent witch. Equally revolutionary was the change in attitude toward the supernatural. Scientists could not examine supernatural forces, precisely because they were not measurable, quantifiable, or repeatable. Astrology was abandoned for astronomy; "natural philosophy" for physics. The scientific method influenced the development of the historical method, which modern historians use to explain the past.

The Scientific Revolution became the most important intellectual innovation of the age, allowing humanity greater knowledge about and control over nature than ever before. The scientific view pushed secularization, using nonreligious criteria to determine society's values and priorities. This shift weakened Christian doctrine's ability to declare witches as dangerous. The scientific method also provided a means to test whether witches actually possessed magical powers over nature. Then and now, all scientific testing has failed to show witches have any affect whatsoever on natural phenomena. These results contributed to the decline of witch-hunting.

THE ENLIGHTENMENT

The ideas of the Scientific Revolution culminated in the Enlightenment, which spread scientific views throughout European culture and society. Many Enlightenment intellectuals, called *philosophes*, saw rationalism and empiricism, the doctrine that all knowledge is derived from sensory experience, as bright lights dispelling the darkness of doubt and ignorance. They hoped for human progress toward better living in this world through the spread of science. The Enlightenment coincided with the end of the witch hunts and, in significant ways, enlightened ideas contributed to their termination.

First, many leaders of society rejected the traditional dogmas of religion. They even began to criticize superstitious abuses of religion, if not religion itself. Some declared themselves to be agnostics. Others became outright atheists. Many of the elites became Deists who accepted a God who created the universe, but not one who regularly intervened with miracles, especially through the incarnation of his divine Son, Jesus Christ. What kept the universe functioning was not the hand of God, but the laws of nature, whose regular functions could be revealed by science and understood by reason. This attitude toward the laws of nature reinforced the skepticism about witches' casting harmful spells.

Even religious leaders who accepted the supernatural dimension contributed to secularism as they "disenchanted" the natural world. Christian teaching once again rejected the reality of magic. The original and traditional Christian attitude toward the supernatural reasserted itself: beliefs in fairies, spirits, charms, and spells were mere superstitious nonsense. Only God's miraculous participation in creation mattered, while the Devil and demons played a confined role within the supernatural realm. By doing this, Christian leaders reduced the conflict with science and acknowledged the success of empirical experimentation. Within the growing secularism, faith largely defended Christianity's essentials, of which witches had never been part.

Second, the enlightened despots and parliamentarians reformed legal systems throughout Europe. These reforms protected the rights of the accused through more careful methods of legal procedure. Rules of evidence in particular began to work against the fantastic confessions of witches. Jurists dropped the concept of *crimen exceptum* that had allowed authorities to violate legal procedures. Slander laws also developed, which, like the old *lex talionis*, discouraged unfounded accusations. And since all accusations of witchcraft causing actual harm were by definition unfounded, the number of cases declined. The cessation of judicial torture surely hindered witch panics. Humanitarianism, or treating other people decently, worked against torture, merely on the principle that one would not want such infliction of pain done to any human being. The witch hunts ended as legal procedures, political, social, and economic changes shifted leaders' interests and abilities to carry out hunts.

Enlightened criticisms of abusive government culminated in the French Revolution, beginning in 1789. By 1800, Napoleon's French armies and the British navy were squabbling over political and ideological power in Europe and around the world. When the guns ceased firing in 1815, the European witch hunts were no more. From the Ural Mountains of Russia, through Europe, to the new states in North and South America across the Atlantic, witch hunting by governments had ceased. Historians and intellectuals began to forget about what had happened, partly out of embarrassment, partly from lack of interest.

Although the Dark Ages had allegedly ended around 1400, witch-hunting cast its shadow over European affairs for the following four hundred years. During those centuries, people were convinced they were doing God's work by accusing, torturing, and punishing alleged witches. The persecution of people for a manifestly impossible crime was laid to rest after 1800. The following chapters bring those dark pursuits back into the daylight.

NOTES

1. "Is there such a thing as an act of harmful magic?" and "Is it a heresy to maintain that workers of harmful magic exist?" [Heinrich Institoris], *The Malleus Maleficarum*, trans. and ed. P. G. Maxwell-Stuart (Manchester and New York: Manchester University Press, 2007), 41, 49; see also Chapter 3.

2. "Judgment on the Witch Walpurga Hausmännin," in *European Witchcraft*, ed. E. William Monter, Major Issues in History (New York: John Wiley & Sons, 1969), 79.

3. Daniel Ogden, ed. *Magic, Witchcraft, and Ghosts in the Greek and Roman World: A Sourcebook* (Oxford: Oxford University Press, 2002), quoting Hadrian of Tyre, 295.

4. Apuleius, *The Defense*, part 2, chap. 26, trans. H. E. Butler, *The Internet Classics Archive* (2000), available at http://classics.mit.edu/Apuleius/apol.2.2.html (accessed 4 December 2008).

5. Minucius Felix, *Octavius*, chap. ix, trans. Robert Ernest Wallis, *Christian Classics Ethereal Library* (2005) available at http://www.ccel.org/ccel/schaff/anf04.iv.iii.ix.html (accessed 4 December 2008).

6. Saint Augustine, *The City of God*, trans. Marcus Dods, George Wilson, and J. J. Smith (New York: The Modern Library, 1950), Book X, chap. 11, 315.

CHAPTER 2

Medieval Origins of the Witch Hunts

The Europe that would carry out the witch hunts formed during the Middle Ages, a period lasting roughly a thousand years following the fall of the western half of the Roman Empire. During this time, various peoples and states slowly rebuilt in western Europe the civilization that had almost perished with the fall of the Roman Empire. In the fifth and sixth centuries, the Germanic conquerors of that empire staked claims to different sections of its territory, founding smaller, fragile, and quarrelling kingdoms. In the eighth century, the Carolingian dynasty, especially under the emperor Charlemagne (r. 768–814), briefly succeeded in consolidating power over the heartland of Europe, aiming to restore Rome's lost might. Charlemagne conquered many German neighbors, forcing them to give up their paganism and convert to Christianity. Even Charlemagne, though, could not control the various Angles, Saxons, and others in the kingdoms of England. Nor was he able to take the Iberian Peninsula back from the Muslims who had conquered it in the previous century.

Charlemagne's dream of a united Christian Europe, then, shattered after his death, with many smaller states that would fight with each other for the next thousand years. The Holy Roman Empire and France fought over the remains of Charlemagne's realm, while England, Scotland, and Ireland struggled over supremacy in the British Isles. The Vikings separated into the kingdoms of Denmark, Norway, and Sweden, while Portugal and Spain finally drove the Muslims out of the Iberian Peninsula as the Middle Ages came to a close. These were the states that would carry out the witch hunts after 1400.

CHRISTENDOM

Although divided into various political states, the religion of Christianity united all these peoples into a community called "Christendom." The cultural unity compelled by Christianity resulted in the last pagans in and around

Europe either being killed or converted by the thirteenth century. Christian authorities insisted on a monopoly of belief, except for a few Jews and even fewer Muslims who were allowed to live within the boundaries of Christendom.

Christianity did not inevitably lead to witch-hunting, however. The split in Christianity during the height of the Middle Ages shows why not. In western Europe, the Bishop of Rome, called the pope, slowly gained administrative and spiritual dominance over the Christian Church. By the eleventh century, the Christians of the Eastern Roman, or Byzantine Empire, objected enough to this papal centralization to accept a schism, or split, from their Christian brethren in the West. The two branches of Christians, the Catholic in the West and the Orthodox in the East, still shared many similar beliefs and practices. One of the differences concerned witchcraft. Orthodox theologians never developed much interest in demonology, the study of demons, and strixology, the study of witches and witchcraft. For them, Christian faith did not need a fear of hostile supernatural agents. Consequently, few hunts took place in Orthodox Christian realms in southeastern Europe.

In Christendom of the rest of Europe, however, theologians increasingly argued about the reality of demons. By the end of the Middle Ages, the inheritance of pagan ideas from Greece and Rome, a rise of both minor and major heresies, and the growing concern about demons united to provide a religious platform on which to build a gallows for witches. When political regimes followed the Churchmen's fears, even more "witches" suffered. A history of the Middle Ages shows the intensifying entanglement of magical thinking and political power, which produced the European witch hunts.

MEDIEVAL BELIEFS AND THE SUPERNATURAL

The Christian Church was the only significant institution to survive the fall of Rome in the West. The fall of Rome meant the collapse of cities and a return to rural life. The vast majority of the population were peasants, workers of the land. Most people lived close to the animals and plants on which their food and lives depended. In small towns or villages, people lived according to the rhythms of nature, rising with the cock crow, lying down to sleep with the setting sun. The normal sounds, even in small towns, were the voices of people, the grunts and snorts of animals, and the bangs and squeaks of the few simple machines, such as the hammer of the blacksmith or the rush of water over the water mill. A small minority ruled, from emperors, kings, dukes, and counts, down to barons and knights. These nobles wielded most of the power and enjoyed most of the wealth.

Another even smaller minority, the clergy, held the first rank of honor. The secular, or worldly, clerics were the bishops and priests, all of them men. Each bishop supervised a large district called a diocese, bishopric, or see. Priests served their bishops in the cathedral churches and other parish churches in towns and villages. Other clergy submitted to special rules of monasticism. Female monastics, called nuns, lived in nunneries, led by an abbess, whereas males, called monks, resided in monasteries, led by an abbot. The regulations of these cloisters meant that monastic clergy held no personal property, ate and slept in common halls, and worked at praying, studying, and holding religious services.

MEDIEVAL CHRISTIANITY

The Middle Ages have often been called the Age of Faith, as well as the Age of Superstition, depending on the labeler's attitude toward religion. Both attitudes are exaggerations. Medieval people probably were neither more nor less faithful or superstitious than people in many times or places in the past. Nonetheless, the Christian Church allowed no other answers to supernatural questions than its own approved ones, no worship except in churches and shrines it controlled, and no devotion to divine beings other than the Holy Trinity.

People today imagine the European Middle Ages to have been full of magic and witchcraft. Certainly a belief in an enchanted world permeated cultural thought then, far more than it does now. Both ancient and medieval people looked for and accepted wonders and miracles regularly. Only after 1400, though, did Europeans worry much about witches.

The primary concern for Christians always remained what happened after death. The work of all clergy aimed to help everyone toward eternal salvation in heaven, especially by providing sacraments such as confession and the Eucharist. Everyone feared going to Hell when they died. Hell gained the image of eternal suffering, either in flames that did not consume, or ice that burned. Some supernatural beings, such as the Devil and his demons, were working hard to seduce and lure people to abandon Jesus and embrace evil. Many medieval people feared the night, forests, and mountains as the abodes of dangerous supernatural creatures who wished them harm.

One source of aid for Christians were the saints, who provided access to miraculous, divine action. In life, they had been holy men and women. In death their remains, or relics, worked divine wonders. These relics might be actual pieces of flesh, bone, and hair, or articles associated with the saint, such as scraps of clothing. Medieval people prayed to the saints, hoping the saints would, in turn, pray for their souls and perhaps change the present through a miracle. Relics would protect against demons while prayers, the sign of the cross, or amulets with relics offered protection against evil. The *agnus dei*, a wax amulet with the symbol of the Lamb of God made from remnants of paschal candles blessed by the pope, became a commonly adopted protector. To an outside observer, these beliefs seem like magic. Christian theologians disagreed, however, claiming that saints and blessed objects operated according to God's benevolence. They may have been supernatural, but they were not magical, as the Church defined it.

It is difficult for historians today to evaluate how much medieval people really believed in magical or miraculous manipulation of the supernatural. Undoubtedly, superstitious attitudes drawn from Greco-Roman and Germanic paganism continued in Christian society. Even today, pagan views can be seen in Christian adaptations (Christmas trees and the Easter bunny) or popular preservations (solstice and harvest festivals). Few historians, however, maintain that pagan worship continued much past the sixth or seventh centuries in areas that had been Christianized under Roman rule.

Before and after that date, though, wise-men and wise-women claimed to perform minor magic in healing, divination, and love spells in many communities. The lack of medical or scientific knowledge meant that society often accepted, even respected, such cunning-folk. They thought of themselves as perfectly Christian, although blessed with special powers of spiritual healing or preternatural sight. For most of the Middle Ages, though, neither the Church nor the State devoted much effort to suppressing them.

Legends and tall tales further nourished concepts of magic and witchcraft in medieval popular imagination. *The Golden Legend*, a story collection of saints' lives, portrays a number of holy men and women defeating demons. The power of Christ and his saints easily triumphed over the tricks of devils, sometimes with as little effort as making a sign of the cross. St. Germanus exposed demons who visited other people's homes disguised as their sleeping neighbors. The legend of Theophilus described a disappointed Sicilian priest who sought help from a Jewish magician who, in turn, sent Theophilus to the Devil. Theophilus signed a pact that gave him wealth and influence, until the demons came to carry him to hell. Only intercession by the Blessed Virgin Mary rescued him. While these moral set pieces often sound like the fictitious fairy tales of today, some people sincerely believed in them through the Middle Ages. They figured in points of sermons, subjects of church sculptures and stained glass windows, and characters in mystery plays. Little evidence, though, shows people fearing the Devil in their day-to-day lives.

Few reliable reports survive of actual, nonfictional interaction with witchcraft or diabolic intervention. Most stories are second-hand hearsay, clearly urban legends of their time. Guibert of Nogent, an abbot of the early twelfth century, provides a few personal interactions with the supernatural. First, his parent's marriage allegedly remained unconsummated for a time because of spells cast by an evil stepmother. He concedes though, that imagination may have exaggerated any actual supernatural power to that supposed magic. Guibert's mother even claimed that she was attacked by an incubus while his father was a prisoner at war. "In the dead of a dark night ... the Devil, whose custom it is to attack those who are weakened by grief, the Adversary himself, appeared all of a sudden and lay upon her, crushing her with his tremendous weight until she was almost dead."[1] Only her cry for help to the Blessed Virgin Mary saved her. Guibert also reported later witnessing two exorcisms.

THE CANON EPISCOPI

The clergy acknowledged that magic was part of the perception of the natural world, yet good Christians were to avoid it. The Church distinguished between acceptable miracles and sinful magic. People were not to defend themselves from perceived magical danger by magical means or submit to supernatural temptations. Sermons, church laws (canons), theological treatises, and penitential books all condemned magic, sorcery, and witchcraft from the early days of the Church. Those who were caught or confessed to such sins might be punished with severe penance, such as fasting on bread and water or undertaking a difficult pilgrimage. The key question became whether practicing magic was sinful either because it meant cooperation with supernatural enemies or being distracted from proper veneration of the miraculous Christian story.

That question appeared to be answered in the most important medieval law concerning witchcraft, the so-called *Canon Episcopi*, or "Bishops Law" in Latin. The oldest version of this law survives in a pastoral-care manual for bishops written by Regino, the abbot of the monastery of Prüm in western Germany around AD 900. Regino had adapted it from a slightly earlier Carolingian capitulary, but tradition dated its origins to the fourth-century Council of Ancyra (or Ankara in modern Turkey).

The *Canon Episcopi* asked that bishops take care, through preaching, that people not believe in such things as riding through the night with the pagan goddess Diana. Those who did accept such, the law declared, had been seduced by the Devil in dreams and visions into old pagan errors. Hence, according to this law, witchcraft and magic had no effective reality. Demonic activity happened only in people's imaginations and dreams, although those perceptions might be caused by real demons. The danger to salvation was not witches, but superstitious belief in magic.

Although its focus is narrow, the *Canon Episcopi* came to be the foundation of Church teaching that there were no actual night rides or even witches. Later canonists repeatedly adapted the *Canon Episcopi* into canon law collections with exactly this interpretation. In the ninth and tenth centuries, later collectors of law, such as Rather of Liège and Burchard of Worms, added to the text of the *Canon Episcopi*. In 1140, Gratian's *Concordantia* ("Concordance of Discordant Canons"), often called the *Decretum*, systematically summed up the laws of the Western Church. He described the *Canon Episcopi* as defining the falsehood of witch practices. Gratian's inclusion and explanation of the *Canon Episcopi* ensured that witches were not a serious concern among most medieval clergy. They were to condemn belief in magic and discourage superstitious attitudes.

Hence, Church leaders and thinkers often expressed skepticism that magic was anything more than a delusion sent by the Devil to turn people from proper Church teachings. Pope Gregory VII wrote in 1080 to the king of Denmark, telling him not to blame the Devil for bad weather. In the twelfth century, the theologian John of Salisbury noted that it was erroneous to believe in the night ride of witches and blood-sucking *lamiae*.

Meanwhile, the laws of early political states, the Germanic kingdoms, had long since prohibited all traffic with magic. The Christian leaders of both church and state agreed on banning supernatural belief and forbidding paganism. Leaders identified pagan religion with magic and false demons, as had been done since the Hebrews in ancient Palestine and Egypt. The state's punishments tended to be more serious than the Church's penance, because of magic's association with poisoning and murder. Civil courts punished the guilty with large fines of money, enslavement, banishment, flogging, or even death. Many laws, though, displayed a certain skepticism, such as the Edict of Rothar from 643, which doubted that magic could cause someone to die from being eaten from the inside out.

Although laws against using magic appear regularly, trials against users of magic remained rare. The *lex talionis*, incorporated into many German law codes, may have prevented unfounded accusations. This principle allowed an accused who was found innocent to bring charges against the accuser for defamation or false incrimination. Because witchcraft was difficult to prove using normal court procedures, few people accused their neighbors of *maleficia* during the Middle Ages.

TRIALS BY ORDEAL

The means of proving crimes in the early Middle Ages would seem rather doubtful today. If guilt could not be confirmed by an eyewitness account or by a confession, medieval courts relied on either compurgation or ordeal. Compurgation meant that an accused found a prescribed number of witnesses (perhaps six or twelve) who would swear an oath to the good character of the accused. The compurgators were not providing evidence or an alibi, just testimony that the accused was not the kind of person to have committed the crime.

Ordeals were more complicated tests of pain to prove innocence. The ordeal of hot iron meant a hot iron bar must be carried a certain number of paces without being dropped. Of course, the hands would be burned, but after a set number of days, if the hands were healing properly, the accused was declared innocent. If the accused's wounds became infected, however, confirmation of guilt and punishment followed. Another common ordeal was that of cold water, also called "ducking" or "swimming" a suspect. Authorities would test suspects by putting them in a blessed body of water. Often the accused would be bound, right thumb to left toe, left thumb to right toe, in order to prevent swimming to stay afloat (see Illustration 8). If they sank, the "holy" water embraced them, and examiners should pull the innocents out before they drowned. If they floated, though, the divine rejected them. They might be executed on the spot, or, more commonly, turned over for trial.

Both compurgation and ordeal were believed to take place under the benefi-
cent care of God, who would ensure that the guilty would be punished and the
innocent freed. Such trials accepted a degree of the miraculous. Quite common
until the twelfth century, they went into decline after improved legal procedures reestablished themselves in western Europe at that time. The cold water
ordeal, however, would rise again during the witch hunts.

So, both the ecclesiastical and the civil courts in the medieval West condemned magical activity. Both punished it through their court systems as either
criminal or spiritual deviance. Yet, only a few legal cases scattered through the
Middle Ages report people using harmful magic. In England in 972, a widow
was executed by drowning for making a doll-image of a man to work him
harm. In France in 1028, an unnamed woman allegedly made Count William
of Aquitaine ill through image magic. A trial by ordeal between champions of
two parties ended with the accused witch's champion failing, vomiting up
charms he had been given by other enchanters. Even after torture, the woman
refused to confess, so Count William spared her life. In Cologne in 1074, a
mob killed a woman whom they believed had driven men mad. Citing these
cases makes them seem more prominent than they actually were. They were
sensational partly because of their extreme rarity.

THE RISE OF MEDIEVAL HERESIES

Although the crime of witchcraft remained rare before 1400, the offense of
heresy became increasingly common. The first new heresies appeared in the
eleventh century, multiplied in the twelfth century, and became a major crisis
by the thirteenth century. Many historians explain the rise of the heresies by
contrasting Christianity's emphasis on a simple life with the rising standard of
living among the upper classes in towns. The growth of towns created a new
class of burghers or townspeople that did not quite fit into the earlier threefold
division of clergy, knights, and peasants. As precursors of the modern middle
class, burghers made their living from trade, finance, and manufacturing, soon
competing with the nobles and clergy for wealth, power, and prestige in medieval society.

Prosperity further introduced social transformation and instability in values
of belief. People were conflicted about how to reconcile Jesus's criticisms of
wealth with their desire for comforts. Growing wealth also flowed into the cof-
fers of the Church, although some Christians thought a wealthy clergy contradicted Christ's teachings. This tension between prosperity and poverty
provoked new heresies for the Christian Church.

Christianity had faced heresies before. A heresy happened when some
believers either exaggerated one aspect of faith at the expense of the whole system or contradicted a key teaching. Because "orthodoxy" was the standard of
belief set by religious authorities, a heresy defied established order. At the start
of any argument about belief, however, it was often unclear which side would

wind up as orthodox and which as heretical. Once the structures of discipline had decided the orthodox position, though, authorities marginalized and eliminated heretics as best they could. In Christian society, political authorities cooperated with ecclesiastical authorities in criminalizing, persecuting, and punishing heretics. This joint persecution had especially taken place as Christianity defined itself in the fourth through sixth centuries in fights over the Trinity. The orthodox victory over Gnostics and others was so complete that no significant religious persecution by Christians took place for centuries. The resurgence of new and old heresies after the twelfth century and the failure to fully defeat those heretics paved the way for later witch hunts. The reality of heresy during the High Middle Ages gave way to the fantasy of witchcraft at the end of the Middle Ages.

The medieval heresies reacted against worldly wealth by promoting a more ascetic lifestyle as a mark of holiness. A movement called *apostolic poverty* followed from the belief that Jesus and his original apostles lived as poor people, without many possessions. For too many Christians, the wealthy and worldly Church failed to provide enough exemplary clergy and inspirational worship. Apostolic poverty's medieval adherents encouraged clergy to live in purity and simplicity, with few possessions. Most ecclesiastical and secular authorities quickly categorized those who supported these views as heretics.

Waldensians

The first organized group of heretics clustered around Peter Waldo or Valdes (d. 1217). Valdes had been a merchant in Lyons in the south of France, but, following a religious conversion, gave up his wealth and preached a life of poverty and simplicity. He organized the "Poor Men of Lyons" around these ideas. His local bishop and the pope refused to recognize Valdes as legitimate and excommunicated him. Excommunication barred someone from receiving the Sacraments, such as Baptism and the Eucharist, or Christian burial. Excommunication also removed legal protections, making someone literally an "outlaw." Hence, the secular rulers could arrest and punish excommunicated individuals. Nevertheless, Valdes and his followers refused to obey the religious and secular authorities. The Waldensians or *Vaudois* set up their own churches and their own system of worship, some of which have survived to today.

Dualism of the Cathars

Another heresy, related to the Waldensians, might actually be better described as a competing religion. This new religion believed in a form of dualism, which conceived of the universe as caught in battle between forces of good and light against those of evil and darkness. Dualism had been a strong faith in ancient Persia, especially as preached by Zoraster or Zarathustra, who founded the dualist religion of Manicheism. The Gnostic heretics who had opposed and sought to change Christianity in its first few centuries had been dualists. A new dualism of the Bogomils had just arisen in the Balkans (perhaps named after the Bulgarians).

Superficially, the battle of light and darkness sounds similar to the ongoing struggle between Christ and Satan over souls described in Christianity, and, indeed, dualism in Europe adopted much from Christian terminology. But the Christian world view declares that the victory of God is certain. Satan can only succeed in as much as God permits the Devil some freedom, and one day even that will be taken away. Dualists see the struggle as more even, perhaps with the outcome at the end of time uncertain.

The Dualists in Christendom were particularly successful and numerous in northern Italy and the south of France, but gained scattered pockets of believers across Europe. Their stronghold was in Languedoc, in southern France. Orthodox clergy called them Albigensians (after the southern French town of Albi) or Cathars (probably from the "religion of pure"). Since these pure ones tried to live more righteously than the Christian priests, bishops, and popes, they built no structure of power and had no taxation. Cathar leaders criticized the propertied Catholic Church and its corrupt hierarchy as having been created by the Devil. From the heretic point of view, the Devil possessed orthodox Catholics.

The Mendicants

The Catholic Church took proactive steps to counter these separatist tendencies, first by establishing new orthodox religious orders dedicated to poverty and preaching. Francis of Assisi (b. 1181–d. 1226), a younger contemporary of Peter Waldo, founded the Brothers Minor, or Franciscans, who preached a message of simplicity and love. The son of a rich merchant, Francis renounced his fineries and dressed in a simple tunic. Dominic Guzman (b. 1170–d. 1221) simultaneously founded another religious order, the Dominicans or Order of Preachers, who excelled in the ministry of teaching. These orders did not confine themselves within monasteries but worked among the people of the newly growing cities. They became the Mendicant Orders, because they originally intended to support themselves through collecting alms, rather than through farming, as most other monks did. Founded partially to fight heresy, they would one day participate in the witch hunts.

Medieval Jewry

Also caught in the net of hostility toward heretics were Jews, Muslims, and other outsiders such as homosexuals and lepers. Official hostility gradually declined against these groups, except, perhaps, the Jews. Jews offered an awkward target, since Judaism had given birth to Christianity, and Church authorities had offered limited tolerance to them over the centuries. However, after the twelfth century, Christians regularly persecuted Jews.

The frequent identification of Jews with heretics demonstrated their danger-
ously marginal status. Christians twisted Jewish terminology, the synagogue
and sabbath, to use against the Cathars. In the language about heresy both *synagogue* and *Sabbath* (in this text shortened to synagog and sabbat) meant a
secret meeting attended by heretics. Christians regularly accused Jews of poisoning wells and conducting ritual murders, such as draining children's blood
to use in blasphemous rituals. Many stories, such as that of the priest Theophilus mentioned above, associated Jews strongly with sorcery.

In some areas anti-Semitism declined simply because there were no more Jews
to hate. England and France had expelled the Jews from their countries before
1400, while Spain and Portugal followed before 1500. Jews were never numerous
in Scandinavia. Italian territories and eastern Europe absorbed great numbers, as
did Muslim-controlled realms. Within Europe, Christians often confined Jews to
ghettoes, restricting their residence to districts of towns usually locked up at
night. Pogroms, or persecution of Jews through killing and destroying of property, began in the late Middle Ages and lasted in eastern Europe well past the age
of the witch hunts. The very existence of Jews incensed many Europeans, leading
eventually to the Nazi's genocidal Final Solution, which attempted to exterminate
Jews once and for all during World War II.

In many senses, anti-Semitism was a true "witch hunt," in that Jews did not
actually endanger Christian society. The imaginary threats they posed, especially when connected to fears of magic, allowed Christians to justify discrimination and elimination of these nominal enemies. Unlike witches, however,
Jews and heretics actually existed. If European society required cultural and
religious uniformity, the diversity represented by Jews and by heretics under-
standably, if cruelly, explained their persecution. Witch hunts, however, lacked
such justification. A concoction of magic, heresy, and diabolism was brewing a
dangerous obsession about magical powers that did not exist.

HERETICS AND THE DEVIL

One medieval explanation for the sudden rise in heretics was to blame the
Devil. The Christian hierarchy denounced heretics with the classic accusations
of secret meetings involving human sacrifice, cannibalism, and unnatural sex
orgies. Heretics allegedly worshiped the Devil, denying the true God. They
formed demonic pacts and worked harmful magic. Heretics were also promis-
cuous, indiscriminately choosing partners at their orgies, without regard to
social status, familial relationship, or gender. These fantastical accusations,
however, had only tortured confessions to support them. Just as the Romans
had once libeled the ancient Christians and druids, now medieval Christians
also charged the heretics with devil worship and inhuman crimes. Similar
charges would soon be made against witches.

Heresy quickly became associated with supernatural, even magical, properties. One of the first mentions of heresy took place in France in 1022. In the

town of Orléans, King Robert II "the Pious" of France tried a group of heretics who allegedly met in secret, conjured demons, held orgies, killed babies that were thereby conceived, and then burned their bodies into blasphemous food. To punish the heretics, the king had them burned alive in a cottage.

In another early example, Abbot Guibert of Nogent interviewed heretics in Soissons in the early twelfth century. He and his bishop were familiar enough with heresy to suspect that these heretics committed sexual sins in their secret meetings, where they also murdered and cannibalized babies. Unable to obtain confessions through questioning, they applied the ordeal of water as later applied to witches. The suspected heretics floated, proving their guilt. While higher authorities discussed proper punishment, a mob broke the accused heretics out of prison and burned them alive, earning Guibert's after-the-fact approval.

Other tales of witches and magic proliferated in the late twelfth and early thirteenth centuries by writers such as Walter Map, Gervase of Tilbury, and Cesarius of Heisterbach. Their tales have little documentary evidence to support them, being no more than second- and third-hand hearsay. Even if such diabolism was mere fantasy, heretics did threaten the established order.

The leaders of the Church dealt with the crisis of heresy through three main methods. First, the Mendicant Orders, as mentioned above, were established to minister to the common people through renewed ideals of poverty and preaching. The preaching friars set personal examples and dealt directly with the faithful. They converted heretics back to catholic orthodox Christianity and helped loyal Christians maintain their faith.

CRUSADES

The second means the Church used to combat heresy was the most extreme and most rarely used, the crusade. Crusades were "Holy War" in that their fighters were considered to be doing a good deed. The crusading ideology had been shaped by the Church by twisting the commandment "Thou shalt not kill" into a promise that those who killed Christ's enemies would win heavenly reward. Their battle cry, used to justify any atrocity, was *Deus vult!* ("God wills it!"). The popes began to encourage crusades during the eleventh century, as religious wars against Muslims started to be fought in Palestine, the Iberian peninsula, and along the Baltic Coast.

The crusading ideal became so important that it transformed both knights and monks, combining the two into religious military orders. The Knights Templars, founded in the early twelfth century, were the first. They lived by strict rules of religious discipline, lacking much personal property, eating and sleeping in common, and engaging in regular, organized prayer. But they were also knights trained to fight and kill in the name of the Church.

The external expansion of Christendom's borders through crusading was complemented by the Church's crusades against its internal enemies, the heretics. The most important of these crusades was that against the Cathars in

Languedoc from 1209 to 1244. The pope encouraged armies from the North of France to invade the South, granting permission to kill heretics at will and confiscate lands and possessions. The ruthlessness that ensued is characterized by the story of the town of Béziers. When the crusaders were about to attack the town, some of them worried that orthodox Catholics who lived there among the Cathar heretics might be killed by mistake. Their commander reportedly said, "God would know His own," so everyone was killed—God lifting good Catholics to heaven and damning bad heretics. The victorious French kings integrated the region under their royal authority in alliance with the ecclesiastical hierarchy.

THE INQUISITION

Since neither mendicants nor crusades eliminated all heretics, a third method came into play, the Inquisition. This method had been invented in ancient Rome, but disappeared when the Roman Empire and its laws fell to German invaders. The Germanic kingdoms originally relied only on oral tradition for their laws. As a result, the Roman court system, with its trained lawyers, collapsed. The subsequent medieval justice system used an accusatory process. A crime victim made accusations to a king or noble with access to a court. Throughout the early Middle Ages, however, those kings and their nobles lacked the finances or training to prove or disprove an accusation. Thus trials involved compurgation or ordeal, as described above.

Roman Law

By the twelfth century, though, Roman law codes began to be reintegrated into the legal jumble that had followed the destruction of Rome. Protolawyers were impressed with the organization and argumentation behind the Roman laws codified in the *Corpus Iuris Civilis*, the last great Roman law code, collected in the sixth century by Emperor Justinian. They reintroduced Roman methods, establishing law programs in both canon and civil laws to be taught in new universities founded by bishops in European cities such as Oxford, Cambridge, Paris, and Bologna. New romanized legal systems replaced germanized ones.

By the twelfth century, governments had become more stable and wealthier and began to investigate crime more conscientiously. The inquisition became the chief example of this approach. Instead of punishing criminals only after an accusation was lodged, the regime began actively to seek out criminals for arrest and punishment. In time, the formal inquisition also became the method of choice for hunting the heretics.

The Inquisition's Model

The ideal inquisition can be broken down into five phases. First, an official tribunal, a panel of inquisitors, would be commissioned for a specific district.

The Dominicans found particular success as officers of the inquisition. A pun tagged the Dominicans as the "hounds of God" (*domini canes*) who harried the heretics. The officials would come to a region, preach about the crime being investigated, and then ask the population to report individuals who had committed the crime of heresy. Denunciations were usually freely offered, but, if not, inquisitors might offer monetary incentives. Second, summons would be issued for suspects and witnesses who had been implicated by the denunciations. Third, the inquisitors would examine these witnesses and suspects. In the process, the suspects might be confined, perhaps chained in a jail cell, and allowed only bread and water. Inquisitors might torture them for information. In any case, the inquisitors took a deposition as evidence against the suspect or someone else. The ideal was to obtain a confession. Fourth was the trial, often quick and simple because a confession required no other proof. Throughout this procedure, the defendant had serious disadvantages. An accused had no right to legal representation, no right to keep silent so as not to self-incriminate, and no right to see or challenge evidence or bring defense witnesses. The *lex talionis*, shared by Roman law and Germanic laws, should have helped protect the innocent, but inquisitors tended to ignore that particular principle.

Finally, the tribunal rendered a verdict. If found innocent, which could and did happen, the accused would go free, although with no compensation for lost income, paid fees, bodily injury, or suffering. If found guilty, the inquisitors were most interested in repentance and reconciliation, bringing the heretic back into the forgiveness and embrace of the Church, to save the lost soul. If the convicted heretic would admit guilt, punishment might be light, no worse than a penance given during any routine sacrament of confession and reconciliation. Other punishments ranged from wearing a large yellow cross as a mark of shame to prison to being burnt alive. That extreme penalty was usually reserved for relapsed heretics, who admitted their errors and then returned to their erroneous ways.

Even a small inquisition involved large numbers of people from a community in supporting roles: secular authorities, local princes who gave permission, local bailiffs, sergeants, watchmen to arrest and escort suspects and victims; messengers and secretaries for information; jailers and torturers, family members, and servants. The inquisitors's control of the trial process made the accused easily vulnerable to conviction. Today we divide up judicial functions among investigation by the police, prosecution by the district attorney, supervision of the trial and sentencing by a judge, and decision of guilt or innocence by a jury. This diversity of participation helps to assure a fair chance to a defendant. In contrast, in the inquisitorial process, the inquisitors played all the roles. To offset this enormous weight of power, the official procedures had originally called for a high level of evidence to prove guilt, such as testimony by two solid witnesses. However, inquisitors often ignored or circumvented these requirements. Abuses of power naturally happened. Inquisitors might use poor translations into and out of Latin to twist the words of the accused into

guilt. There was no concept of innocent until proven guilty. Everyone was suspect. The guilty would be found.

The denunciations that started the inquisitorial process were another problem. Soliciting the local population for accusations often resulted in local
squabbles and feuds being elevated to the level of heresy. People would inform
on their neighbors because they had quarreled about a cow breaking a fence or
a dog killing a chicken. Accusations also targeted people who in general had a
poor reputation, called *infamia*. Members of the socially acceptable majority
might accuse infamous persons merely because of their unusual antisocial
behavior. Vulnerable outsiders ranged from well-connected bullies, to cranky
old spinsters, to traveling folk, who ranged from merchants to the destitute
homeless. Worst of all, hearsay and circumstantial evidence often opened the
door to torture, euphemistically called "putting to the question."

Torture

Putting to the question, like the recent term used by American officials,
"enhanced interrogation techniques," cloaked the pain inflicted during torture,
perhaps the most notorious horror associated with the inquisition. Gratian's
codification of canon law in 1140 had banned torture by the Church, but it
was being used again in less than a century. A number of circumstances
brought torture into play. Roman law, which had been rediscovered and
revived, accepted torture as part of criminal investigation (although ancient
Roman torture had usually been limited to slaves). The Romans had regular-
ized the process of the inquisition, which relied on confessions. Even more
important, Roman law discouraged using the traditional trial by ordeal in
courts. In 1215, the Fourth Lateran Council banned ordeals. Prescientific
courts then faced the challenge of finding clear proofs for crimes. Without witnesses, physical evidence rarely could be analyzed in an age without crime
scene investigators and forensic science. Without a way to investigate the facts
of the crime, confessions remained the best way to assign guilt. Torture forced
many to confess.

Unfortunately for justice, torture brings out many false confessions. Many
innocent people will say anything to stop the pain. Even techniques of questioning that do not inflict physical hurt can confuse an accused person into untrue
statements. A psychological bond develops between the interrogator and the
interrogated. The authority figure can apply alternating care and callousness,
sympathy and anger, respect and disappointment, to break down the suspects to
where they seek only to please. As psychologists know and studies of modern-
day police interrogations have shown, accused people can even build false memories out of lies and faked evidence provided by authorities, thereby convincing
themselves of their own guilt and making a false confession.

Even without torture, normal people suddenly thrust into the criminal
machinery, variously restrained, confined, isolated, intimidated, and surrounded

can break down and confess to things they did not do, in an attempt to restore normality. Other people who are slightly abnormal confess out of guilt for other crimes, out of desire to be famous or notorious, or out of disconnection from reality through mental illness. Older authority figures can intimidate young persons into confession. Medieval inquisitors did not bother with the many discrepancies and outright contradictions that appeared in confessions. The similarities were enough to focus on and prove a person's guilt. At the time, some legal theorists who conscientiously wanted to avoid wrongful conviction thought confession protected the accused. They actually asserted that false convictions did not happen because what people said under torture was always true. Sadly, that is not the case.

There were limits to and rules about torture, at least in theory. Various legal handbooks and torture manuals by canon and secular lawyers offered both uniformity and creativity. Questions should be standardized and not lead the accused. Officials, such as judges and secretaries were to observe and record the sessions. Certain people, such as pregnant women, children, or nobles were usually exempted. Every opportunity was to be afforded to the accused to confess, and thereby avoid torture. Church rules called for the intensity of pain to only gradually increase, usually through "degrees." A first degree might start with being prepared for a session, to the second degree with an instrument being laid on the person, and then to a third degree of actual pain. Or the degrees might range from least to worst instrument and method. No bloodshed or permanent damage was to be left on the accused. If someone withstood torture, they might gain a presumption of innocence.

Local court officials, however, often enjoyed wide leeway of interpretation, leading to frequent surpassing of "humane" restrictions and protections. Actual tortures varied by region and individual taste. Although victims were not supposed to suffer permanent damage, many devices if used as designed could not help but leave scars, inflict enduring harm, or kill. Torture was only to be applied once, but officials "repeated" or "continued" sessions that extended for days, weeks, and even months. The accused were to repeat their confessions without torture in open court, but authorities often held the threat of renewed torture to guarantee that the confessions stuck. Some officials insisted on torture to use pain to break the power of the Devil over his minion. Other magistrates thought that those who withstood torture proved their guilt, being granted the fortitude by Satan. Shedding tears, or not, might be interpreted as evidence of guilt or innocence, depending on the time and place. The legal notion of the *crimen exceptum*, an exceptional and most dangerous crime, excused the consciences of court officials to do anything necessary to protect the public welfare. Heresy was one such crime; witchcraft would be later.

Torture is not mere questioning, but the infliction of pain either to get answers or to punish. Human creativity in cruelty has fashioned many torture devices and practices sometimes described and illustrated in the law books of those times. Many tortures were accomplished with simple machines and equipment. Crushing tortures used twisting ropes or screws to cut off circulation. Thumbscrews and legscrews worked like any vice, the workshop tool that clamps or holds an object. The torturer's screws had grips, often lined with metal bumps or spikes, that fit around the appropriate limb: fingers, arms, or shins. The torturer then slowly tightened the screw, squeezing the flesh. Even a light amount of pressure could bring excruciating pain. Although a conscientious torturer would not cause bleeding in the tissues or breaking of bones, many often broke the rules and brought about lasting damage.

Other tortures stretched the body beyond normal limits. Because of its easy availability, the strappado remained one of the most popular torture devices through the periods of the inquisition for heresy and the witch hunts. The strappado was essentially a pulley. A torturer tied a victim's arms behind his back and then bound the wrists to the rope of a pulley on which he hoisted the victim. A simple hoisting caused severe pain without any lasting damage. The examiner could add extra pain by hanging blocks from the victim's feet or jerking on the pulley to make the victim bounce (see Illustration 12). Dislocation of the shoulders, elbows, and wrists by extreme application, could permanently maim, however. Similar effects could be done simply on a ladder or using the infamous rack.

A significant number of tortures by their nature meant permanent disfigurement and should, therefore, have been avoided. Nevertheless, authorities rationalized their way around cruelty because of their belief in the seriousness of the situation, whether with heretics or witches. Beating with cats-o-nine-tails, rods, or switches; burning with oil, water, irons, or fire; and pulling out hair or toe- and fingernails, certainly left scars, if not worse. Other tortures might be justified by merely imposing momentary discomfort. Examiners applied such temporary pain with expanding mechanical "pears" in bodily orifices; force-feeding food or water; withdrawing nourishment; imposing body positions as standing, crouching, kneeling, and holding arms outstretched; or putting the prisoner in an environment that was too hot, too cold, or filthy. The individual's body could suffer when the eternal soul and the common good of society was at stake.

Although people questioned under torture might be innocent, another aspect of torture was punishment for those found guilty in a court of law. Justice demanded, they thought, that a guilty person suffer for committing a crime. The death penalty was very common for many crimes, not only for heretics and witches. The execution was to be as painful and showy as possible, hence the common use of burning at the stake. The fortunate ones would be strangled first. Otherwise death came slowly as the flames destroyed tissues, and they were suffocated by the smoke. Hanging by strangulation was also common, the body being burned afterward to purify the "unclean" remains of a criminal. Other vicious and common methods of execution, from boiling in water, impaling, or breaking on the wheel, were used less often with heretics and witches. For convicted witches, nonlethal, yet painful, penalties included cutting off body parts, branding, whipping, beating, imprisoning, fining, and withholding food or water.

Throughout the medieval and early modern periods many punishments and executions were public rituals, attended by crowds, and formalized with parades, prayers, and speeches by the sentencing officials and the condemned. Such formalities maintained order during an act of violence, the horrible execution, forbidden to individuals yet sanctioned here by the state. Everyone needed to know what crimes had been committed and the just deserts received by the guilty.

THE FIRST INQUISITIONS FOR HERETICS

The inquisitorial process formally began when Pope Gregory IX in 1231 issued *Excommunicamus et anathematisamus* ("We Excommunicate and We Curse"). This papal bull excommunicated all heretics and turned them over to the "secular arm" or political authorities for actual punishment, since Church ministers were not supposed to harm anyone physically, but rather were to care for people's souls. The interesting euphemism for this handing over to punishment was "relaxation." Punishments included life imprisonment, excluding heirs (children and grandchildren) from clerical benefices, exhuming one's corpse, and demolishing homes. Pope Gregory IX sent inquisitors Stephen of Bourbon to France and Conrad von Marburg to Germany.

Conrad is partly famous as the confessor of St. Elizabeth of Hungary, whom he had flogged regularly, to help spiritual growth. Conrad began an inquisition against heretics in Germany. He was soon carried away with fanaticism and denounced numerous people. His investigation uncovered rituals where worshipers kissed a supernatural pale man or the rear of a cat in place of the traditional kiss of peace. Conrad even had the powerful Count of Sayn tried for heresy, but, not surprisingly, the court found that powerful noble innocent. Shortly after, in 1233, Conrad was assassinated. He had become so hated, that the Germans declined to avenge his murder.

Conrad's reports reveal that heresy had begun to be associated with magic and devil worship. Pope Gregory IX strengthened this connection two years after *Excommunicamus et anathematisamus* with his document *Vox in Rama* ("Voice in Rama"). It was based on credulous reports Gregory had received from Conrad of Marburg. Gregory warned the Archbishop of Mainz and the Bishop of Hildesheim about reports of the Devil and magic. In lurid detail about their worship of Lucifer, he described the cold kiss of the Devil, who took the form of a toad (perhaps the size of a duck or even an oven), a pale, thin man, or a cat (the size of a dog). Lights went out, and heretics joined in a depraved orgy. The heretics blasphemed the sacred Host by throwing it into privies. These activities surpassed any previous heretical accusation and fed an irrational fear of the Devil.

Soon after this, Pope Alexander IV worried that sorcery might distract his inquisitors from crushing true theological heresy. But under pressure, in 1258

Pope Alexander issued *Quod super nonnullis* ("Since about Several"), which allowed inquisitors to prosecute sorcery where it was obviously a manifestation of heresy. This opened a loophole that allowed inquisitors to investigate witches unchecked. Sorcery was already a crime in most countries, but the presence of an inquisition practically guaranteed a higher rate of conviction.

Some Waldensians in their Alpine valleys survived the onslaught. They were much more difficult to reach, had fewer lands to seize than the Cathars, and worshipped closer to standard Christianity. Their ongoing existence, though, fed into the witch hunts. Some later witch hunters reasoned that the Waldensian heretics had converted into witches. Indeed, in French a common term for a witch was *Valdensis* or *Vaudois*, which derived from Waldensians.

As for the Cathars, the Christian crusade against them had been very successful, eliminating most within the region, although not all. So the Church now applied the inquisition, drawing in other heretics as well as eliminating the last few Cathars. One focus of inquisitors in the early fourteenth century was the small village of Montaillou just north of the Pyrenees. One day in 1308, the inquisition rounded up the entire adult population for questioning. Another inquisition was conducted there from 1318 to 1325. The eager inquisitor for this investigation was the local bishop, Jacques Fournier, who later would become Pope Benedict XII (r. 1334–1342).

The careful record of this inquisition detailed widespread Cathar and Waldensian beliefs: strong belief in the power of the Devil, a fear of witchcraft, and some evidence of folk magic, such as casting simple spells. The local noble Béatrice de Planissoles had learned from a converted Jewess how to use the first menstrual blood of her daughters, umbilical cords, and nail clippings to cast spells of love, luck, or protection. In spite of this, her most serious crime was heresy. Of the more than one hundred people accused in Montaillou, only five were burned at the stake for the crime of heresy. Later, Pope Benedict XII would admonish an inquisitor to use discretion in getting at the truth in cases of women allegedly making diabolic pacts. If guilty, the women should be punished, but with penance and "in a spirit of mercy, in as much as their contrition merits and you acknowledge their return to a rational frame of mind."[2] Eagerness to root out the heresy of magic with torture and flame had not yet taken hold.

The Dominican priest Bernard Gui was perhaps the most famous inquisitor. Gui was active as inquisitor in Toulouse from 1307 to 1324, rising to be Bishop of Túy. He himself reported he had burned 548 people and had ordered eighty-eight dead bodies dug up so he could properly punish the corpses of the heretics. Some of his victims, though, only had to wear the penitential shirt with yellow crosses as punishment. In 1323, Gui finished a manual to guide other inquisitors: *Practica inquisitionis haereticae pravitatis* ("Practical Tips for the Inquisition of Heretical Depravity"). His main efforts were against Cathars, but he also targeted Jews and witches. His list of possible criminal actions for those suspected of sorcery and summoning of demons included the following:

children or infants put under a spell or released from one; lost or damned souls; thieves ...; quarrels or reconciliation between spouses; making barren women fertile; things given to eat, hairs, nails and so on; foretelling future events; female spirits whom they call Good People who go about, they say, by night; enchantments and conjurations using songs, fruit, plants ...; any superstition, irreverence or offence connected with the sacraments of the Church ...; making leaden images....[3]

In his manual, Gui offered useful advice on procuring information about these crimes. He advocated extending supervision, confinement, and even torture of suspected heretics over a period of several years.

Other heresies continued to spring up, often connected to one another. The *Fraticelli*, or Brethren, in northern Italy focused on apostolic poverty. In the thirteenth and fourteenth centuries in Germany and Austria, a group called Luciferians may have actually worshiped the Devil as their God, although they were more likely Waldensians whose views were grossly twisted by their accusers. Supposedly, grasshoppers landing on their mouths spurred their sexual debauchery. Authorities burned more than thirty in lower Austria in 1315. In England, John Wycliff inspired the Lollards, another heretical group. Lollardy traveled to Bohemia, where it stimulated an enduring heretical movement promulgated by Jan Hus, a professor. The Catholic authorities invited Hus to the Council of Constance to discuss his views but instead arrested him and burned him at the stake in 1415. His followers, the Hussites, raised rebellion back home in Bohemia, defying both king and bishops. Claiming to have the true faith, even Hussites turned on other heretics, such as the group called Adamites. Named after the first human in the Bible, Adamites allegedly went around nude and practiced sexual abandonment until the Hussites wiped them out by slaughter and burning. Many groups felt the need to defend the boundaries of their orthodoxy against heretics.

THE HERESY OF THE KNIGHTS TEMPLAR

One unusual victim of the inquisition methodology was the religious order of the Knights Templar. Templars were monk-knights who combined religious discipline with military activity to fight in crusades. The Templars had lost their main crusading area of Palestine after the Muslims reconquered it in 1291, but had persevered and reestablished their organization throughout Europe. They claimed to raise support for more crusading efforts, often through the lucrative transaction of making loans.

One important noble who needed revenue was King Philip IV of France (r. 1285–1314), since he was preparing for war with England. Looking for a new source of income, Philip began his own investigations of sorcerers, usurers, and Jews. His attempt to tax the Church lands provoked a serious fight with Pope Boniface VIII (r. 1294–1303), who insisted that papal permission was needed to tax the Church in France. Philip orchestrated his clergy and laity to declare the pope deposed, accusing him of being a sorcerer with a familiar or demon in animal form. Philip's agents even tried to kidnap the pope. Although the kidnapping failed, Pope Boniface died soon after. Philip was not quite finished with him, however. Philip put the late pope on trial for being a sorcerer who worked with a familiar, conspired with the Devil, and employed various diviners and soothsayers. Although the Church ignored the inevitable guilty verdict, Philip's campaign helped to discredit papal authority in France and spread fears of magic.

Soon afterward, King Philip IV began to see the Knights Templar as a danger. Whether his fears were legitimate or based on his desire to exploit their wealth, his investigation exposed strange doings in Templar secret rituals. In initiation rites, members reportedly denied Christ; spat on the cross; presented themselves naked to be kissed by the Master on the base of the spine, stomach and face; and finally submitted to sexual acts. The new pope, Clement V, discussed Philip's investigation with the Templar Grand Master Jacques de Molay, who found the charges ridiculous and hoped a papal investigation would clear the Templars. But the papacy and Clement had been relocated from Rome to the city of Avignon, right on France's border. During this so-called Babylonian Captivity, the papacy depended on French support between 1309 and 1377. Thus, as the papacy hesitated, Philip seized the initiative. Royal authorities arrested several thousand Templars all over France during the night of October 13, 1307. The raid was so efficient that only thirteen Templars managed to escape.

Subsequent inquisitorial examinations by French bishops using torture extracted more strange tales that connected the Templars to witchcraft and demons. Most bizarre were tales of Templars' worshiping a strange idol of a bearded man. This would have amounted to a serious crime of heresy. Many of the accused monk-knights confessed to crimes, starting with the spitting, then the kissing, to the sodomy, finally, to the heresy. Dozens died from the torture. Then the confessions began to be filled with tales of more obscene kisses, cannibalism, incest and orgies, and worship of a black cat, taken to be a demon.

At the official trials in 1309, many of the Templars tried to recant their confessions, but fifty-four of them were immediately convicted and burned at the stake as relapsed heretics. Other burnings followed. The papacy's own belated investigation cleared the Templars of heresy and immorality, but the king of France pressured the pope, who by 1313 suppressed the Order of Templars everywhere. Philip had Jacques de Molay, grand master of the Templars, burned alive in 1314. Jacques died shouting his innocence above the flames. Philip seized most of the Templars' properties in France. In Portugal, Castille, England, and Germany most Templars who survived merged with the Order of the Hospitallers, whose main base in Rhodes off Asia Minor continued the fight against the Muslims. Thus the Templars passed into legend, later giving rise to unfounded tales involving buried treasure, secret cults, and the Holy Grail.

The significance of the Templar tragedy for the witch hunts is its demonstration of how easily torture and goals of destruction can produce the ends desired. Torture easily "confirmed" crimes from minor to major. Adding charges of strange sexual practices and the worship of animals of supernatural nature could escalate into accusations of witchcraft. If such respected, connected, and powerful people as the Templars could be burned alive, no one was safe.

THE RISE OF DEMONS

Diabolism, the belief that demons were organized by the Devil and worked serious harm in this world, became a key ingredient in brewing the witch hunts. Although the Devil and his demons had been part of the Christian view since the time the gospels were written, only after 1200 did theologians really begin to devote their attention to understanding the role of demons in human affairs. Why the Devil mattered more is unclear, whether such concern arose from explaining heresy or as an unintended aspect of a scholarly construct. In any case, the theories that medieval demonologists developed reached the highest levels of the Church. The obsession with demons helps explain why witches replaced heretics as a concern.

In the process of both preaching and hunting heretics, the Dominicans had taken the lead in scholarship on heresy, promoting a number of leading academics. One Dominican, Albertus Magnus (b. ca.1200–d. 1280), acquired a renowned expertise in magical lore. Albertus not only studied the natural world, he also was reputed to study alchemy, Egyptian mysticism, and sorcery. According to legend, he held a demon oracle in a brass sculpture of a human head. Theologians increasingly wove the Devil into their systems of salvation, trying to explain the nature of evil and how the Devil controlled it.

Even more important to demonological scholarship was Albertus Magnus' student, Thomas Aquinas (b. 1225–d. 1274). Most famously, Aquinas helped establish Scholasticism as the leading intellectual tool of medieval theology. Scholasticism's method of argument was modeled on the logical principles taught by Aristotle. When Aristotle's writings had been revived in the eleventh century, the Church had at first been suspicious, often outlawing, excommunicating, and censoring those who used a mode of thinking promoted by a pagan philosophy. But scholars like Aquinas showed how, rightly used, scholastic argumentation could support the teachings of the Church. Aquinas believed that correct reason and logic could never contradict the true faith of Christianity.

Part of Aquinas's systematic study, of course, examined the Devil and magic. In doing so, Aquinas and other scholastics introduced some innovations into magical thought that had been laid out by Augustine. Aquinas argued that the assaults of demons on humans were real, not illusion. Demons were not necessary to cause sin—humans could do that on their own—but demons did actively tempt people. The Devil and his demons could cause impotence and so break up a marriage. They could possess a person, although technically that person's free will still remained. The Devil's magic could only be overcome by the works of the Church, exorcism, and prayers.

One serious challenge for demonology, though, was the physicality of demons. Much theological debate over the centuries had questioned whether demons were spiritual beings. While demons could cause physical effects, like raising storms, they themselves supposedly had no corporeal form. The succubus, a demon in female form, or the incubus, a demon in male form, had sexual intercourse with its victim. If they lacked physical bodies, how then did they have sex with people? All theologians would not agree on one answer. Aquinas, following Augustine, seemed to argue that angels and demons assumed the appearance of physical form, as more of a virtual representation to allow most humans to interact with them. By contrast, the Devil became incorporate in the secret meetings with his few followers and involved physical contact ranging from the kiss on the anus to copulations.

The Devil's physicality became a part of the changes in demonology that fed into the witch hunts. Descriptions circulated about the Devil as fully anthropomorphized in his contacts with his followers, appearing as a dark man, fully human. The classic diabolic attributes of horns, tale, hairiness or scales, cloven hooves, and pointed tail appeared relatively late in the stories of witches, although artworks in churches portrayed such demons. And although technically the Devil was sexless, he most often appeared as male, because his embodiment as incubus was a key part of his evil work with weak women. The Devil could get women pregnant, although not with his own semen, the argument went. Instead, as a succubus, a demon had sex and captured the semen from the male victim and then transformed into the incubus to deposit the fluid inside a female victim.

Aquinas and his colleagues were worried about the sin of demon worship, which perverted the function of *latria*, the true worship due to God. Offering *latria* to demons condemned anyone's soul and meant apostasy, or total departure from Christianity, and a de facto pact with the Devil. This demonic pact of course was a capital crime, punished by death. Another school of philosophy, nominalism, which emphasized how words define reality, raised concerns about witchcraft being idolatry. Some historians also argue that theologians' emphasis on using the Ten Commandments to frame instruction about moral thought encouraged demonological thinking. The Second Commandment's prohibition of worshiping false gods drew particular attention from theologians, who considered demons to be false deities, like the pagan gods of old. In all, varied religious attempts at explaining sin helped to blame idolatry of demons for heresy.

THE AVIGNON POPES AND WITCHES

During the Babylonian Captivity of the popes in Avignon, the Church focused more attention on witchcraft. One pope, John XXII (r. 1316–1334), became obsessed with sorcery. This obsession may have stemmed from his contested election, domination by the French king, or even fear of assassination by poison or sorcery. Pope John reportedly used a magical curved horn to test his food for poison. In 1318, he ordered the investigation of a handful of courtiers, including priests, a physician, and a barber, who were found to possess books on the dark arts of communication with spirits, as well as mirrors and rings used to predict the future and invoke demons. He accused them of attempting to extend or shorten life spans and attempting to cure illnesses with a mere word. The pope turned them over to the inquisition, which found them guilty. The next year he imprisoned Bernard Délicieux for owning a necromancer's manual. Another victim was Bishop Hugo Géraud of Cahors, accused of using wax images and poison against the pope. Pope John personally questioned him, until the bishop confessed. The pope then had him degraded and turned over to the secular arm, which dragged him through the streets by a horse's tail to the place where he was burned at the stake. Several other members of the court were accused, such as the pope's own barber/surgeon who confessed to trying to use poison stored in rings, spells, and charms smuggled into the court in loaves of bread. Fearful about a growing threat, Pope John issued *Super illius specula* ("Upon His Watchtower"), outlining the connection of many kinds of magic with demons because of a hell pact.

Pope John XXII also figured indirectly in one of the first significant witch trials, that of Alice Kyteler in Ireland. The trial originated with Richard Ledrede whom the pope had appointed as Bishop of Ossory. One of Richard's parishioners there, Alice, had been married four times and was suspected in the death of some of her husbands. When her current husband and his children suspected her of making him ill through witchcraft, they accused her of sorcery to Bishop Richard. Her servant, Petronilla of Meath, provided testimony against her mistress after being whipped six times. Petronilla told how Alice had met the demon Robert, or Artisson (Son of Art), at a crossroads and concocted potions with roosters, spiders, black worms, and the hand of a thief. Alice's demon lover, Petronilla testified, appeared as a black dog or three black men, and Alice rode through the air on a wooden beam and participated in an orgy. Alice escaped the trial by fleeing to England, although her son William Outlaw, who confessed to a lesser charge of harboring heretics, did penance and paid a fine. Poor Petronilla was burnt for sorcery. This trial represented a dramatic change in which witchcraft became the focus of the charges of magic, unconnected to any actual existing heresy. Although few other witch trials would take place in Ireland, this one set an interesting precedent in the detail of description of demonic magic and conspiracy.

During the next few decades after Pope John XXII died, the number of witch trials temporarily declined. Inquisitors still hunted sorcerers, but not with any real energy or success. Evidence survives for only a few dozen trials between 1330 and 1375. As the fourteenth century continued, however, inquisitors and popes laid the groundwork for a new intensity. While the number of heretics slowly declined, concern about witches increased.

The inquisitor Nicholas Eymerich (or Nicolau Eymericus) helped to solidify worries about witches. Eymerich, a Dominican, gained several decades of experience with the inquisition in his native Aragon after 1356. His *Contra demonum invocatores* ("Against Those Who Call up Demons") from 1369 spelled out many of his concerns about sorcery, based, he said, on magical tomes he had read before destroying them. Even more important was his *Directorium inquisitorum* ("Directions for Inquisitors") in 1376, which quickly became even more widely used than Bernard Gui's manual. Eymerich allowed that some "Low Magic," such as palm reading or astrology, was merely sinful. Like Aquinas, he stated that if the magical activity rose to the level of cooperation with demons, then it was *latria*, equivalent to apostasy. He argued against the *Canon Episcopi*'s lax attitude, saying that since the women on the night ride invoked demons, they were guilty of heresy whether or not they actually rode. Eymerich considered witches to be worthy of punishment because of their turning away from God. He did not suggest, though, that that they formed a vast diabolic conspiracy.

As the Babylonian Captivity ended and the so-called Great Schism (1378–1417) began, accusations of witchcraft began to be used even against popes. Three popes, each in Rome, Avignon, and Pisa, claimed to be the one true pontiff and attacked the others as illegitimate. The Council of Pisa in 1409 charged Pope Benedict XIII of the Avignon line with necromancy, which could mean using corpses for divination, but probably just entailed any sort of magic. The Council alleged that he possessed books with both prayers and spells. Tomes of magic might be considered to be magical in themselves, possessed by demons. Also in 1409, Pope Alexander V, the new Pisan pope, named an inquisitor to go after the "new sects" of "some Christians and perfidious Jews" who were "sorcerers, diviners, invokers of demons, enchanters, conjurers, superstitious people, augurs, practitioners of nefarious and forbidden arts" because "all of these stain and pervert the Christian people, or at least the simpler-minded of them."[4]

While the Church hierarchy quarreled, professors at the University of Paris issued a notable declaration about the growing concern over witches. In 1398, they condemned sorcery. The professors listed twenty-eight articles of dangerous activities, mostly about divination and invocation of demons. Their list declared such activities to be vanity, falsehood, and insanity. Anyone who believed in or practiced such errors were idolaters and apostates worthy of excommunication and eternal punishment, lest other Christians be led astray. The learned faculty might have been reacting to trials going on in Paris (see Chapter 4), but certainly were building on the growing ecclesiastical worries about the occult. The renowned intellectual theologian Jean Gerson may have encouraged these prohibitions. Gerson wrote several pieces on demons and magic. His work became widely influential, especially in Spain.

In any case, a growing preponderance of intellectual argument supplied tinder for the fire of a fear surrounding sorcery and witches. Most common people through the Middle Ages and into the early modern age feared witches, if they believed in them at all, because of *maleficia*. They blamed witches for the cow's not giving milk, the hail storm's destroying crops, the trip that broke a leg, or an infant dying. They did not understand, nor care, by what mechanism a neighbor might be giving the evil eye. Such suspicions usually remained within bounds, rarely rising to violence or charges brought to the authorities. Demonic ideas, though, clearly affected the elites and intellectuals and trickled down to the common folk. Other pressures of these changing times would help heap logs onto the pyres.

THE END OF THE MIDDLE AGES AND THE BEGINNING OF MODERN EUROPE

By the mid-1300s, the Middle Ages were closing and the Modern Era opening. During this time of transition, some historians note a growing mentality of fearfulness. The leaders of the Church seemed too preoccupied with fights over the papacy to care about the common people. Reformers went unheeded. Waves of plague continued to strike Europe after the first big torrent of the Black Death in 1348 that killed perhaps a third of the population in a few short years. Some people reacted with practices such as special dances to ward off the epidemic. St. John's, St. Vitus, or Tarentella dancers would wander through towns, stripping, gyrating, and collapsing, in the hope of warding off divine vengeance. Another practice was self-flagellation, whipping oneself. Male and female flagellants paraded from town to town, lashing themselves both on covered and exposed flesh. As always, wars continued to wreak fear and havoc on countryside and city alike.

Other historians have noted that Europe suffered a measurably colder climate at the end of the Middle Ages, sometimes called a "mini-ice age." From about 1300 to 1700 the average temperature dropped a few degrees. This led to shorter growing summer seasons and longer, wetter winters. That meant less food and more hunger.

Hard times increased the numbers of beggars wandering the roads or haunting the alleyways. Whether as strangers or long-time members of the community, the poor made easy targets for blame and resentment. The rise of capitalism also brought instability. By its nature, capitalism changes lives. As businesses succeeded or failed, they promoted movement: bringing in new people and wealth or driving away the jobless and leaving behind poverty. Fights over property became more serious, often with men wanting to control lands inherited by women and orphans. Remarriages likewise provoked more conflicts about inheritance among members of blended families composed of step- and half-siblings. Because women tended to live longer than men, suspicion about their secret ways increased.

People wanted to get ahead, move into the new middle class, even into the upper class, but many were left behind. Those who had achieved wealth wanted to keep it; those who stayed at the bottom of society needed someone to blame for their lack of success. Even with the continued growth of towns, most people lived in the countryside until the Industrial Revolution of the nineteenth century. Rural folk resented the seemingly prosperous urban elites.

In these times of change and crisis, people wanted reassurance about life's meaning. Individuals have often relied on magical explanations to relieve anxiety when no other rational or effective means are available. Better to grasp at nonsense than live in fear. Class jealousy, resentment at being stuck lower on the social scale, nourished mutual accusations of witchcraft. The poor might have hoped that the Devil could give them revenge for petty or serious slights against their status and character.

The political, economic, social, and cultural transition from medieval to early modern times offered the setting for hunts. Strixology, literature on the study of witches and witchcraft, proliferated. Strixologists spread both theoretical explanations and lurid examples of witchcraft across national boundaries. Attentive persons of high and low status called for the destruction of witches. National, regional, or local governments took action through legal procedures, with the cooperation and blessing of religious leaders. Court cases established legal principles and practices that offered few protections to the innocent. Torture guaranteed that confessions to bizarre deeds abounded. Publicity around the horrid and lurid crimes spurred the wielders of judicial power to repeat the cycle of persecutions.

At the end of the Middle Ages, then, intellectual opinions of clerics, political decisions of princes, and popular apprehensions of commoners were all building toward a hunt for witches. After 1400, the crime of witchcraft shifted from a rare, isolated, and minor matter to a common, widespread concern of intense importance. Admittedly, that beginning date is somewhat arbitrary. It could be moved back somewhat in some countries, moved forward in others. Similarly, the end date of 1800 is long after hunting witches had ceased in certain territories, but it marks the cessation in others. The intensity of hunting would also vary by time and place. Governments never did devote substantial effort for very long to eliminating witches. Nevertheless, the direct responsibility for hunting rests with the individual regimes that authorized trials and executions. The next chapters describe how particular political and religious authorities hunted witches in Europe and abroad.

NOTES

1. Guibert of Nogent. *A Monk's Confession: The Memoirs of Guibert of Nogent*, trans. Paul J. Achambault (University Park, PA: The Pennsylvania State University Press, 1996), 40.

2. P. G. Maxwell-Stuart, ed. *The Occult in Medieval Europe: A Documentary History* (Basingstoke, UK: Palgrave Macmillan, 2005), 146.

3. Bernard Gui, *The Inquisitor's Guide: A Medieval Manual on Heretics*, trans. Janet Shirley (Welwyn Garden City, UK: Ravenhall Books, 2006), 150.

4. Alan Charles Kors and Edward Peters, eds. and revised by Edward Peters, *Witchcraft in Europe 400–1700: A Documentary History*, 2nd ed. Middle Ages Series (Philadelphia: University of Pennsylvania Press, 2001), 153.

CHAPTER 3

Witch-Hunting in the Holy Roman Empire

The large collection of principalities organized under the Holy Roman Empire suffered the worst witch-hunting in Europe. Perhaps as many as three in four of all victims came from that ramshackle political structure, described by Voltaire as neither holy, nor Roman, nor an empire. The Empire included what are today the countries of Germany, Austria, Luxembourg, Liechtenstein, the Dutch Netherlands, Switzerland, the Czech Republic, and parts of Italy, France, Poland, and Denmark. Emperors in the tenth century had founded the state, which quickly became the most powerful in Europe. After 1250, the centralized authority of the Holy Roman Emperors dwindled, since the emperors depended on election by seven representative Electoral Princes in order to assume the throne. Instead, real power increasingly lay with the princes who ruled in the hundreds of territories within the Empire. These territorial principalities ranged from tiny patches ruled by knights, through modest counties, and city-states, to great electorates reigned over by prince-bishops, dukes, and kings. By the sixteenth century, the Holy Roman Empire of the German Nation had lost most of its non-German-speaking lands, and the central power continued to deteriorate until its final dissolution in 1806.

This diversity of political organization significantly influenced the severity of witch-hunting. A strong central government might have more easily supervised legal procedures, judicial appointments, and capital punishment, to restrain the excesses of hunting. Instead, the weakness of the central regime allowed hunting to unfold according to the choices of local authorities. Thus, some regions rarely saw any witch persecutions, while others suffered repeatedly.

This discrepancy helps to put witch hunts, overall, in perspective. Witch-hunting followed from conscious decisions of elites to set up criminal procedures to cope with the alleged crime of witchcraft. Government authorities at the same time, however, regularly dealt with other crimes, such as prostitution, murder, or theft. The focus here on witchcraft should not leave the impression that everyone was obsessed with witches. In fact, witch hunts were not common or regular anywhere, even during the most intense period of 1400–1800.

Regimes everywhere in the empire had the freedom to develop vicious and intense hunts, or none at all. Some areas, especially in the North and East, never did. Most did so rarely. Territories in the South and West suffered more hunting than other areas, and more often. Yet even some of the worst places for hunting, namely territories where prince-bishops held both political and religious authority, experienced hunts only for a few years or a few decades between 1400 and 1800. The worst phase, as elsewhere in western Europe, took place between 1560 and 1660. Some governments readily caved to pressure from the elites and the common people to deal with witches; others resisted, or never even felt pressured. Still, if witches were being hunted, they were hunted first, longest, and most cruelly in the Holy Roman Empire.

Religion stands out as one reason why. The power of prince-bishops and the pseudo-ecclesiastical status of the "Holy" Roman Emperor tangled church and state in Germany more than in most other countries. In the late medieval period, reform movements within the Church automatically also included the imperial structure. Then, with the Reformation, Christianity divided people in the Holy Roman Empire to an even greater extent than in other countries. Only in the Empire did large numbers of people belong to all three major branches of Christianity (Roman Catholics, Lutherans, and Calvinists) after the Reformation. These changing religious structures bred fearfulness and uncertainty about salvation. Blaming witches provided a simple response to those anxieties.

Anabaptists, a collection of various new Christian sects, added to the religious competition and confusion. Their name derived from their support of baptism for adults rather than infants, as all other Christians practiced. They also rejected clerical and aristocratic hierarchies, as had the heretics of Apostolic Poverty from the Middle Ages. For this and other beliefs in radical simplicity, the other Christian branches united in persecuting the Anabaptists, with hundreds consequently suffering heresy trials, torture, and burning at the stake. The Anabaptists themselves hardly hunted witches, or anyone, at all. For one reason, they did not wield political power anywhere for very long. Additionally, their own persecution gave them a unique perspective. Lastly, they lacked a strong belief in demonology.

In hunting the Anabaptists, authorities in the Holy Roman Empire drew on the long tradition of persecutions of both heretics and Jews. These persecutions lasted longer in German territories than other western European states partly because heretics were not eradicated as early. The Germans were fighting against powerful Hussites in Bohemia and a few Waldensians in Switzerland in the fifteenth century. Jews also continued to live in the Empire, as compared to England, France, Spain, and Portugal which had all expelled Jews by 1500 (as pointed out in Chapter Two). The multiplicity of "outsiders" as targets in Germany only made it worse, rather than easier, for all victims, including witches. Where Anabaptists were zealously hunted, though, such as in the Netherlands or the Tyrol, witch hunts remained limited. Authorities usually persecuted either witches or Anabaptist heretics, rarely both at the same time.

Another unusual factor in the German hunts was the role of universities. By the late Middle Ages, the Holy Roman Empire had many schools of higher education, whose professors stayed current with the latest intellectual trends. Familiar with the general growing concern for witches, as presented in demonological and strixological writing, German scholars embraced attitudes about a diabolic conspiracy of witches. Many local government officials and magistrates, themselves ignorant about such new legal cases or witchcraft, consulted these alleged experts. They often received replies that encouraged harsh measures against these enemies of God and society. One declaration by the legal faculty at Jena confidently advised witch interrogators in one case, that, "if she does not confess right away, because of the strong evidence against the same, to question her with torture, and with appropriate pressure, and to carefully record her testimony, whereupon what is right will come about."[1] Thus, scholarly discourse supported torture and hunting.

Since the majority of the Empire's inhabitants were ethnically German, some historians have suggested that national character played a role in making the witch hunts there so severe. But the Germans' inclination toward hunting witches probably derived more from their political and religious fractures, as described above, than from ethnicity. Strixology flourished first and best in the Empire because of unique historical circumstances. Over the same centuries, however, Germany's neighboring countries also embraced the witch-hunting ideology with nearly the same enthusiasm and diligence as the Holy Roman Empire. Everywhere, too many people were willing to believe in unnatural powers of the Devil to work evil.

THE FORMATIVE FIFTEENTH CENTURY

The date of 1400 for the beginning of the witch hunts in Europe is only an approximation. As seen in Chapter 2, few witches were being put on trial in most European countries at that point. The early trials stand out for their rarity and often for unusual participants, whether high aristocrats, heretics, or end-of-the-world prophets. Around 1400, however, the ideology that supported hunting and wider trials that could be called "panics" or "crazes" started to grow. The imperial territories deserve special attention because many of the ideas and actions which came to characterize witch-hunting formed there.

THE COUNCIL OF BASEL

A significant turning point for witch-hunting was the Council of Basel (1431–1439). The town of Basel lay in the southwest corner of the Empire, today part of Switzerland. The Council's main purpose was to continue reform in the Western Church through conciliarism, where representatives of the clergy and laity worked together with the popes to supervise behavior and belief. The Council also tried to solve the fight with the heretical Bohemian Hussites. The patriarchally inclined popes, though, did not like the idea that representative councils should play a role in governing the church and forming doctrine. So Pope Eugene IV (r. 1431–1447) repeatedly tried to shut down or transfer the Council of Basel. Many participants in Basel resisted, however, believing that councils were necessary to reform the Church. They defied the papal commands. As moderates left, the radicals became increasingly predominant and even elected an anti-pope (believed legitimate by the electors, but considered a false claimant by the Church and historians). Unfortunately for the fight against heresy and the push for reform, the Council of Basel failed to achieve much, eventually dissolving under criticism from all sides.

Nevertheless, the Council of Basel was perfectly timed to become a center of information about witches. Various theologians and demonologists met and discussed the latest news of hunts, observations of magical phenomena, confessions of witches, and conclusions about what they saw as the Devil's work. These conversations were tangential to the main business of the Council. Still, the subsequent writings of participants helped to launch the new science of strixology, a genre moving beyond general demonology to focus explicitly on witches.

Some of the witch stories circulated at the council came from a judge named Peter of Simmental, near Bern (today the capital of Switzerland). Peter reported his judicial actions against a peasant man named Stedelen (or Staedlin) who had committed *maleficia* and had admitted under torture that he was part of a sect of Devil worshippers. Some of Stedelen's actions fit into the standard curses and spells performed in any folk-magic framework. For example, Stedelen confessed to having buried a lizard under a threshold to cause infertility in the home's residents, and to having sacrificed a black rooster at a crossroads and tossed it into the air for a devil to catch, who then caused hail storms. Stedelen and others met at a church to pay homage to Satan, renounce their Christianity, and cannibalize dead babies cooked into soup or transformed into magic potions. The theme of secret meetings and cannibalism stirred old fears. Stedelen's diabolic powers for a while allegedly prevented his capture. He emitted a horrible stench to slow down captors, could transform into the shape of a mouse and hide, and once, while invisible, even shoved the judge Peter down some stairs. Many of these stories were recorded by one of the council's participants, Johannes Nider, in his *Formicarius* ("The Ant Hill") in 1438. First as a manuscript, then as a printed text after 1475, *Formicarius* ran through many editions.

Nider's *Formicarius* laid an important foundation for future strixology, although it was originally conceived as a broad collection of moral lessons and examples. Nider was a Dominican professor at Vienna University. At the Council of Basel, he had been involved in both proposals for Church reforms and negotiations with the Hussites. The *Formicarius* collects five "books" of anec-dotes and tales that illustrate the problems of sin in the world. Much of the last book concerns witchcraft. Some historians blame Nider for overemphasizing the susceptibility of women to the Devil, due to their melancholy and deceiving nature. Nider, however, also included many examples of men, since demons easily tricked all humans. Other early strixologists at Basel brought ideas concerning witches back with them into France (see Chapter 4), and over the centuries many scholars would continue to cite or borrow from Nider.

LUCERNE AND LAUSANNE

One early area of concentration for witch burning in Europe began in the 1430s around Lucerne and Lausanne. Though geographically near one another, they nevertheless offer sharp contrasts that illustrate the diversity of hunting. In Lucerne, secular judges managed the hunts. The civic magistrates identified crimes of *maleficia*, such as accusations that witches caused hailstorms. A few decades later, they began to see conspiratorial pacts with the Devil. The magis-trates mostly accused women, many of whom had reputations as bad neighbors with loose sexual morals.

On the other hand, Lausanne's hunts were supervised by the local bishops using inquisitorial methods. The bishops suspected more men than women as witches. Quite early, ecclesiastical judges such as these adopted the demonological ideas of a "sinagoga," later called the sabbat, where witches met with the Devil to plan crimes, blaspheme Christian sacraments, eat flesh, and have orgies. The terms above also illustrate the connection still made between Jews and sorcery.

BAVARIA AND THE TYROL

The Council of Basel surely buzzed with the latest gossip from Bavaria. In 1428, the young Duke Albrecht had fallen in love with Agnes Bernauer, the daughter of a barber. They married secretly in 1432. In October of that year, while the son was away on a trip, the duke's father accused Agnes of bewitching his son with a potion. He tried to execute her by throwing her off a bridge into the Danube River. When she swam to shore, a guard held her under the water with a pole until she drowned.

The fear of witches did not only come from the learned and political elites in the Empire. One example is Hans Vintler, a Tyrolian poet, and his poem *Blumen der Tugend* ("Flowers of Virtue"), written around 1450. One section of this poem illustrates folk traditions about believing in the Devil and going out on night rides. In the south of the Tyrol lay the prince-bishopric of Brixen. Its bishop, the famous humanist Nicholas of Cusa (r. 1450–1464), dealt with two old women who thought they had made a pact with a spirit to gain wealth. Nicholas recognized these women as deluded, although he did not quite know

...r to counsel them. Clearly witches were becoming a concern through much of the fifteenth century, but only a few territories, mostly in Alpine lands, took action with a small number of trials.

"THE HAMMER OF WITCHES"

With the victims still numbering in the mere hundreds, witch-hunting might have remained a very minor footnote in history. This changed at the end of the fifteenth century, partly due to the infamous book, the *Malleus Maleficarum* ("The Hammer of Witches"). Many historians see its publication in 1486/1487 as the single most significant turning point in the witch hunts. Its origins lay with the Dominican Henry Krämer, an aspiring inquisitor in southern Germany. In 1484, he convinced Pope Innocent VII to publish the bull *Summis desiderantes* ("Desiring with Supreme Ardor"), which seemed to command that the inquisition hunt witches through much of Germany. On the way back to Germany from Rome, Krämer stopped first at Constance, where he failed to get much interest in organizing a hunt, but he soon found more success in the prosperous town of Innsbruck.

He advertised for information about witchcraft from the local population. On the basis of his sources, he arrested and put on trial seven local women in October 1485. The authorities, Duke Sigismund of the Tyrol and Bishop George of Brixen, soon intervened, however, shut down the proceedings, and strongly suggested that Krämer leave the territory. The disappointed inquisitor did not let his failure slow him down. Krämer, using the pen-name *Institoris* (a Latinized verion of his name, meaning "peddler"), wrote down his collective interpretation and knowledge about the danger of witches. The title of his work was inspired by inquisitorial manuals written earlier in the century, *The Hammer of Heretics* and *The Hammer of Jews*. Krämer also improperly affixed to his title page the name of the humanist scholar Jacob or James Sprenger, dean of the University of Cologne, probably hoping to add some scholarly legitimacy.

Although hastily written, *The Hammer* tries to provide a systematic explication of the danger of witches. The problem was serious, Krämer wrote, because the "evils which are performed by witches exceed all other sin which God has ever permitted to be done...."[2] In *The Hammer*'s opinion, anyone who even denied the reality of witches was a heretic. *The Hammer* cites many authorities to bolster its points, from Aristotle and Augustine, to Aquinas and Nider. Part 1 explains how witches really existed and threatened the Christian commonwealth. Part 2 details the wide-ranging methods of witches and how to defeat them. One of their nastier crimes was to steal men's "virile members" by casting a spell called a glamour. Part Three presents model judicial procedures for carrying out hunts, including advice on torture and sentencing. Interestingly, the *Malleus* prefers that secular courts take on the task of witch-hunting, perhaps because religious courts leaned toward mercy, thus delaying the destruction of these horrible creatures.

Many historians also blame Krämer for encouraging witch hunters to target women more than men as witches. Even his spelling of "maleficarum," with an *a* in a feminine gender instead of the usual masculine-gender "maleficorum" with an *o*, seems to emphasize his hostility toward women. Krämer's misogynistic arguments list many reasons why women were more likely to be witches than men. They were less clever, vainer, and more sexually insatiable. While these were not new criticisms against women, Krämer helped to entrench them in strixological literature. The book went through dozens of editions over the next two centuries. Krämer even wrote a shorter manual in German to help magistrates who could not read the original Latin.

Once Krämer had vacated Innsbruck, the confused Duke Sigismund needed to make some sense out of these witchcraft accusations. Ulrich Müller (or Molitor), provided some clarity with his short text *De Lamiis et Phitonicis Mulieribus* ("On Witches and Female Oracles"). This work takes the form of a three-way dialogue between Molitor; Sigismund, as the skeptic; and Conrad von Stürtzel, the ducal secretary. They debate about the powers of the Devil and of witches: what is real, what is illusion? Can spirits affect the natural world? The dialogue largely supports the traditional view, which doubted that women actually traveled to sabbats or raised storms and maintained that the Devil manipulated people's gullibility through images and illusions (see Illustration 2). God had the ultimate power, and the Devil could do no harm without divine permission, while witches could do no harm without the Devil's help. Although Molitor's work retreated from the extreme position of Institoris', it still condemned women as more likely to be witches.

A third work which also discussed the problem of witches quickly followed. In 1508, Johann Geiler von Kaysersberg, a preacher in Strasbourg influenced by Nider's *Formicarius*, published *Die Emeis* ("The Ant Colony"; see Illustration 3). His writing in German helped to broaden the discussion to nonscholars. Illustrations attributed to Hans Baldung Grien further suggested the reality of witches (see Illustration 4). The result, however, was exchanges of ideas, rather than creation of hunts. Few governments at the time took up the encouragement of strixologists to destroy witches, as enemies of God. Attention to the more important upheavals of organized religion in Europe due to the Reformation may have contributed to a delay in interest.

THE REFORMATION

Martin Luther's Reformation, which began in Germany, remade the relationship of Church and State. Luther sought a better way for fallen humanity to receive divine grace and achieve salvation. His doctrine of "justification by faith alone" simplified both the sacraments and the hierarchy of the church. Along the way, Luther also explored the issue of witches. The Devil was very real to Martin Luther. He allegedly threw his ink pot at the Devil's appearance in his monastic cell, where it still stains the wall today. He also told of how witches tormented his own body with ailments and how his mother reacted to a neighboring witch "with deference and try[ing] to conciliate her, for the neighbor had through witchcraft caused her own children such sharp pain that they cried themselves to death."[3] As Luther aged, his stories and fears of witches became stronger. Luther wrote several sermons against witches and endorsed the execution of at least four witches at Wittenburg during 1541. Fear of diabolism, therefore, only increased among Lutherans.

At the same time, Emperor Charles V (r. 1519–1556) was trying to rule the Holy Roman Empire benevolently, at least when not trying to hunt down Luther and his Protestant heretics. One of his best efforts was the reform of the laws, known as the *Constitutio Criminalis Carolina* or Caroline (after the Latin for Charles) Code, in 1532. This legal reform took many of the older, conflicting, and confusing laws of the medieval empire and reorganized them into a more clear and comprehensively organized system.

Article 109 dealt directly with witchcraft, narrowing the definition of the crime to that which caused someone's death. If murder was not part of a charge of witchcraft, other laws were supposed to be applied. The regulations also required local courts to seek professional advice in serious crimes, by consulting university professors, for example. The Caroline Code allowed torture, although it did try to establish boundaries. Torture was only permitted with sufficient cause, such as a genuine complaint of a specific crime, and needed to be authorized by a judge. Torture should last only one day, and the confession was to be repeated in court several days later, without any threat of further torture, although a judge could ask questions. Conviction also required evidence obtained by means other than torture.

These reasonable measures would have reduced the severity of hunts, had they been followed. Local magistrates, however, often did not heed them. First, local laws might have superiority over imperial laws. One example was the notorious 1572 law code in Saxony. It made any form of magic, whether harmful or not, a capital crime punishable by burning at the stake. These Saxon laws were widely imitated in other territories' law codes. In addition, the Holy Roman Empire lacked a competent system for enforcing its laws, and its courts of appeals were slow and cumbersome. The local territorial princes bore responsibility for enforcing imperial law; the emperor had no police force or army that did not depend on the good will of the princes. Regionalism therefore allowed a variety of legal approaches to hunting witches, from hunting them ruthlessly to ignoring the alleged problem.

RENAISSANCE INTELLECTUALS AND WITCHES

Intellectuals fostered by the Renaissance examined issues of magic and witchcraft. One, Heinrich Cornelius Agrippa von Nettesheim (b. 1486–d. 1535), spoke up in favor of magic and against witch-hunting. Agrippa had studied and traveled widely, serving rich and powerful people as an astrologer and physician. His interest in the occult led to his book, *De occulta philosophia* ("On Occult Philosophy"), written in 1510. This book outlined how to achieve a more noble life by understanding magic through the planets, numbers, spirits, and natural wonders. Those ideas convinced many people to regard him as a great sorcerer. Legends of magic became attached to Agrippa, and his large black dog, his supposed familiar. He rejected evil magic, such as necromancy, in which a necromancer ensorcelled a dead person's spirit back to a corpse in order to reveal occult knowledge. He did note how women were more vulnerable to deceits of demons, because they "are desirous of secrets, and less cautious, and prone to superstition, and they are more easily deceived, and therefore give up themselves more readily to" evil spirits.[4] His position as a wise magician elevated him from the common witch, however. Learned philosophers who dabbled in "High Magic" could usually do so without much fear of being prosecuted, much less persecuted. Women who were common witches more frequently succumbed to prosecutorial zeal.

One such unnamed woman in Metz fell victim in 1519, accused of witchcraft by the Dominican Nicholas Savini. The inquisitor had accused her largely because her mother had been deemed a witch and a demon may have been her father. Agrippa came to her defense and asserted that such a rationale granted too much power to the Devil and deprived the Holy Spirit of any potential for saving grace through baptism. Agrippa actually won the woman's freedom, although he himself then felt pressured to leave town, while the inquisition continued to investigate other suspected witches. The sermons of another priest, John Roger Brennon, helped to bring the witch hunts in Metz to an end shortly after. And out of this experience came Agrippa's book, *De incertitudune et vanitate scientiarum* ("Of the Uncertainty and Vanity of the Sciences") in 1527 which was critical of the inquisition. He argued for a more skeptical pursuit of knowledge, based on reason rather than scriptures and faith. As a result, officials accused Agrippa of heresy and he suffered both bouts of jail and exile.

Two other contemporary scholars, Theophrastus Bambastus von Hohenheim (b. 1493–d. 1541), known as Paracelsus, and Erasmus (b. ca.1466–d. 1536) left more ambivalent legacies regarding witch hunts. Like Agrippa, Paracelsus gained a reputation as a sorcerer. He studied magic and the occult, just as he did nature, as a way to learn about God's creation. While he promoted white magic as a useful gift from God, if its dangers could be avoided, he condemned black magic, which he associated with women, Jews, and Gypsies, all of whom were especially vulnerable to Satan's temptations. Once again, learned sorcery was distinguished from the low-class diabolic magic of witches. The contemporary stories of Dr. Faustus, a sorcerer who made a pact with the Devil and was carried off to hell, may have been elaborated with rumors about Paracelsus and Agrippa. The Dutch Christian humanist Erasmus is most famous for promoting tolerance and the use of reason and moderation. Yet he feared a witch conspiracy. He also gave credence to some of the tales of witches appearing in his day, calling them a new form of heresy. Thus the more fearful ideas of Luther, Paracelsus, and Erasmus won out over the skepticism of Agrippa.

John Weyer

One other powerful voice in the middle of the sixteenth century tried to stem the growing wave of hunting. John Weyer, also known as Joannes Wierus or Johann Weir (b. 1515–d. 1588), had been an ardent student of the humanist Agrippa for several years before studying medicine in Paris. In 1550, he became the personal physician to Duke William of Berg, Jülich, and Cleves. Weyer studied the human mind, later leading Freud to praise him and his work as helping to found modern psychiatry. Weyer offered his sensible advice in cases dealing with nuns who exhibited symptoms of possession, determining that they should "be separated and conveyed each to her parents or her nearest relatives by blood and marriage, so that individually they may be more readily and more reliably instructed and healed."[5] He was skeptical of the efficacy of torture. His book *De Praestigiis Daemonum* ("On the Tricks of Demons") from 1563 became a best seller, with many editions within a few years and immediate translation into German and French. His second book, *De Lamiis* (1578), repeated and elaborated his arguments.

Weyer's long studies investigated various aspects of magic. He drew distinctions between sorcerers and magicians or conjurors who did tricks for entertainment. As for witchcraft, Weyer accepted the reality of demons, but "the pact is illusory and that it is fabricated and confirmed by the deceptive appearance of a phantasm, or a fancy of the mind or the phantastical body of a blinding spirit; it is therefore of no weight."[6] His most important contribution was his conclusion that women who believed themselves to be witches were mentally ill, not bound to the Devil.

The reaction against Weyer was enormous, provoking a counterattack by many strixologists. Thomas Erastus, a medical professor from Heidelberg, argued against Weyer's ideas of mental illness in his *Dialogues against Paracelsus* in 1572. According to Erastus, witches actually and consciously made a pact with the Devil and thus needed to be punished. Although Erastus could apply empirical observation to contest some of the extreme claims about witches, he knew they existed because, as a good Protestant, the Bible told him so.

Within a few years, Jean Bodin in France and King James of Scotland (see Chapters 4 and 5) also explicitly attacked Weyer's arguments. Enemies in the principality of Berg, Jülich, and Cleves tried to have Weyer convicted of witchcraft, but Duke William protected his trusted advisor. Only a few contemporaries, like Reginald Scot in England (see Chapter 5), would rely on Weyer's learning and argumentation. Ultimately, the interest provoked by Weyer's book may have actually encouraged hunting for the next few decades. Even Duke William's successor became obsessed enough with witches to inspire the Italian Francesco Maria Guazzo's promotion of hunting (see Chapter 6).

THE WAVE OF THE LATE SIXTEENTH CENTURY

Beginning around 1560 and for the next several decades, witch-hunting multiplied in various parts of the Holy Roman Empire. The first generation of the Reformation was passing, and the second would turn to witches. Ongoing religious tensions, poor weather and harvests, plague, warfare, and economic change all contributed to worries among both rich and poor. It was always political elites, though, who encouraged, allowed, and carried out any hunts. These elites based their decisions on local circumstances, political gain, personal piety, and the opinions of strixologists. New editions of *The Hammer of Witches* and other strixological works fueled ideas against witches. Prince-bishops were at the forefront of many hunts, responsible as they were both for politics and for faith within their realms. Descriptions of a few hunts will serve as examples.

In 1575, in the province of Salzburg, a parish priest fell victim to the fears of witchcraft. People were looking for someone to blame for many recent thunderstorms. They found a candidate in the bad-tempered seventy-year-old Eva Neidegger, who cooked for the pastor, Rupert Rambsauer of Bramberg by Mittersill. She had already been denounced in 1573, only to gain her release on bail. The next year, though, new storms brought more demands for her arrest. Under torture with thumbscrews, she implicated Pastor Rupert, who was said to have twice caused hail inside a closed room. An ecclesiastical court defrocked him for using the Mass to raise storms. Handed over to the secular court, both pastor and cook were burned on the pyre on March 13, 1575.

STOECKHLIN IN OBERSTDORF

Chonrad Stoeckhlin, a self-proclaimed witch finder, provoked another hunt in Augsburg. This so-called Shaman of Oberstdorf wanted to prove his abilities and so accused Anna Enzensbergerin in 1586. He soon, ironically, became caught up in a wave of persecutions. As the number of accused reached several dozen people, a female relative implicated him.

According to his forced confession, his witchery began when a friend, Jacob Walch, returned to visit him after his death. Walch's spirit helped Stoeckhlin repent of sins, but also acquainted him with night phantoms, with whom he flew to strange places. These helped Stoeckhlin to increase his abilities as cunning-man, a practice he pursued as a sideline to his trade as a horse wrangler. His questioners were suspicious about the dead friend, the phantoms, the night flying, and the meetings in strange places. They reinterpreted them as demons and the sabbat. Tortured, he admitted to the worst suspicions of the authorities. Altogether, the trials held at Rettenberg dealt harshly with two dozen women, while the accused men escaped condemnation, except for the unfortunate Stoeckhlin. He and the twenty-four women were executed. Dozens more, including Walpurga Hausmännin (see Chapter 1) followed in other cases before the hunt ended in 1592.

BAVARIA

In neighboring Bavaria, Duke William V (r. 1579–1597) embraced witch-hunting as one more dimension of his personal religious fervor. He wore a hairshirt under his clothing, flagellated himself, and regularly undertook pilgrimages. His witch trials started out slowly, clustering in intensity in the late 1580s. In one, a local parish priest wanted to ignore the accusations that a farmer's wife, Geiger of Steingaden, had bewitched cattle. Authorities overruled him and sent her to the ducal council, where torture convicted her.

The Bavarian hunting ideology received endorsement from the local University of Ingolstadt. On April 28, 1590, the professors released a learned opinion that witches were a serious danger and advocated their persecution. By the end of the year, Duke William had granted administrative orders for judges to persecute witches, calling on all his subjects to come forward with suspicions. Any acts of supernatural or superstitious nature fell under the crime of diabolic witchcraft. By the time the duke was finished, he had executed about two thousand people.

Factions within the Bavarian government, however, disagreed about witch-hunting. Some zealots wanted to increase persecutions, while more pragmatic politicians sought to avoid hunting. The zealots reached a high point in 1600 with the punishment of the Pappenheimer family. The members of this family had been homeless vagabonds, trying to earn meager livings as cleaners of latrines and cesspits. Rounded up in a sweep against vagrants, they found themselves implicated in witchcraft. Under torture, Anna, her husband Paul, and their three sons confessed to many fantastic charges of witchery. They had flown on sticks, produced magic potions, raised storms, had intercourse with the Devil, and dismembered and cannibalized corpses, as well as committing numerous robberies, arsons, and murders. Any rational accounting of the numbers would have recognized the impossibility of these confessions, but with witchcraft the impossible became credible.

The ducal regime executed the Pappenheimers on July 29, 1600. Before a crowd of thousands, officials carted them first to the place of public punishment. The youngest, a child of eleven, watched the proceedings and was burned several weeks later. Officials ripped at the Pappenheimer's flesh with red-hot pincers. The torturers then committed a rarely performed insult to motherhood: they cut off Anna's breasts, then rubbed the bloody lumps around her two older sons' mouths. The suffering Anna and her family were then trundled in a cart another half-mile to the formal execution. There the men were broken on the wheel, Paul Pappenheimer impaled, and all tied to stakes and burned alive. A half-dozen other people connected with this hunt were burned in November. A few implicated women of more respectable social status had their cases dismissed after defenses by friends and lawyers. This overreach into the upper class helped to end the hunt.

A Bavarian law of 1611–1612 by Duke Maximilian I, the *Landtgebott wider die Aberglauben, Zaubery, Hexery und andere sträffliche Teufelskünste* ("The

Territorial Ordinance against Superstition, Magic, Witchcraft, and other Criminal Arts of the Devil") set forth clearly and boldly the danger of witches. Scholars, magistrates, and judges had been debating for decades whether the danger of witches was serious enough to expend so much effort. This law decided that witches were dangerous. The law was taken seriously enough to be reissued in 1665 and 1746. It technically lasted until 1813. Duke Maximilian himself encouraged hunts and personally overturned the acquittal of a woman and three children in Ingolstadt in 1625. Other public officials neglected to hunt witches seriously.

JAKOB BITHNER

To the south of Bavaria, Lutherans and Roman Catholics managed to join forces against the common enemy of the witch. A Lutheran became the chief inquisitor in the Roman Catholic province of Styria in the late sixteenth century. Beginning about 1578, the territorial provost, Jakob Bithner, conducted dozens of trials looking for witches. He did not desire a widespread panic, however, discounting the more exaggerated tales of the Devil and sabbat orgies. He mostly targeted the wandering homeless and beggars. Some claimed, usually after torture, to be able to get money from the Devil or to raise storms. One, Jakob Glogger, who claimed to be able to break through handcuffs, actually did succeed in escaping.

Bithner confronted a popular uprising of peasants in 1590. A Roman Catholic priest in Oberwölz, Martin Lindmayr, had spoken out against witches. His zeal had provoked his own (possibly Lutheran) parishioners to accuse him, in turn, of weather magic. They roughed the priest up, threw him out of town, and sued him in court. Judges threw the case out, however. The elites knew their interests were best protected by their own control of hunting, not allowing popular panic to seize the upper hand.

HUNTS IN TRIER

Ruthless hunts ravaged the Electorate of Trier from about 1581 to 1593. The territory seemed to have suffered from bad weather, destruction of crops by rodents and locusts, and lawlessness of wandering robbers. Some of the most extreme reports of devastation recorded in popular histories of the witch hunts come from this area. For instance, an often cited case from 1589 about one village concluded that only two old women were left alive after a hunt, although the men were unharmed.

One hunt in Trier, which enflamed large numbers of children openly into confessing to witchcraft, rose to include the local elites. A noble boy implicated himself in an attack on the elector and prince-archbishop John VII von Schöneburg (r. 1581–1599), then, under the pressure of exorcism, the boy accused Dr. Dietrich Flade, one of the most prestigious figures ever convicted of witchcraft. Flade was a judge, the mayor of Trier, the rector of the university, and a privy councilor to the prince-archbishop. Up to this point, Flade himself had been hunting witches as part of the general persecution, although he had tried to be particularly scrupulous about evidence. As more than a dozen accused witches, probably prompted by questioners, began identifying him under torture, Flade decided to flee the province.

Flight only made him appear more guilty. Authorities captured him and returned him for examination. His appeal to the prince-bishop and examination by his own university faculty members did not save him. Put on trial in August 1589 and tortured five times, he confessed. When he named names, however, he tried to weaken his accusation by saying that he could not be certain that the people he had seen as witches were those actual individuals or merely beings stealing their outward appearance. Trier's authorities burned Dietrich Flade and several other priests and officials on September 18, 1589, although the archbishop graciously allowed him to be strangled before the flames were lit. Two years later, the death toll of this one hunt reached around 300.

PETER BINSFELD

A powerful motivator for these events was the local assistant (suffragan) archbishop, Peter Binsfeld. In 1589 and 1591, Binsfeld published his *Tractatus de confessionibus maleficorum et sagarum* ("Treatise on the Confessions of Witches and Wise-Women"). The book became a widely read explanation of the danger of witches. Binsfeld claimed that God would not allow an innocent person to be executed. He also granted full credence to the testimony of children, allowing their stories and tortured statements to be used against themselves and others. His book was quickly translated into German in Munich, greatly influencing the legal system in Bavaria.

Meanwhile, the scholar Cornelius Loos (who also used the scholarly name Loosaeus Callidius; b. 1546–d. 1595) had been teaching in Trier. Although born in the Dutch Netherlands, Loos had converted to Roman Catholicism. Still, he doubted the claims about witches, especially after he read the work of John Weyer. Loos wrote *De Vera et Falsa Magica* ("On True and False Magic") wherein he denied the reality of devils. Authorities confiscated the book before it could be published and imprisoned Loos in the local Abbey of St. Maximin in March 1592. To gain release, Loos recanted and begged for forgiveness on his knees to Peter Binsfeld. He then fled to Brussels, where he again criticized the witch hunts. Belgian authorities arrested Loos as a heretic and briefly imprisoned him again, contributing to his early death.

After the 1590s, the waves of persecution in Trier slacked off for a few years. Protestants continued to identify the superstitious aspects of magic with the rituals and sacramentals of Roman Catholicism. This position merely hardened Roman Catholics, who used the insult "protestant" against those who did not believe that witches were a real danger.

BARBARA RÜFIN

The Ellwangen hunts of 1611 may have been sparked by severe storms and plagues along with the preaching of Jesuits. The provost of the territory, Johann Christoph von Westerstetten, would soon become prince-bishop of Eichstätt (r. 1612–1636). As a witch hunter, Johann Christoph had almost 400 people burned in seventy-three sets of executions. The hunting began in April 1611 when the seventy-year-old Barbara Rüfin was arrested for desecration of a Host. While she sat in prison, accusations of her witchcraft reached the authorities. Even her husband, son, and daughter-in-law accused Rüfin of trying to poison her son (and a few cows) because she did not like his marriage. After two weeks of gathering evidence, the authorities stretched her on the rack in bouts of twenty minutes. After two days and a total of seven sessions, she broke down and confessed to the usual *maleficia* and to having sex with the Devil. She also named accomplices. Freed from torture, she tried to renounce her confession, but authorities tortured her again until she "freely" admitted her witchery. On May 16, the executioner first beheaded her with a sword and then burned her corpse. The authorities also confiscated her property.

The circle of witches expanded outward from Barbara Rüfin. After Michael Dier (or Dirren) witnessed her execution and protested her innocence, officials arrested, tortured, convicted, and executed him. The inquisitors were particularly effective in creating a set of eighty-four consistent questions which elicited conforming confessions. Early questions asked about the accused witch's sexual behavior, trying to connect improper sexual activity with witchcraft. The ultimate seducer was the Devil. Later questions investigated blaspheming against the Host by using it in potions and harmful *maleficia*. Other questions clarified the sabbat, which would identify fellow witches. The last question warned the accused witch that she "should think of the salvation of her soul, since she cannot escape the authorities; it is better to suffer a slight earthly punishment than eternal damnation in the hereafter."[7] Inquisitors pursued dozens of names pulled from each confession. These names were kept on file to use for years afterwards. The circle of accused widened to include two priests, the church organist, the wife of a judge, and then the judge himself. The brutality of the system is illustrated by the example of Magdalena Weixler, the wife of a prominent scribe. She protested her innocence to her husband after her arrest in 1614. To obtain better treatment, she vainly tried to bribe the guard with jewelry, then with sex. Although the guard was later convicted for bribery, Magdalena had already been executed.

Such witch hunts readily left themselves open to corruption. The guards in Ellwangen seem to have been particularly criminal in their exposure of evidence and extortion of the accused, all for personal gain. Balthasar Nuss or Roß, a professional witch-hunter who worked for the Abbot of Fulda, boasted of consigning more than 200 witches to the flames. Unfortunately for him, authorities arrested Nuss for corruption and executed him in 1618 after thirteen years in prison. Bavarian authorities also arrested judge Gerhard Sattler of Wemding, who had persecuted witches in 1609–1610. The regime convicted him of corruption and beheaded him in 1613. These examples should have led people to worry about the honesty, effectiveness, and decency of witch-hunting. Fear of hostile diabolic witches continued, however, even after the exposure of official corruption.

HUNTS DURING THE THIRTY YEARS WAR

The intensity of witch-hunting soared during the Thirty Years War (1618–1648). This devastating conflict marked a turning point in German history, if not the witch hunts. Its origins lay in the efforts of the Habsburg dynasty to increase control over their own territories and the empire as a whole. Although a Habsburg regularly succeeded in being elected Holy Roman Emperor, the office itself had continued to decline in actual authority. The Habsburgs had better success in inheriting provinces through marriage, although the newly acquired people often resented the new "foreign" dynasty. The most troublesome territories were Bohemia and Moravia, where the Habsburgs' interest in enforcing Roman Catholicism only worsened existing tensions. Bohemia and Moravia had been centers of religious reform movements since the Hussites of the fifteenth century. As the Habsburgs pushed for Counter-Reformation Catholicism, the Bohemians defied them with "defenestration" or tossing the Habsburg representatives out of a window in the Prague Castle.

Most neighboring states joined in the Thirty Years War, which resulted from this defiance. Rampaging armies inflicted enormous suffering on the Germans, seizing food and supplies, forcefully recruiting men and boys, waging destructive battles, and plundering ruthlessly. Adding to the natural fragility of the agricultural system were crop failures due to bad weather, since the 1620s were notorious for being cold, wet, and rainy. People later remembered 1628 as "the year without a summer." Crop failures drove up prices and created food shortages. The demands of armies, whether paid for by taxes or by plundering an enemy, fueled inflationary crises. The horrors of a long war only amplified the usual fears and panics of people attributing their misfortune to witches. Although the decisions and failures of the territorial princes were actually at fault for most of the suffering, blaming witches was more convenient.

The heightened enthusiasm of Counter-Reformation Catholics to fight for their version of Christianity added to the fanaticism. Any deviation from perceived Roman Catholic orthodoxy was heresy, and heresy had long since become associated with diabolic activity. The Protestant attack on the celibacy of Roman Catholic priests carried over into an overheated concern about sexual temptations of all kinds. Anyone whose sexuality deviated from approved norms ran the danger of being drawn into witch hunts.

A number of prince-bishoprics reenergized witch-hunting at the end of the 1620s. In Eichstätt, the prince-bishop George Frederick von Greiffenclau (r. 1626–1629) burned between 200 and 900 witches, mostly women. In

Würzburg, the phrase "Würzburgish Work" became a synonym for excessive zeal in torturing and burning witches, as demonstrated by Würzburg's prince-bishop, Philip Adolf von Ehrenberg (r. 1623–1631). In Cologne, Ferdinand von Wittelsbach (r. 1612–1650) and his notorious witch hunter Franz Buirmann executed the province's chancellor, the chancellor's wife, the wife of the bishop's personal secretary, and even the executioner.

HUNTS IN BAMBERG

The hunts in the prince-bishopric of Bamberg can serve as a detailed example of this wave by ecclesiastical territorial rulers. Already in 1507 a legal reform called the *Bambergensis* had ranked crimes of religion as the most heinous. During the first phase of the Thirty Years War, Prince-Bishop John Godfrey von Aschhausen (r. 1609–1622) had determinedly recatholicized his diocese, to remove any taint of Protestantism left by his predecessor. He invited in the Jesuits, founded new schools, sent derelict priests to their own special prison, the *Pfaffengewölbe* or "Priests' Vaults," and hunted witches. He had about 300 witches executed.

John Godfrey's successor, John George II Fuchs von Dorrnheim (r. 1623–1632) gained the nickname *Hexenbischof* ("Witches-Bishop"). The centerpiece of his reign was a thorough hunt for witches. His principality's law allowed the confiscation of witches' property. This encouraged the bishop to strike at the upper classes, who possessed most of the wealth. Also, the victims were responsible for all court costs, so the system practically paid for itself. For torture sessions, victims were even liable for the travel expenses of the torturer, his helpers, and horses. At the execution, victims, or rather their surviving relatives, might be charged for everything from the rope, nails, wood, and ignition used at the stake, to the fee for every kind of punishment from beheading and placing a head on a spike, to putting up a ladder to hang a body. Even suicides had to pay for their own body's removal. Hundreds of thousands of florins flowed into the prince-bishop's treasure chests.

One of John George's prisons became known as the *Hexenhaus* (Witches' House). Its walls were covered in Biblical texts, both for edification of and protection against witches. Those brought in for investigation could suffer torture only with the personal consent of the bishop, but that permission he usually gave freely. The examiners might apply hot pincers to the groin, soak the accused in baths of hot lime, or provide herring soaked in salt and pepper as food, without access to any water. Tortures of applying burning feathers on sensitive body areas or dunking in frigid or hot water killed six people. Normally torture was not supposed to kill, but here little care was given. In the rare cases where a subject was found innocent, he or she had to promise not to reveal the methods of investigation.

John George's assistant bishop, Frederick Förner, wholeheartedly supported his superior. Förner wrote a manual for experts and gave more than thirty sermons to instruct the common people about the danger of witches and how to protect themselves. Regular participation in the sacraments was essential, of course. Sacramentals, such as holy water, sacred bells, or consecrated oils, were useful too. Calling on the help of a guardian angel, making the sign of the cross, venerating relics, praying to saints, calling on the Blessed Virgin Mary, and fasting were recommended. Amulets containing snippets of scripture likewise offered aid to the worried.

John Junius

The most famous victim of the hunts in Bamberg was the mayor of the town, John Junius. His troubles started when another important personage, Dr. George Hahn, the bishop's vice-chancellor who had been directing the hunt, was accused and arrested. During Hahn's trial, which lasted from December 1627 to July 1628, investigators also prosecuted his wife, Ursula; his daughter, Maria; his son, George; and their servants. All ultimately burned at the stake. Before they died, however, the Hahn family implicated many others, including priests and mayors, and John Junius.

Officials first examined Junius on June 28, 1628. They found on him a "Devil's Mark" shaped like a four-leaf clover. Two days later, they began the torture sessions. First came thumbscrews, then legscrews, and finally the strappado. The scribe-recorder to these sessions wrote that the investigators noted how Junius felt no pain. Junius likewise refused to admit any witchcraft, blasphemy, or other criminality. Investigators found his endurance under torture and refusal to confess to be unnatural. On July 5, they actually convinced him to confess while not under torture. He admitted to having sex with a demon. He also confessed that he had used a magic powder to kill his own horse, but not his children (as he said the demon had instructed him). Then the authorities marched Junius through the streets of Bamberg, to induce him to identify more witches. When his list seemed too short, they hoisted him on the strappado again.

His letter from July 24, smuggled out to his daughter, reflects some of the horror of these matters. Contrary to what the scribe officially recorded, he felt indescribable agony. On the advice of a guard, he confessed to stop the pain, although he believed himself to be an innocent martyr. He wrote his daughter that his confession was "sheer lies and inventions, so help me God. For I was forced to say all this through fear of the torture that was threatened beyond what I had already endured. For they never leave off with the torture till one confesses something; no matter how pious he really is, he must be a witch. Nobody escapes...."[8] The bishop gave him the special grace of being decapitated with a sword before they burned his remains on August 6.

ERNEST VON EHRENBERG

The hunt even reached the bishop's cousin, Ernest von Ehrenberg. The bishop tried to reform this young man from his rather riotous life by scaring him with an inquisition. Investigators held his trial without him being invited, using testimony extorted from his friends under torture. Officials arrested him and showed him the torture chamber, at which he fainted. Because reform efforts by Jesuits and Franciscans failed, they suspected the Devil was at work. The prince-bishop finally ordered his execution. Von Ehrenberg learned of his condemnation only as he was being brought into the execution chamber. He cursed his escorts and fought against them until exhausted, after which the executioner sliced his head off with a sword.

The story of a nine-year-old boy provides another example of the horrors of the hunts in Bamberg. He is unnamed in the records, ostensibly to protect his identity. Authorities interrogated him for several weeks, during which time he confessed, without torture, to all sorts of demonic activities. He admitted that a demon named George, with horns and goat feet, had both threatened him and shown him to transform his friends into mice and back. After this, the boy said he agreed to learn witchcraft. He underwent a mock baptism in a creek, learned to fly on a pitchfork, and met with demons and others at witches' dances.

His hostile acts included cutting down crops, making powders and potions to poison people and blind an ox, stealing wine, pinching people in their beds at night, killing livestock with freezing weather, spoiling grain, and making flies and rabbits. He described how: " I first had to beat to death a dog, take some of its flesh and blood, mix it up with a secret dye given to me by my demon, and then smear this mixture all over the dog's body. When I did this, I was supposed to dedicate the sacrificed dog to my demon by saying certain words. I tried it and when I finished, a rabbit jumped out of the dog's carcass and hopped away."[9] His demon, George, could visit him in prison, just as other demons consoled other witches there. George also helped the boy briefly escape, through a crack in the wall, to attend a wedding feast. Such crimes should have led to his execution, but the records of it have not survived.

Accusations against the important councilor G. H. Flöck provided a turning point in this hunt. Flöck fled to Nuremberg, but his wife Dorothea Flöckin then became ensnared in the investigation. Flöck and his relatives tried to secure her release by appealing both to Emperor Ferdinand II (r. 1616–1637) and to the pope. Both these important people wrote letters in support of Flöckin. The bishop, however, rushed her trial and had her executed before the letters could arrive. Emperor Ferdinand then intervened more strongly in the hunting policies of the Bishop of Bamberg, urged by his Jesuit confessor and further motivated by political concerns about the election of his son as successor. After Ferdinand's officials investigated the court records, Ferdinand issued an imperial order that property could no longer be confiscated from victims. Although the emperor continued to put pressure on the bishop to slow the hunts, hunting nevertheless continued until the Swedish army invaded the see and took over administration. By that time, the "Witches-bishop" John George II of Bamberg had killed more than 900 victims.

The intervention by the imperial regime finally helped to bring an end to this wave of hunts by 1630. Similarly, the intervention of the *Reichskammerger-icht* (Imperial Chamber Court) at Speyer and the *Reichshofrat* (Imperial Aulic Council) in Vienna also helped to mitigate hunting. These central authorities, however, were too weak and too rarely involved to end the hunts decisively. The invading Swedish armies, which roamed and plundered all over the Empire after 1632, also meant that less attention could be spent on witch-hunting. The exhaustion of the participants, though, after such intense activity of both warfare and trials, probably contributed most to the cessation.

Many scholars at the time, however, continued to urge energetic pursuit of witches during the Thirty Years War. One of the most successful was Benedict Carpzov who published *Practica Rerum Criminalium* ("Practicalities of Crimi-nal Matters") in 1635 as a commentary on the laws of Saxony. His treatise veri-fied witchcraft as one of the worst of all crimes, a *crimen exceptum*. Carpzov himself was a witch hunter, who declared that mere supposition was as good as solid evidence to permit torture. Interestingly, he thought that only Christians could be witches, since he saw witchcraft as a form of apostasy from the true faith. Carpzov's notoriety for hunting was so great that another contemporary believed Carpzov had signed death warrants for more than 20,000 people.

ARGUMENTS AGAINST HUNTING

More reasoned men began to protest against such hunting. One such was Hermann Löher. His *Hochnötige Klage* ("Highly Necessary Complaint") declared that torture had no value. Hostile reactions, though, forced Löher out of the region to exile in Amsterdam. Two Jesuits had more success. Adam Tanner, a Jesuit professor of theology who lectured at the University of Ingol-stadt, criticized the hunts in his four-volume work, *Theologica Scholastica* ("Scholastic Theology") of 1626/1627. Tanner admitted that witches existed and were the worst enemies of the commonwealth. Yet he worried about the use of torture on the innocent, as clearly happened so many times. Moreover, Tanner doubted that members of honorable, high-placed families accused of witchcraft could actually have turned to Satan. He hoped that a specially trained commis-sion could act with spiritual counseling rather than the rack to bring confes-sions. Instead, two inquisitors threatened to torture him. Upon his death from natural causes, superstitious panic ensued when people found a strange device among his possessions. Looking through the eyepiece, they thought they saw a demon. It was, in fact, a microscope, with a mosquito under examination.

Another Jesuit, Paul Laymann, wrote *Theologia moralis* ("Moral Theology") in 1625. It focused on the issue of confessors who in the final sacramental con-fessions of those found guilty of witchcraft heard them protest their innocence. Confessors who believed the condemned to be innocent then found themselves trapped by their own complicity in a system that sent innocents to death. Lay-mann's examination of witch-hunting in Cologne only confirmed his opinion that the methods of hunting witches only made society less well-off, not more secure.

Most influential was the work of the Jesuit priest and professor of moral theology at Paderborn, Frederick Spee von Langenfeld (b. 1591–d. 1635). His 1631 book *Cautio Criminalis* ("Warning about Criminal Prosecutions") drew on his own experiences during the hunts in Würzburg. Spee did not equivocate as Tanner and Laymann had, but directly attacked the witch hunts, urging an end to all hunts and noting how many innocent people suffered. He cautioned that if Germans "consistently insist on conducting trials, no one of any sex, fortune, condition, or rank whatsoever who has earned himself even one enemy or slanderer who can drag him into the suspicion and reputation for witchcraft can be sufficiently safe in these times."[10] Spee had originally published this dangerous text anonymously, but his identity was suspected by church authorities from Rome to his local community. The cautious Spee moved from place to place, until he died of plague spread by the fighting of the Thirty Years War.

Spee's cautionary text nevertheless gained a growing readership as it became translated into German, Dutch, French, and Polish before the end of the century. One reader, Heinrich Schultheiß, the commissioner for witches in Paderborn, argued for the harsh pursuit of witches. On the other hand, Queen Christina of Sweden (see Chapter 7) may have been moved to use her Swedish armies in the empire to help discourage witch-hunting. As years passed, Spee's powerful warnings helped to turn the tide of opinion against the hunts.

Two more incidents show that reason could prevail against fear of witches. In the territory of the Rhine ruled by the Count Palatine in 1628, Ursula Zoller, the ten-year-old daughter of an executed witch, was put on trial. The count's officials were not quite sure what to do with such a young girl, so they solicited opinions from officials and clergy in neighboring principalities. The responses ranged from spanking her and sending her home, to sending her to prison, to trying her and executing her once she reached the "adult" age of twelve. The Count Palatine ultimately decided to send the girl to a church school.

Another accused witch escaped the worst because of her prominent connection. A neighbor accused Katherine Kepler, mother of the famous astronomer Johannes Kepler, of witchcraft in 1615. She allegedly sparked crippling pains and foggy visions in several people and made pigs cry themselves to death. Authorities imprisoned and threatened her with torture for more than a year. Her son's intervention rescued her from the stake by 1621, although she died a year later. Authorities in both these cases declined to persecute witches to the full extent of the law. A few more decades were needed before the laws themselves changed in the Empire.

WITCH-HUNTING IN SWITZERLAND

The southwest corner of the Holy Roman Empire that became Switzerland led the way into modern witch-hunting. The Alpine cantons of Switzerland first began to withdraw from the Holy Roman Empire in 1291. They finally achieved independent sovereign status at the end of the Thirty Years War in 1648. Many of these territories tried to base their government on popular rule, involving townspeople and peasants in elections against hereditary nobility, a democratic type of government unique in Europe. Switzerland's success as a state did not depend on ethnic unity. People in the small nation spoke four different languages: German, French, Italian, and Rheto-romanish, a language derived from ancient Latin.

The first serious witch hunts in all of Europe began in the Swiss valleys of the Simmental in the 1390s and in Lucerne and Lausanne in the 1430s (see above). After a lull, various cantons became heavily involved again in the late fifteenth and sixteenth century. As in the rest of the Holy Roman Empire, regional tensions and diabolic fears allowed some hunts to be intense and powerful. Some areas burned most of the guilty; others merely banished the majority.

With the Reformation, the small Alpine state splintered into serious religious divisions. Many clung to Roman Catholicism, while others embraced Calvinism, which established its base in Geneva. There were even pockets of smaller groups, including Zwinglians, Anabaptists, and even medieval Waldensians. In Zürich, the center of the reformer Ulrich Zwingli, more than two dozen witch trials and eight deaths occurred during the early sixteenth century.

Calvinist hunting was informed by the belief that the Devil actively tempted people in the world. "The Devil made me do it" was a legitimate excuse by Calvinists who had committed sin. Calvinist theologians willingly adopted the writings of both Lutheran and Roman Catholic demonologists. They worried especially about the diabolic pact being a mockery of the Christian covenant between people and God. They saw the Christian's acceptance of the resurrected Jesus as redeemer led to heaven, while a witch's allegiance to the Devil as provider of worldly power led to hell.

DEVIL'S MARK

As proof of such a diabolic contract, the Calvinists popularized the Devil's Mark. Demonologists invented the Mark as a tangible sign left by the Devil of his compact with the witch, partly to provide physical evidence that could be used in court. The only other evidence was the Devil's black book, in which people signed their names, but that corroboration never could be found. To find the Devil's Mark, officials needed to look no further than the accused. Officials would search for it by shaving all hair off the accused and examining every nook and cranny of the body. Since such an examination took place in a public place, such as a court, it brought enormous shame and humiliation. Examiners might also apply pricking, sticking a needle into the suspected spot. If needle-sticking did not result in pain or bleeding, the examiners confirmed the spot as a Devil's Mark. Not surprisingly, poking needles could easily become a form of torture.

The Calvinists readily accepted torture, believing that it forced the witch to break the Devil's hold on their free will. Calvinists likewise readily presumed that anyone accused was guilty, since their general outlook on humans and sin considered the Devil's influence to be pervasive. Calvinists were also more likely to hold public trials than secret inquisitions. Openness did little to protect the accused, however, since popular sentiment so easily accepted the diabolic danger. Furthermore, Calvinist magistrates tended to arrest the poor, feeble, and outcast members of society, especially women.

Although Calvinist officials used torture to extract confessions and accusations, substantial numbers of accused people managed to win their freedom again. For one, Calvinist torturers scrupulously adhered to standards. They restricted torture to three bouts on the strappado over the course of three days. For another, judges such as Germain Colladon (from the 1550s to the 1580s) seem to have realized that torture extorted confessions that better reflected pain and fear of the investigator's questions, rather than truth. Unfortunately for the accused witches, his views took time to prevail.

HUNTS IN GENEVA

Despite Calvin's declaration of hostility toward witches, his stronghold, Geneva, saw fewer than a dozen trials during his time there. Stories of Calvin's extraordinary hostility toward witches far exceed the number of actual trials. Over the next century, though, as many as 477 total trials took place in Geneva, although the rate of executions remained low. The authorities mostly accused women, viewing them as more likely to rebel against God because of the alleged weakness of female character. Many witches in Calvinist territories were tried, technically, as *engraisseurs*, or spreaders of plague who worked with the Devil, but only possessed power for this one evil task. Authorities killed supposed plague spreaders more frequently than normal witches.

HUNTS IN BERN AND THE PAYS DE VAUD

The Protestant regime in Bern, which ruled the Pays de Vaud, became notorious for the number of its witches. Already before the Reformation, a hunt in 1448 had burned a physician for cannibalizing infants. Serious hunting began after 1550 and mostly ended by 1650. During this period at least a few witches were burned every year. Typically, a small spurt of accusations of a half-dozen people would agitate a region for a few months, followed by single arrests for a few years, then a repeat of a small hunt. The largest hunt burned twenty-seven witches at Chillon castle in 1613. Unrestricted application of torture (atypical for Calvinists) resulted in a 90 percent conviction rate. Neighboring Roman Catholic Fribourg, in contrast, carefully regulated the use of torture and only convicted one-third of the accused. An estimated 1,200 people died as witches in the area around Bern.

One notable victory for the innocent in Swiss territories was the accusation of Marie Joly in the diocese of Basel in 1592. Locals accused her of causing harm to people and animals, but after being questioned by authorities for two days on the strappado, Marie still maintained her innocence. Upon her release, her accusers from the village were forced to pay for the costs of the investigation.

HUNTS IN LIECHTENSTEIN

The tiny country of Liechtenstein, squeezed today between Switzerland and Austria, actually came into existence because of a witch hunt. In its capital of Vaduz, the local count carried out hunts between 1648 and 1680 that killed as many as 300 people. As the hunting reached into upper class families, several nobles complained to the *Reichshofrat*. An investigation confirmed an unreasonable brutality to the hunt, which led to the count's arrest and imprisonment. The little province was soon sold to the Liechtenstein dynasty, which still rules there today.

Cantons near Vaduz also suffered comparable hunts. These hunts came to the attention of the Roman Inquisition (see Chapter 6), which labored to regulate, and even end, them. Geneva saw its last executions by the 1650s. Still, trials remained a possibility in some Swiss cantons through the eighteenth century, although widespread hunts diminished to sporadic individual persecutions. For example, a hunt in Zug in 1737 freed Max Stadlin and his daughter, Euphemia, after they resisted torture. His wife, Anna Maria, was not as fortunate. She suffered torture and admitted to witchcraft, only to recant afterwards. So, they tortured her again for a total of six times, after which she recanted no more. They then executed her. The lone witch could still fear persecution in Switzerland before 1800.

WITCH-HUNTING IN THE NETHERLANDS

Like Switzerland, the United Provinces of Netherlands belonged to the Holy Roman Empire at the beginning of the time of the witch hunts. Throughout the Middle Ages, France and the Holy Roman Empire fought over the rich and prosperous territories of the Lowlands, which included what would become today's "Benelux" countries of Belgium, the Netherlands, and Luxembourg. The Lowland territories experienced only a little hunting until the mid-sixteenth century. For example, urban governments in Utrecht and Amsterdam executed fewer than a dozen witches before 1555. The Reformation brought sects of Anabaptists into the region, whose persecutions occupied the attention of the Catholic Habsburg authorities, perhaps to the exclusion of witch-hunting. Then, rapid expansion of Calvinism transformed the Dutch-speaking provinces into a Reformation stronghold by the middle of the sixteenth century. Witch-hunting was embraced along with Calvinism. In Gröningen in Gelderland officials killed twenty witches in 1547, as well as five others in 1562.

An interesting case in 1550 arose from the accusations of Jochum Bos in the village of Nijkerk. In his travels, Bos had become aware of magical lore and began boasting of his abilities to find witches. He used his knowledge to accuse twenty-three-year-old Neele Ellers and four older women of bewitching fifteen-year-old Geertgen Goosen and others. Ellers' family in turn accused Bos of slander and tried to intimidate him into withdrawing his accusations. The authorities took Bos, Ellers, and the four other accused women to the local capital of Arnhem. There Bos, by then notorious for his drunkenness and womanizing, suffered his own share of accusers. Rather than be tortured himself, he recanted. Here, the ability of the *lex talionis*, which permitted the accused to demand sufficient evidence, was a mitigating factor. Such moderation, however, was soon lost. The taint of witchcraft remained on Neele Ellers. In the 1590s, she and many of her family were accused again, arrested, and executed in Utrecht.

Cases of accusers being accused were not isolated. Soothsayers Jacuob Judoci de Rosa in 1547 and Dirck Pieterszn in 1551 both wound up punished themselves after having identified witches. Accusations of a diabolic conspiracy, however, remained rare; alleged crimes were typically *maleficia*, rather than diabolic pacts. Usually the accused was already known in the community for *infamia*, a bad reputation and thus already condemned in popular opinion, if not a court of law. Still, a good defense could lead to an acquittal for the accused and guilty verdicts for the accusers. Overall, witch-hunting at this time in the Netherlands remained rather restrained.

Philip II and Rebellion

In the second half of the sixteenth century, the Netherlands rebelled against Spanish rule, leading to the provinces becoming a sovereign nation by 1648. The fervently Roman Catholic King Philip II of Spain (r. 1556–1598) had inherited the territories from his father, Emperor Charles V. Philip II wanted not only to benefit from the taxes and revenues of these wealthy Dutch towns and territories, but also to convert the people to Roman Catholicism once again. This motivated the Dutch to declare independence as the United Provinces of the Netherlands, in 1581. After roughly eighty years of conflict, Dutch independence was internationally acknowledged at the end of the Thirty Years War.

In the meantime, witch-hunting had intensified from both Calvinist and Roman Catholic interests. Philip II enabled witch hunters through his condemnation of Protestantism as a heresy. The instruments and methodology of the Spanish Inquisition came to the Lowland countries. In 1570, torture could be used against suspected heretics, although serious evidence was necessary to permit torture, and a second torture session was only allowed under the license of professional lawyers. Restrictions on trade and shipping, due to warfare, coincided with minor hunts in 1585 and 1591. By 1592, the Spanish regime equated witchcraft and demons with heresy and passed a law to exterminate it.

The main Dutch court in Holland rejected the law the next year, adding to their rebellion against Philip II. Perhaps trade gave the Dutch Netherlands more resilience to inevitable economic downturns caused by flood, famine, plague, or war and less reason to look for scapegoats in witches. Other provinces soon quickly followed, ending witch burnings in the United Provinces by 1608. Serious hunting, however, continued in the occupied areas under Spanish authority (see Chapter 6).

Fear and resentment toward witches lingered in the Netherlands, but Dutch officialdom tried to discourage further persecutions. The religious diversity of Christians in the Netherlands led to one of the first genuinely tolerant states. Dutch Calvinists, as the majority, permitted the Mennonite Anabaptist, Roman Catholic, and Lutheran minorities to practice their faiths in peace. Some of the powerful arguments that helped to end witch-hunting came from intellectuals living in the Netherlands. One was the refugee scholar René Descartes (b. 1596–d. 1650), from France. His "Cartesian doubt" required proof for something so fantastic as witches. His promotion of the scientific method showed that witches could not be proven to be real. The tenets of rationalism fortified the skeptics of witch-hunting.

Benedict de Spinoza

Another refugee who settled in the Netherlands, the philosopher Benedict de Spinoza (b. 1633–d. 1677), also argued for rationality. Spinoza's family members were Marranos, Jewish converts in Portugal (see Chapter 6). Suspected by the Portuguese Inquisition of lacking proper sincerity in their Christianity, the Spinoza family had emigrated to Amsterdam. Spinoza cherished the intellectual freedom of the Netherlands. He undertook a number of broad philosophical inquiries, some of which bordered on pantheism, the belief that the divine and the world were joined. In such a divine universe, the Devil had no place; he simply did not exist. Jewish rabbis declared Spinoza a heretic in 1656, but Dutch authorities were not inclined to prosecute him. At that point, they had long since stopped burning anyone.

Balthasar Bekker

Nevertheless, some Dutch Christian clergy stubbornly continued to argue that witches remained a danger, even though witch hunts had ended. Balthasar Bekker (b. 1634–d. 1698) sought to contradict this idea. His book *De Betoverde Weereld* ("The World Bewitched") of 1691/1693 argued against witches, using both a close reading of the Bible and the history of demonological thought. Bekker, who had been influenced by Descartes, also argued against superstition, which included most magical practices. His interpretation of the Bible was different from most of his colleagues. For him, the Devil was not a real danger to be feared, but was rather a symbol for sin. The Devil and demons could not influence people, nor could humans interact with them. Bekker even questioned the literal reading of Christ expelling demons, as found in the Gospels. This interpretation moved him away from standard Christianity toward deism, a belief which removes God and the Devil from constant and intimate intervention in this world.

Bekker's book found a ready reception, both locally and internationally, selling thousands of copies and being quickly translated into French and German. In reaction, pamphlets attacking Bekker also poured out (see Illustration 14). Bekker's local colleagues forced him out of his position and expelled him from the Dutch Reformed clergy. Still, neither he nor his book ended up burned in the Netherlands, and he helped turn the tide of popular opinion decisively against belief in witches.

WEIGHING AT OUDEWATER

What remained of witch-hunting in the Netherlands was an oddity that can be enjoyed even today: scales in the town of Oudewater, used to test witches by weighing them. The practice of weighing witches allegedly dated back to a privilege granted by Emperor Charles V, although such a document can no longer be located. The idea of witches having little or no weight had been suggested by some strixologists to explain how little broomsticks could carry them through the air. The town of Oudewater had a scale that was normally used to weigh sacks of grain or wheels of cheese. The town began to weigh people as a way to help protect them from witch accusations. Town officials used their scale to certify that most people weighed as much as they were expected to. For a fee, the weighed persons could then have documented proof that they were not a witch, and they could show this documentation as they traveled to more hostile territories. The weighing at Oudewater began in the mid-seventeenth century just as witch-hunting was ending in the Dutch Netherlands. Official weighing in Oudewater continued as a legal means of testing witches until the mid-eighteenth century, possibly as late as 1823. Today the scale is a popular tourist attraction.

THE DECLINE OF HUNTING IN THE EMPIRE

Occasional bouts of hunting continued in some German territories during the late seventeenth century. A theology professor at the local university, the Jesuit Bernhard Löper, started a hunt in Paderborn lasting from 1656 to 1658. He began with trying to exorcise two nuns from demonic possession, then gained dozens of possessed victims of witches. Confusion and hesitation on the part of the local bishop, Dietrich Adolf von der Recke (r. 1650–1661), allowed civil disorder to break out. Adolf's own hunt claimed several victims. By contrast, his successor, Ferdinand von Fürstenburg (r. 1661–1683), ceased hunting witches. He supported the views of the *Instructio* of the Roman Inquisition, which limited the scope of hunts, restricted investigations, and moderated punishments (see Chapter 6). Prince-Bishop Ferdinand executed only one person for witchcraft and largely ended the hunts for good in Paderborn.

THE WITCH MAYOR OF LEMGO

At about the same time in the nearby Protestant County of Lippe, a serious hunt broke out in the town of Lemgo. The town's mayor, Hermann Cothmann, soon acquired the nickname as the *Hexenbürgermeister* (Witches' Mayor) for his zealotry in hunting witches. When Cothmann was twenty-five, his own mother had been condemned as a witch in a hunt that claimed the lives of thirty-seven other people between 1653 and 1656. In 1665, Cothman's own hunt began when a seventeen-year-old named Elisabeth turned herself in as a witch. She claimed to have traveled in a coach to a sabbat, where she and several other citizens of the town met with Satan. Cothman properly acquired the supportive legal declarations from theologians at Rinteln. Elizabeth was allowed to return home and later to flee the town, but others soon found themselves caught up in the mechanisms of the justice system. The widow Plöger, under thumbscrews, confirmed the girl's testimony, and people who had escaped a first hunt fell victim in the second. The hunt slowly expanded to include ninety victims before it ended in 1681. By 1715, the town council had become embarrassed and ordered the "Black Book" of records of the hunt to be cut up, shredded, and burned.

THE WITCH'S TOWER OF LINDHEIM

Lindheim, in the Würzburg region, suffered its third and worst hunt in 1661–1663. A hunt in 1632 had killed three, and another in 1650–1653, several more. The 1663 hunt arose from the suspicions of the magistrate, a former soldier named George Ludwig Geiss. Magistrate Geiss took advantage of the absence of the local mayor, Baron Oynhausen, to accuse a midwife of killing a child and using the corpse to produce potions. Local officials exhumed the child's body and found it intact, but Geiss managed to continue the prosecution anyhow. He favored a special torture in his prison, called the Witch Tower. He suspended victims above a slow burning fire. More than two dozen people were finally executed, including the dead baby's parents.

The hunt ended through the efforts of a miller, John Schüler, and his friends. Geiss had implicated Schüler and his wife in the death of their stillborn son, allegedly by a midwife who had bewitched the child and later used its body in potions. The Schülers, in contrast, blamed the death on natural causes. They even exhumed the baby from its grave, which proved that the body was intact and not made into some witch's brew. Geiss still maintained the validity of the confessions he had gained from torture. He used a tortured confession from another purported witch to implicate Schüler's wife, whom he then tortured to accuse her husband. Geiss managed to torture Schüler himself for several days, although he could not get the miller to stand by his extorted confession. Schüler's friends rescued the miller from the Witch Tower by breaking in through the roof. His wife, unfortunately, refused to join in the escape and was burned a week later. Schüler's friends contacted lawyers; brought back the mayor, Baron Oynhausen; and appealed to the Imperial Court in Speyer. The court ordered the hunt to cease. The mayor fired Geiss, who left town, taking his "fair" share of the legal fees with him. Later, he allegedly fell from his horse and died in a gully soon called the "Devil's Ditch."

ZAUBERER-JACKL

Salzburg experienced a strange hunt in 1680–1689. It centered around the outlaw Jakob Koller, who was better known as *Zauberer-Jackl* (Magic-Jackie). In 1675, when Jackl was fifteen, authorities burned his mother, the beggar Barbara Koller, known as "Schinderbärbl" (Tanner-Barbie), for witchcraft. During the investigation, she accused her son of magic, but authorities could not find him to arrest him. Jackl soon led a band of local beggars and vagrants, many of whom were children. He provided them with money and food. To create a community, he fashioned magic rituals, drawing blood and using it to sign members' names in a book. Jackl himself was said to possess a cap, or possibly a salve, that could make him invisible. If that did not work, he could transform himself into various farm animals, although he could also become a werewolf and fly on a pitchfork. Zauberer-Jackl allegedly could call up swarms of rats and bugs as allies. His reputed crimes included the murder of pregnant women, theft, and desecrating religious statues and pictures.

In hunting down this notorious witch, authorities arrested and charged nearly 200 people. About two-thirds of the accused were male, almost three-quarters were minors under eighteen, and nearly all were beggars. Most, 139, were found guilty and executed, usually through strangulation, with the corpses then burned. The *Fallbeil*, an early form of the guillotine, ended the lives of many of the younger victims. A handful of others died in prison or were exiled. A few "simple-minded" children were sent to orphanages. Neighboring Bavaria and the Tyrol also caught and put on trial various young people allegedly connected to the magic band. Zauberer-Jackl himself, though, escaped capture, to disappear into history.

By this time, many university professors had come to doubt the existence of a diabolic conspiracy of witches. In 1673, the University of Tübingen discouraged the prosecution of a woman accused by children of poisoning. A few years later, ten-year-old Bartholomew Sieben confessed to poisoning the schoolmaster's son and accused his step-grandmother Anna Hafnerin of teaching him witchery. The University of Tübingen suggested moderation, mere flogging as punishment, rather than execution. Unfortunately for the accused, in 1683 local people generated a panic that got Sieben and Hafnerin arrested, tortured, and executed for witchcraft. Their accused crimes, however, did not include a diabolic pact. After a mob killed another member of the family, authorities banished other family members for their own protection. The authorities tried to calm the situation down, discouraging local fears about the dangers of witches.

CHRISTIAN THOMASIUS

One scholar, Christian Thomasius (b. 1655–d. 1728), argued decisively against witch-hunting and torture. Thomasius had risen in academic circles to become rector, the equivalent of a president, of the University of Halle in the Brandenburg territories. In 1694, local authorities examining Barbara Leberenztin asked Thomasius, as a university scholar, to render a legal opinion about her guilt. He took the time to study the strixology of Carpzov, Bodin (see Chapter 4), and DelRio (see Chapter 6). Thomasius, however, came to quite opposite conclusions, agreeing more with Spee. He complained about excessive prosecutorial zeal in the case and admonished the entire legal system to take caution in hunting witches.

Thomasius' own colleagues on the theological faculty, who still maintained the dangerous reality of witches, demanded that he revise his official opinion. Thomasius and his colleagues began to argue back and forth in a series of academic debates. When his colleagues tried to quash and burn his writings, King August II of Poland and Saxony (r. 1697–1733) allowed him to continue. Thomasius' two books, *Dissertatio de Crimine magiae* ("Dissertation on the Crime of Magic") of 1701, and *Dissertatio de origine ac progressu processus inquisitorii contra sagas* ("Inquiry into the Origin and Progression of the Inquisitorial Process against Witches") of 1712, reemphasized the traditional interpretation that demons could not take material form and thus could not really harm humans or make a diabolic pact (see Illustration 10). To believe otherwise, he maintained, derived either from insanity or the brutality of torture.

Thomasius died in 1728, the year in which the Prussian government executed a witch for the last time. Prussia had already reformed the procedures for dealing with witches beginning in 1714. By then, any sorcery case that involved the death penalty had to be referred, in writing, to the king. Only the monarch could then issue a death warrant. By 1721, the Prussian government eliminated the death penalty for all crimes of magic. The enlightened despot Frederick II or the Great (r. 1740–1786) eliminated torture and praised the late Thomasius for recommending this. Other governments followed.

Some academics and authorities still continued to argue in favor of the danger of witches. One notable academic controversy erupted in Bavaria in the mid-eighteenth century. In 1759, a Protestant Priest, Sterzinger, sparked a debate by holding a lecture at the Academy of Sciences in Munich, during which he attacked the idea of hunting witches. In the subsequent "Bavarian

Witch War," Church authorities both in Rome and Bavaria disputed his position, once again contending that belief in God also required belief in a Satanic pact with witches. The *Kehlheimer Hexenhammer* ("Hammer of Witches from Kehlheim") of 1769 repeated the old arguments of Institoris. By that time, the days of the hunts had passed. Shortly after 1800, torture and laws against witchcraft were deleted from the legal codes in Bavaria.

THE LAST TRIALS

The last significant witch trial in Germany took place in the Würzburg region in 1749. Eighty-year-old Sister Maria Renate Sanger of the Premonstratensian convent of Unterzell allegedly helped cause the possession of a young nun. Her superiors interrogated Sister Maria with torture and a list of 240 questions derived partly from the *Malleus Maleficarum*. She confessed to having had sex with demons since the age of eight, having presided over a sabbat by the age of twelve, and recently having abetted the Devil's attack on the young nun. The bishop found her guilty and then had her beheaded and her body burned.

The last legally authorized execution in the Empire took place in 1775 in the territory of the prince-abbot of Kempten. A local doctor, John Joseph Gassner, blamed illnesses on witchcraft. He helped to implicate a homeless and probably mentally ill woman, Anna Maria Schwägelin, several times betrayed by men who had abandoned her after promising to marry her. She had been heard to say that she would rather be in the Devil's service than abide in the local homeless shelter and workhouse. During her arrest on February 20 for vagrancy, she had raved and cursed the Blessed Virgin Mary. This foul curse led authorities to suspect witchcraft and a pact with the Devil. Their investigation led her to confess to having attended sabbats and committed other evil acts with her former lover. The prince-abbot himself ordered her to be beheaded on April 11.

The final execution in western Europe took place in Switzerland on June 17, 1782. The alleged witch, Anna Göldi, had worked as a servant in many households over the years. Her two illegitimate pregnancies ended in the infants' deaths, leading authorities to prosecute and punish her for infanticide in the 1760s. In 1780, at the age of forty-six, Göldi entered the service of a physician named Tschudi, to look after his three children. After a squabble, nine-year-old Anna Maria Tschudi began to spit up pins. Even after the parents fired Göldi, little Anna Maria continued to spit up stones and pieces of metal and then suffered fits and lameness. The pitiful girl blamed the former servant. Authorities investigated, arrested, and tortured Anna Göldi until she confessed. The executioner beheaded her with a sword.

After this miserable case, the witch hunts were over within the territories of the Holy Roman Empire. Shortly afterwards, in 1806, the Empire itself collapsed. Between 1400 and 1806, tens of thousands of innocent persons had died for the supposed crime of witchcraft. The voices of Nider, Krämer, Binsfeld, Carpzov, and superstitious peasants convinced numerous regimes and their officials to take action. They supported an aberration in Christian thought that attributed lethally effective powers to witches, although other voices, most notably Agrippa, Weyer, and Spee, denied the ability of humans to magically affect nature and thus asserted the essential wrongness of hunting witches. Their voices were not always heard in their lifetimes, but eventually they won out.

NOTES

1. Peter Morton, ed., *The Trial of Tempel Anneke: Records of a Witchcraft Trial in Brunswick, Germany*, trans. Barbara Dähms (Peterborough, Ontario: Broadview Press, 2006), 82.

2. *The Malleus Maleficarum of Heinrich Kramer and James Sprenger*, trans. and ed. Montague Summers (1928, 1948; reprint ed., New York: Dover Publications, 1971) [Part I., Q. 14], 74.

3. Martin Luther, *Luther's Works, Table Talk*, vol. 54, ed. and trans. Theodore G. Tappert (Philadelphia: Fortress Press, 1967), 188.

4. Henry Cornelius Agrippa von Nettesheim, *Three Books of Occult Philosophy*, ed. and annotated by Donald Tyson; trans. James Freake (Woodbury, MN: Llewellyn Publications, 1993), 696.

5. Johann Weyer, *On Witchcraft: An Abridged Translation of Johann Weyer's De prestigiis daemonum*, trans. John Shea and ed. Benjamin G. Kohl and H. C. Erik Midelfort (Asheville, NC: Pegasus Press, 1998), 241.

6. Johann Weyer, *Witches, Devils, and Doctors in the Renaissance: Johann Weyer, De praestigiis daemonum*, trans. John Shea, ed. George Mora. Medieval & Renaissance Texts & Studies, 73 (Binghamton, NY: Center for Medieval and Early Reniassance Studies, State University of New York at Binghamton, 1991), 173.

7. Christoph Hinckeldey, ed. *Criminal Justice Through The Ages: From divine judgement to modern German legislation*, Medieval Crime Museum, Rothenburg ob der Tauber, 4 (Heilsbronn, Germany: Druckerei Schulist, 1981), 190.

8. Lara Apps and Andrew Gow, *Male Witches in Early Modern Europe* (Manchester, UK: Manchester University Press, 2003), 163.

9. Hans Sebold, *Witch Children: from Salem Witch Hunts to Modern Courtroom*, (Amherst, NY: Prometheus Books, 1995), 132.

10. Friedrich Spee von Langenfeld, *Cautio Criminalis, or a Book on Witch Trials*, trans. Marcus Hellyer, Studies in Early Modern German History (Charlottesville, VA: University of Virginia, 2003), 221.

CHAPTER 4

The Witch Hunts in France

At the beginning of the witch hunts, France was struggling for survival as a state. The Valois dynasty survived the Hundred Years War, however, and went on to become the strongest monarchy in Europe. Over the next centuries, French kings would continue to try to increase their power from Paris outward into every corner of the kingdom. During the most intense period of witch hunting, the centralizing and secularizing regime in France increasingly came to dominate regional and local governments. The clergy were brought to obedience through the concept of a "Gallican" Church, which put French interests ahead of universal, catholic Christendom. The only resistance to royal absolutism centered in secular courts run by the nobility. This took longer to overcome. By the end of the witch hunts, France was wrestling with its transformation into the first modern state in Europe, gained through the French Revolution. The growing strength of the central government affected how witches were hunted in France. French absolutism eventually eliminated witch hunting, because it concentrated authority in the king. While the hunts lasted, however, the kingdom of France experienced enough hunts to make its death toll second only to the Holy Roman Empire.

As in the Holy Roman Empire, most hunting was led by local and regional courts, not those of the monarchy. Many of these courts were conducted by learned and noble judges who exercised broad authority. These were secular courts, not those of bishops or of the Inquisition. Aristocratic control sometimes allowed local hunts to get out of hand, although appeals to provincial and royal courts often moderated their severity.

The most important appeals were to the *parlements*, regional panels of judges and representatives who would hear cases and adjudicate laws. The most important *parlement*, that of Paris, covered the largest territory and acted as a sort of Supreme Court. It only allowed about one-fifth of the witch-hunting cases that came before it to end with an execution. Other provincial *parlements* also reduced killing, although to a lesser degree. For decades, though, most French courts accepted witch trials as part of the legal system, even though witch hunting had never really been codified into French law. Only the kings themselves would eventually shut down hunting, overruling any local interests in keeping the pyres burning.

What made French witch hunting somewhat unique were its targets and punishments. France seemed to experience a rather large number of werewolf and demonic possession cases, the latter especially involving nuns during the seventeenth century. Although women comprised the majority of targets in most provinces, the persecution of men outweighed women in Burgundy and Normandy. One punishment often used for witchcraft was consignment to the galleys, large warships powered by oars rather than sails. Since the work was hard and dangerous, the government usually forced convicted criminals to man the oars. This punishment only applied to guilty male witches, of course. Most convicted female witches were hanged or strangled, with their bodies burned, though some were banished or publicly whipped. The French were a little less inclined to burn witches than the Germans.

WITCH TRIALS THROUGH THE HUNDRED YEARS WAR

As related in Chapter 2, France had experienced a great deal of heresy in the Middle Ages. As the actual threat of heretics diminished after 1350, the Inquisition helped to fuel an interest in witches. Older history books point to this important transition in the records of trials at Toulouse in the early fourteenth century, which supposedly contained early mentions of the sabbat and other witch activity. More recent historians, though, have exposed these documents as forged by nineteenth-century historians eager to make a reputation or prove the cruelty of the Church, so the information is wrong. Nevertheless, the intellectual and legal framework for eliminating heretics, as seen in the Holy Roman Empire, did shift to hunting witches.

The first serious trials in France began during a period of political instability. Philip the Fair (r. 1285–1314) had greatly succeeded at expanding the power and authority of the monarchy, as shown in his crushing of the "heretical" Templars and his intimidation of the papacy. After his death, however, disputes about inheritance of the throne, together with tensions with England, led to the outbreak of the Hundred Years War (1338–1453).

This war was episodic. It did not entail constant violence over a century, but rather periodic brief moments of slaughter and destruction in certain provinces, followed by long periods of relative quiet and recovery. Nevertheless, the war weakened France and almost destroyed the monarchy. In 1420, King Henry V of England was even crowned and recognized as King of France. The rightful heir of the French king, called the "Dauphin," struggled to hold onto power in the southern part of the realm. By 1453, though, the Dauphin, now King Charles VII (r. 1422–1461), and his French armies had defeated the English.

Concurrently, during these twelve decades of war, new strixological concepts sparked the witch hunts.

THE HUNT IN PARIS, 1391

Witch-hunting started with a few minor trials. The first French witch trial by secular, rather than ecclesiastical authorities, led to the burning of two women: thirty-four-year-old Jehanne de Brigue, called "La Cordière," and Macette de Ruilly. Both were accused of conspiring with a devil named Haussibut to kill Macette's husband. The *parlement* of Paris hesitated and studied the evidence for quite a while, suggesting that such a charge was still unusual in nature. Confessions wrung from the ladder and rack, together with evidence of some charms and a communion Host, finally convinced the court to find the women guilty. They were burned on August 19, 1391, in Paris.

Another late medieval witch trial focused on princely courts and accusations of attempted murder. In 1397, madness overcame King Charles VI (r. 1380–1422). He and others blamed witches in general. The king accused his own physicians of witchcraft and even pointed the finger at his brother, Louis, Duke of Orléans. Louis had allegedly touched a weapon against the corpse of a hanged criminal cut down from the gallows; had stored a ring in the corpse's mouth; and had made powders from its bones and pubic hair. Louis survived this accusation and his descendents became kings under the name of the Valois dynasty.

JOAN OF ARC

The most famous politically based witch accusation was against Joan of Arc (b. 1412–d. 1431). Joan's unique story stands out in historical annals. As a young teenager from the border regions of France and the Empire, Joan felt inspired by the voices of Saints Catherine and Margaret and the Archangel Michael to bring about the coronation of the Dauphin as King of France. People actually believed her incredible story. In early 1429, the Dauphin put her at the head of an army that successfully relieved the siege of Orléans, turning the tide of the Hundred Years War once more to the French advantage. By summer, the Dauphin had been crowned King Charles VII in the Cathedral of Rheims, with Joan at his side. She continued her campaigning, now to liberate France entirely from English forces. Burgundian allies of the English captured her in May 1430, however, and turned her over to the English and to the Inquisition.

The Inquisition considered charging her with witchcraft. Ultimately, though, the charges only included the lesser charge of divination. They burned her at the stake not because she was a witch, but because she recanted her confession and refused to give up wearing men's clothing. Popular tradition in England, however, continued to see Joan as a witch, as shown in Shakespeare's play *Henry VI, Part One*. The French, in contrast, hailed her as a national heroine.

In 1920, Joan achieved the official status of sainthood in the Roman Catholic Church.

BLUEBEARD

One of Joan's compatriots, Baron Gilles de Rais (b. 1404–d. 1440), the Marquis de Laval, sometimes called Bluebeard, had a much more elaborate case of witchcraft developed against him. When he served with Joan of Arc as marshal of France, he appeared noble, generous, and pious, with his founding of chapels and funding of Masses. Shortly after Joan's death in 1432, he began secretly to dabble in alchemy and sorcery.

In 1440, the Bishop of Nantes brought charges against Gilles de Rais, perhaps because of accusations by family members who feared that he was squandering the family fortune. Officials arrested him, eleven other men, and two women as coconspirators in a bizarre and horrible set of crimes. Torture of several accomplices and of Gilles himself helped produce lurid evidence. Gilles was alleged to have kidnapped children fourteen years earlier (before he knew Joan of Arc) for use in magical potions. He had cut their throats and committed sodomy on them. He then supposedly used the blood of children and pregnant women to write spells in order to predict the future. In total, he had burned and hidden the bodies of about 140 victims, although some original estimates ran to as high as 800.

As part of these ceremonies, Gilles de Rais may have celebrated the Black Mass. Both the sabbat and a Black Mass were heretical perversions of the Christian liturgy of the Eucharist. The Devil himself personally presided over the sabbat, which was held in a wild forest glen or mountaintop, whereas a human priest conducted the Black Mass, often in an actual church. In a Black Mass, the presiding priest would merely invoke the Devil, not expecting the demon to be physically present. During the ceremony, bloodletting, killing, and sex might take place in the sacred space. In doing these deeds, though, the priest violated his sacramental vows with blasphemy. Although Black Masses are commonly associated with Satan worship and witchcraft today, they actually appeared only rarely in the trial records of the witch hunts.

After his torture, Gilles confessed to many of the crimes at three separate courts: the Inquisition's, the bishop's, and the Duke of Brittany's. The authorities hanged him and two of his compatriots at the end of October 1440, although his family was allowed to rescue his body from a dishonorable disposal in flames and bury it elsewhere.

People have debated about the case ever since. Was de Rais guilty of playing with magic or of the incredible crimes piled up against him? Did he confess because he had been mentally or physically broken by imprisonment and torture, had actually committed the crimes, or hoped he would get a milder penance? That many of his accomplices escaped punishment gives the matter a suspicious air. Some historians have argued that he was targeted for his wealth or secrets known about important personages. Gilles de Rais's case remains an unusual and notorious witch trial. A high-ranking personage accused of such bizarre cruelty would not occur again in France for several centuries.

DAUPHINÉ 1421

Trials against common people for witchcraft were already increasing in France by the time Gilles de Rais was hanged. For example, trials beginning in 1421 in the province of Dauphiné (so named because it belonged to an earlier Dauphin, the heir to the French throne) had revealed pacts with the Devil, who appeared in the form of dark animal-shaped spirits or of a little black man. One accused witch, Pierre Vallin, confessed after torture that he had submitted himself to Beelzebub sixty-three years earlier, kissing the demon's thumb. Vallin said he met Beelzebub at a synagogue and copulated with the demon, who took the form of a girl. Pierre's *maleficia* included raising storms and murdering his own daughter. The Inquisition found him guilty, confiscated his property, and turned him over for punishment to the court of the local noblewoman, Elinor of Grolea. Her officials sentenced Vallin to confess his crimes publicly in the castle courtyard. A local judge also tortured him further, to try and extort a few more names of his coconspirators. He resisted and was probably executed soon after.

THE COUNCIL OF BASEL

Important ideas about witches also began to circulate at the Council of Basel (1431–1439; see Chapter 3). Since the Council of Basel took place in the French-speaking corner of the Holy Roman Empire, its ideas easily spread into France. One participant, Nicholas Jacquierius (b. ca.1400–d. 1472), or Nicolas Jacquier, added to strixological lore with his *Flagellum haereticorum fascinariorum* ("A Scourge for Heretical Witches") from 1458. As an inquisitor in Tournai and Bohemia, Jacquier had plenty of experience with heresy and witchcraft. Jacquier argued that the contemporary problem with witches differed from the deluded wretches of past ages who believed in the witchery of the night ride, as described in the *Canon Episcopi*. He based his proof for the reality of demonic sex based on evidence of *maleficia*, confessions, and witnesses to the sexual activity. He described their evil activities at their "synagoga" an early and clearly antisemitic reference to the sabbat). Even if the events witches caused were only imaginary, Jacquier declared, witches were still heretical and deserved the harshest punishment. He thought the problem so serious that even a recantation of heresy should not save witches, as it might a different sort of heretic.

Another participant at the Council of Basel, Martin le Franc, worked for both the legitimate pope, Nicholas V, and Duke Amadeus of Savoy, who became the antipope, or false claimant to the papacy, elected by the Council of Basel in its late, radical phase. In 1440, Martin wrote a long poem, *Le*

Champion des Dames ("The Defender of Ladies"), as an argument both for and against the virtue of women. In some passages, a misogynistic character lists arguments about women as witches, including the notion that witches flew to their meetings with the Devil. One manuscript even contains the first known picture of a witch flying on a broomstick (see Illustration 1). The poet ultimately champions women and attacks the reality of witches, saying "There is no aged woman so stupid/Who has been guilty of committing the least of these deeds,/But in order to have them burned or hanged,/The enemy confuses human nature."[1] Despite Le Franc's defense, the belief grew that the Devil actually enabled witches to do harm.

The learned judge Claude Tholosan, another attendee of Basel, participated in trials in the Dauphiné, that resumed between 1428 and 1447. His *Ut magorum et maleficiorum errores* ("Concerning the Errors of Magicians and Witches") of 1436 fleshed out the growing accusations against witches. He believed ten thousand witches could travel to a sabbat, although he was somewhat skeptical about witches' flying. He identified witches as a new and dangerous sect.

Various strixologists applied this argument of novelty to get around the *Canon Episcopi*. Persecutions in Carcassone around 1450 led Jean Veniti to write his *Tractatus contra demonum invocatores* ("Treatise against Those Who Invoke Demons") in 1470. Veniti concurred that the witches were a new sect, and thus the old interpretations no longer applied. The intellectual distinctions hardly mattered, though, as people continued to hear more stories and warnings about witches in their midst. As the danger of witches gained currency, more witches would be identified.

ARRAS THROUGH THE FRENCH WARS OF RELIGION

The significant hunts in Arras or Artois from 1459 to 1462 brought France into out-of-control persecution. They started with an investigation into the heretical Waldensians (or Vaudois) that entangled a local hermit, Robert (or Robinet) de Vaulx. Robert's vocation of poverty and suffering made him suspected by the Inquisition. Under torture, Robert implicated a local prostitute, Deniselle of Douai, and a poet, Jean la Vitte. Under torture, Deniselle also named Jean as a witch. The poet tried to resist confessing by cutting out his own tongue, but the authorities finally got him to name the first two, and others. He soon died in his cell.

These and later confessions began a series of accusations that the Devil had organized a sect of Waldensians who met regularly in gatherings called "synagoga," either on Thursdays or around the Christian holidays. Some of the witches would fly through the air, born aloft either on broomsticks or the excrement of a horse or mule. At the meeting, the witches ate awful food, which tasted like manure. The Devil himself would then lead an orgy, taking various forms, both natural and unnatural, visible and invisible. His sexual member felt cold upon penetration.

The suffragan, or assistant, bishop of Arras, the Dominican Jean "bishop of Beirut" Jacques du Boys, as well as the dean of the local chapter of Dominicans preached regularly about witches. He asserted that as much as a third of the population of Christendom were witches. On May 9, 1460, the authorities burned five people, including Deniselle. Several individuals tried to retract their confessions before burning, proclaiming that they had been promised simple penance in return for their confessions. On July 7, more were burned, although those who did not retract confessions were spared this time. The widening circle of arrests, ranging from prostitutes to visiting merchants, began to make businessmen in neighboring towns very nervous. Many appealed to the Duke of Burgundy to conduct his own investigation. The duke's consultations with theologians of the University of Louvain gave him little to go on, but he nonetheless sent his heralds to sit in on the inquisitorial procedures.

While this slowed the pace of the trials, it did not stop them. By October 22, 1460, a dozen wealthy men were put to the stake. They had been tortured, whipped, imprisoned, and fined. One of the victims, Huguet Aubry, had appealed to the *parlement* in Paris. That court belatedly intervened. The *parlement*'s judges released many of the accused and brought others directly under their authority in the massive medieval prison in the heart of Paris, the Conciergerie.

The Parisian *parlement* slowly carried out its own investigation. The court's final verdict in 1491 came long after most of the participants were dead. Not surprisingly, the *parlement* adjudicated that the inquisitors had abused their prosecutorial authority. A few were fined, while a memorial cross for the falsely burned witches was set up in town. This one victory came too late for the victims and was little heeded by those who continued hunting witches.

THE FRENCH WARS OF RELIGION

In the late sixteenth century France faced a political crisis similar to the crisis of the Hundred Years War. This time the English were not involved, but Frenchmen fought Frenchmen in French Wars of Religion lasting from 1562 to 1598. The breakdown in the social order during these wars added to the atmosphere of fear and scapegoating favorable for witch hunting.

These religious wars in France grew out of the ideas of the Reformation. In France, the most influential reformer was the Protestant Jean or John Calvin, whose French Calvinists became known as Huguenots. For Calvinists, Satan the tempter was very present and had to be resisted with prayer and upright behavior. The Calvinists were thus notorious for legislating moral behavior, using the force of law to bolster the weakness of the soul. Calvinists won many converts among the successful merchant families in urban centers.

Religious intolerance and hostility became political upon the death in a jousting tournament of King Henry II in 1559, seemingly predicted by the prognosticator Nostradamus (b. 1503–d. 1566). After Henry's death, different religious factions, dominated either by Roman Catholics or Protestants, fought over who would control the crown. The Protestants fell victim to the Massacre of St. Bartholomew's Day in 1572. Members of the Catholic faction murdered thousands of Protestants in cold blood, in Paris and throughout the country-side. But the main Protestant claimant to the throne survived, namely Henry of Navarre, a small realm on the border with Spain.

Although historians once suggested that witch hunting was another method wielded by one side against the other during the civil wars, that does not seem to have been the case. When they did accuse witches, Calvinists generally hunted fellow Calvinists, whereas Roman Catholics largely hunted other Roman Catholics. For instance, many good Catholics suspected that Queen Catherine d'Medici and her son, King Henry III, resorted to witchcraft to hold onto power. Both sides, though, used accusations of witchcraft and magic to prove their moral and doctrinal superiority over the other side.

Calvinist interpretations of the Bible acknowledged the danger of witches and their deserved death. For example, Lambert Daneau, a Calvinist pastor near Orléans, wrote a dialogue on witchcraft in 1564, *Les Sorciers* ("The Witches"). It acknowledged the difficulty in believing in the fantastical crimes attributed to witches, but ultimately came down on the side that witches were real and dangerous. Other Calvinists followed that line of reasoning. While Calvinists agreed with Roman Catholics about the danger of witches, they disagreed on other issues. The reformist Huguenots attacked the Catholic priestly structure as useless. They charged that ideas like transubstantiation, the alleged changing of a wafer of bread into Christ's body through the consecration of the Eucharist, involved magic. Calvinist hostility toward the rituals and rites of the Roman Catholic Church caused them to see Catholics as traffickers in witchcraft and demons.

Roman Catholics, in turn, saw the Calvinists as heretics who needed to be brought back into obedience to the Church. The Spanish Jesuit professor in Paris, Juan de Maldnado or Maldonat, lectured in the 1560s and 1570s on how demons and witchcraft multiplied when heresy was allowed to prosper. Both sides, then, saw the Devil was at work in the world, shaping the opposing religion. Both thought they must fight the Devil to restore the Divine order.

JEAN BODIN

In this time of civil disturbance, some intellectuals were trying to offer ideas for future stability. One such was Jean Bodin (b. 1530–d. 1596). Bodin was both a Carmelite monk and a law professor at Toulouse. He rose to be a member of the Estates-General and a royal attorney. Bodin secured his place as one of the leading intellectual figures of the age through his work on political theory, *Six libres de la république* ("Six Books of the Commonwealth") in 1576. His rigorous explication and defense of absolute monarchy advocated strong royal power, but also supported checks on its total absolutism through representation of the people. This book gained enormous popularity in Bodin's own lifetime. Some of his ideas seem less brilliant nowadays. For instance, Bodin noted that women were the most inferior of humans, even below children, servants, and apprentices.

Four years later, in 1580, Bodin published a text on witchcraft, *De la démonomanie des sorciers* ("On the Demonomania of Sorcerers"). Although largely ignored by today's political historians, in Bodin's own day this treatise was comparable in its popularity and influence to his book on political theory. Some saw it as the flip side of his argument about the importance of public power, because Satan's witches provided a perverted model of the divine order and the ideal human family within the state. Bodin specifically refutes John Weyer (see Chapter 3). He attacked Weyer's credentials, arguing that Weyer had no special training in law and so was not capable of using it to argue. Bodin criticized Weyer's medical knowledge as well, denying that melancholy humors caused women to believe they were witches. He likewise disputed Weyer's analysis and translation of scriptures. Bodin even went so far as to suggest that Weyer himself be prosecuted for being a sorcerer, for teaching sorcery through his book, and for being a blasphemer and protector of witches. Bodin also included the late Cornelius Agrippa and his alleged demon dog in the same category.

For Bodin, witches were real, were inspired by the Devil, and should be punished, even if, ultimately, the Devil was at fault. His conviction was based on hearing confessions of those accused of witchcraft. Bodin had been early convinced by the trial of fifty-year-old Jeanne Harvillier in 1578. Jeanne had confessed without torture that her own mother had signed her as an infant over to the Devil. Jeanne claimed that from the time she was twelve, the Devil initiated her into his society. Appearing as a dark man dressed as a gentleman, he had repeatedly had intercourse with Jeanne, later even in the same bed as her sleeping husband. The Devil had her poison people and attend the sabbat. That one judge hesitated to burn Jeanne at the stake, preferring to hang her instead, prompted Bodin to write his text.

Bodin feared that women were especially vulnerable to Satan's temptations. Witches were such a danger that the concept of a *crimen exceptum* applied, namely the idea that guilt could be established with very limited evidence, including the refusal to confess under torture. Witches should be killed in particularly long and painful ways, such as roasted over a slow smoky fire of green wood, because evil people needed longer to be killed.

NICOLAS RÉMY

Another intellectual proponent of witch hunting, Nicolas Rémy (or Remy or Remigius), soon reinforced Bodin's treatise. Rémy was the procurer general of Lorraine from 1591 to 1606 and traveled around the province helping local courts initiate witch trials. His publication, *Demonolatriae libri tres* ("Three

Books on Demon Worship") in 1595, called for the eradication of magical beliefs and the extermination of witches. He thought it "not unreasonable that this scum of humanity should be drawn chiefly from the feminine sex, and that we should hear mostly of women simplists, wise women, sorceresses, and enchantresses ... [since] women are more prone to believe in witchcraft."[2] Witches were particularly vile, passing sorcery to their offspring.

Rémy offered some of the most detailed accounts of sabbats until those of Delrio (see Chapter 6). Sabbats usually took place on Wednesday or Saturday. The attendees ate foul, bitter, and dirty food; danced to frenzied and discordant music until exhausted; had painful and disgusting sex; and were forced to kiss the Devil's odorous goat-shaped posterior. Rémy claimed that the participants hated the whole awful experience, but their oaths and fear of the Devil kept them from repenting.

To break the Devil's power over those who resisted repentance, Rémy readily applied torture. He discouraged certain techniques, such as shaving, tossing cold water in the face, swimming, or the ordeal of hot-iron, as unfit for the modern age. He did, however, recommend close imprisonment, hard questioning, and proper torture to free the witches from their sin. Head clamps (also called ortillons), the strappado, the ladder, and the rack were approved applications. Witches guilty of obeying the Devil deserved the worst torments of execution, to match the heinous nature of their crime and, very importantly, to deter others. Rémy's judges often had the children of witches stripped naked and flogged while they watched their parents burned. But Rémy worried that lenience would allow the children to carry on diabolic crime. He preferred to execute them, first applying red-hot tongs and then burning them alive or even crucifying them. Suicides of accused witches facing such punishments merely proved their guilt, allegedly being driven to such extremes by demons. Rémy boasted when sixteen witches committed suicide by hanging rather than face the sure conviction by his "justice." He bragged about having executed 800 people, although the actual number was probably much lower.

Torture brought people to such a condition that they despaired of living and confessed about seductive demons. A modern viewing of his record shows how some people easily confessed in order to protect friends and family, whereas others readily implicated a wide range of associates. Without torture, witnesses rarely mentioned intervention by the Devil, usually confessing only *maleficia* against neighbors. For them, accusations served as an outlet for pent-up frustrations. Saying a neighbor was a witch focused anger and resentment about day-to-day squabbles.

HENRI BOGUET

A third major contributor to strixology in France toward the end of the civil wars was Henri Boguet. His *Discours des sorciers* ("Discourse on Sorcerers" or "An Examen of Witches") of 1602 also enjoyed several editions, becoming the unofficial witch-hunting manual for France, although his experiences came from the Franche-Comté (Free County) of Burgundy, or the Jura region, which did not entirely come under French rule until 1674. Caught between the Holy Roman Empire and France, this border province revealed elements of both systems of witch hunting. Because Boguet was a judge and hunter for the Abbey of St. Claude, he was able to report on dozens of cases he had personally participated in, many of which ended in the death of the accused in prison by hanging, or by burning.

Boguet's discourse begins with his observations on the possession of eight-year-old Loyse Maillat in 1598. The stricken girl accused an old woman, Françoise Sécrétain, who had begged to spend the night at the girl's house. The old woman had secretly given Loyse bread that resembled manure, which then caused Loyse's possession by five demons named Cat, Dog, Wolf, Griffon, and Jolly. Judge Boguet, although he noted the superficial appearance of innocence, found the woman to be a witch. Her rosary had a defective cross, and she never cried during confession. But after they stripped, shaved, and searched her body for marks, the old woman broke down and confessed to having had sex with the Devil, attending the sabbat, flying there on a white staff, and causing hail that killed both people and cattle. Boguet had Sécrétain dispatched before the year was out. Over two decades later, Maillat wound up executed herself.

Boguet's analysis of the sabbat revealed some of the diverse opinions concerning that meeting. *Transvection* or flying occurred by riding on stereotypical brooms or white staffs as well as on animals like goats and sheep, on a tall black man, or even on the wind of a storm. Some also merely traveled on foot. The Devil could convene sabbats any day of the year, but he often blasphemously chose great religious feast days. Sabbats were, of course, held at midnight, because the darkest night pleased the Prince of Darkness. They ended at the first cock crow, which frightened Satan. At the sabbat, witches worshiped the Devil in the form of a tall black man or a goat by offering him candles and kissing his buttocks. They danced back to back, wearing masks. In Boguet's version, the orgy comes before the feast, with the Devil enjoying himself in the forms of incubus and succubus. The participants eat, yet leave the table as hungry as they came. They confessed to the Devil their evil deeds, and he encouraged them to do more. A perverted Mass concluded the events, at the end of which Satan vanished in a flash of fire. The witches then took the ashes to make potions and returned home.

Boguet's advice to judges about punishment probably ensured his book's popularity. He liked stripping, shaving, and examining for the Devil's Mark, but disapproved of ducking. He thought torture might be without effect, due to witch's charms that allowed them to be insensitive to pain. Nevertheless, Boguet thought torture was justified if the accused was suspect by common rumor, had lied at all, or showed "light indications." These flimsy indicators might be avoiding eye contact, shedding very few tears, having no cross on a rosary, using blasphemous language, or being related to other witches. Boguet preferred to execute witches by burning them alive, without the benefit of strangulation. Even children were to be burned because of "the enormity of the crime, which is the most abominable of all crimes that can be imagined. For the atrocity of this crime is the reason why the ordinary provisions of the law are not applicable to it; and therefore in the case of atrocious crimes children are often put to death for the fathers without any regard being had to their ignorance."[3]

Boguet connected an outbreak of werewolves to his hunt. Lycanthropy, or the notion that people transformed into wolves, was a rare phenomenon of witchcraft. Actual cases were alleged to have taken place only in France, a few provinces of the Holy Roman Empire, and Livonia. Boguet recorded how Benoît of Bidel claimed that he and his sister had been attacked by a wolf who had human hands and lacked a tail. Local hysteria then targeted the Gandillon family. Boguet's observations of their bestial behavior in prison convinced him of their guilt, although he held doubts on theological grounds. He reasoned that Satan embodied the actual werewolf metamorphosis on behalf of a sleeping witch. These scruples notwithstanding, he consequently executed three members of the Gandillon family.

Boguet did not doubt that France faced serious danger from hundreds of thousands of witches. Some historians suggest he projected his concerns about the religious conflict of the age onto his witch victims. In any case, his command and those who followed his advice led many innocents to the grave.

The sudden appearance of Bodin, Rémy, and Boguet's major texts, in addition to texts from Germany, inspired witch hunting at the end of the sixteenth century in many parts of France. These works recorded the worst hunts that had taken place during the period of the Wars of Religion and laid a foundation for more to come in times of peace. Of course, some areas experienced almost no hunts. But in regions where the people looked for witches to blame and the authorities allowed or encouraged them to do so, the worst phase of witch hunting in French history occurred over the next few decades.

MICHEL DE MONTAIGNE

While the strixologists Bodin, Rémy, and Boguet dominated the intellectual milieu, one voice did speak up for a more cautious approach. Michel Eyquem de Montaigne's (b. 1533–d. 1592) famed *Essais* ("Essays") of 1588 were widely read for his social criticism on the issues of the day. One of those essays, *Des Boîteaux* ("Concerning Cripples"), directly addressed the witch hunts and discussed the accusations that abounded in his neighborhood. This essay references the famous case of Martin Guerre, who supposedly suffered impotence through witchcraft. At issue was the question of how to determine truth. From his own experience, Montaigne ridiculed stories of witches as merely the imaginary figments of ignorant peasants. His famous sentiment expressed at the end of the essay warns that "after all, it is setting a very high price on one's conjectures to burn a man alive for them."[4] One small skeptical push for facts about witch hunting, though, could not stop the tide.

WITCH-HUNTING UNDER ABSOLUTISM

The French Wars of Religion ended with the victory of King Henry IV or Henry of Navarre (r. 1589–1610). Henry had originally been part of the Protestant faction but had converted to Roman Catholicism in order to gain acceptance by the majority French population. In his Edict of Nantes, though, he tried to protect religious freedoms for the Huguenots. Supported by his success and the desire of many French for prosperity and order, Henry strengthened the French monarchy along the absolutist lines suggested by Bodin.

Once the ascendancy of the central government had been achieved, witch hunts were moderated. The panic associated with hunting did not align with practices of good government. Also, the prosecution of actual crimes, such as theft and murder, better served the purpose of confirming royal justice than identifying isolated women as spell-casters. The *parlement* of Paris served as a useful conduit for restricting hunting. After a hunt in the Campagne Ardennnes region in 1587–1588 killed hundreds by using the "swimming" test, the *parlement* of Paris ordered review of all witchcraft cases. By 1624, the *parlement* of Paris had claimed the right to hear all appeals for witch trials, and it generally acquitted those who did make it before the bench. In 1639 the *parlement* of Paris actually convicted three local judges for abusing their power in persecuting witches.

The end of the Wars of Religion and the assertion of absolute power for the king, however, did not remove all fears of witches. King Henry IV sent Pierre de Lancre and Jean d'Espaignet to the south of France in 1609 to investigate witch activity in the Pays de Labourd, a province in Henry's home kingdom of Navarre, on the French side of the Pyrenees. D'Espaignet was the presiding judge in the *parlement* of Bordeaux and had written about hermetic magic based on the ancient writings of Hermes Trismegistus rediscovered in the Renaissance. Pierre de Lancre (b. 1553–d. 1631) was a lawyer and a member of the *parlement* of Bordeaux. As inquisitor, de Lancre's called for the growing absolute monarchy of King Henry IV to crush the conspiracy of witches.

The land of Labourd, though, was very different from the rest of France. Although it lay not far south of Bordeaux, the people who lived there were mostly of Basque ethnicity, not French or Spanish. The Basques were an ancient people, perhaps the oldest in Europe, who managed to preserve their language and many of their customs despite enormous pressure from nationalistic regimes in Madrid and Paris. For the two investigators, it was as if they had left Europe for a New World. When they arrived, they found a witch hunt in progress.

De Lancre's inability to comprehend the unique culture complicated his treatment of the hunt. He thought the Basques, with their "foreign" language and customs, were as awful as the savages in America. He also disapproved of women helping during the Mass by carrying the chalice and ornaments or dressing the altar. He saw the long absences of men on fishing expeditions as merely encouraging women's carnality. He took advantage of the fishermen's absence to carry out his inquisition, convinced that the entire population were witches.

Through an interpreter, de Lancre personally investigated forty-six suspects. He particularly targeted people under thirty, teenagers, and children as young as ten. He also interrogated twelve priests, who revealed participation in various blasphemous acts, including celebrating the Black Mass. The followers of the Devil had allegedly once even held a Black Mass in his own bedroom while he slept. That the Church's own priests were in league with the Devil particularly worried de Lancre.

But others did not share his concern. The opposition of local clergy grew against him, and the return of the fishing fleet finally ended the hunt. The enraged fishermen threatened de Lancre, so he fled the area. He claimed his final death toll to be about 600 burned. That high number cannot be confirmed by the trial records, which are now lost. His book about the trials, *Tableau de l'inconstance des mauvais anges et démons* ("Description of the Fickleness of the Evil Angels and Demons") in 1613, became a major hit.

The point of de Lancre's book was to show how Satan and his changeable demons overturned the normal, stable, decent social order. He described the sabbat in detail, aided by evocative engravings of the chaotic activities made by Jan Ziarnkov of Poland (see Illustration 13). De Lancre believed that thousands, even a hundred thousand witches, could gather at a sabbat. His witches were so bold that they even held the sabbats in daytime. How such a huge gathering could escape notice from unbiased observers, de Lancre does not explain. The sabbat includes the usual magical transportation thereto, plus cannibalism, distribution of poisonous powders, and the Devil's marking his male and female witches.

Sexual activity drew de Lancre's special attention. At these sabbats the Devil copulated with women and ejaculated cold semen. His penis could divide into two or three parts, depending whether he wanted to violate the vagina, anus, or mouth. Perhaps worst of all, men and women danced together. Indeed, it was worse than mere dancing, being "acts of incest and other hideous crimes and trespasses which, we can truthfully say, have come to us as a result of the pernicious proximity of this country to Spain, for the Basques and the people of Lambourd are neighbors."[5]

The book's popularity sparked more persecutions. De Lancre blamed a witch outbreak in Navarre in 1610 on the insufficiently persecuted Basque witches. An inquisitor conducted an inquisition in Navarre from 1608 to 1611. That hunt turned out to be comparatively mild. At first, more than 5,000 people, including 1,300 children, confessed to witchcraft. Of these, Spanish Inquisitors trimmed the numbers down to about 300 individuals for whom they planned a great auto-da-fé or public burning of heretics (see Chapter 6).

By the time of that two-day-long event on November 7–8, 1610, however, the death toll only numbered one suicide, five dead in prison, and just six who actually burned at the stake.

This defeat did not deter Pierre de Lancre, though. He continued his activities in France, even uncovering the notorious werewolf Jean Genier. De Lancre wrote additional books encouraging witch hunts, refuting his opponents, and implicating Jews as most hated by God. De Lancre's opinions inspired a widespread hunt in neighboring Languedoc from 1643 to 1645. Hunts could run unchecked far from the capital, as royal authority lapsed during the restless time when regents ruled for the child-king Louis XIV. That would soon change.

HUNTS IN CANADA

As the witch hunts reached their heights in Europe in the early seventeenth century, France became a colonial power. In their colonies in the New World, the French confronted peoples of very different religions, which the Roman Catholics considered paganism and Devil worship. The French immediately sought to convert the natives to Roman Catholicism. However, French power in their colonial regions was not nearly as strong as that of the Spanish or Portuguese in theirs (see Chapter 7). The French could only lead by example, at first.

The native "Indians," in turn, had some authority actually to attack the French. When epidemics plagued the Hurons between 1634 and 1641, they blamed the Jesuits in the area. Indeed, the Jesuits may have been at fault, unknowingly bringing germs from Europe that infected the natives. The Hurons, though, accused the Jesuits of magic and tortured several. Their torture, though, sought not to extort confessions as in the European system, but was intended both to destroy the magical power and to inflict horrible pain on the enemy.

The French immigrants in Canada imported their own magical superstitions along with their customs. Witch mania remained relatively rare and stayed focused on *maleficia* and demonic possession. In Montreal, for example, René Besnard allegedly used a ligature to render sterile the marriage of his rival with the woman he loved. Ligature meant casting a spell by tying knots in a string which would make a man impotent, symbolically strangling his manhood. The bishop actually annulled the marriage on the grounds of magically cast impotence, demonstrating the power of superstitious thought. In 1658, a court found Besnard guilty of witchcraft. Instead of being sentenced to death, he only had to pay a fine and go into exile. Two years later near Quebec City, demons allegedly haunted the sixteen-year-old servant Barbe Hallé, appearing to her in various forms of men, infants, and beasts who spoke through her mouth. Mother Catherine of St. Augustine helped to cure Barbe by the unusual method of shutting her in a linen sack. Catherine was then herself tormented in the next two decades by demons against whom she conducted exorcisms.

Both these cases show the contemporary power of magical thinking, but neither sparked a wider witch hunt. Besnard probably deserved some punishment for his open hostility to the marriage, and banishment was better than death or prison. After his punishment, both victims made new marriages and succeeded in having children. While Barbe Hallé and Mother Catherine won notoriety for their dealings with demons, the courts condemned no one for sending the demons through witchcraft. Courts likewise failed to persecute numerous self-professed diviners and faith healers who had arrived in the New World and offered their services to farmers and millers who consulted them. By the end of the eighteenth century, with French Canada under English rule, charges of fraud were more likely than charges of witchcraft. Of the handful of trials in Canada, perhaps only one in 1661 ended with an execution, and that involved the heresy of Huguenot Protestantism. The real threat of Indian wars replaced the need for finding witches.

THE FRENCH POSSESSED

Demonic possession seen in Canada manifested itself in France to a greater degree than elsewhere, often in nunneries. As early as 1491, a convent in Le Quesnay near Arras allegedly overflowed with possessed nuns. The nuns had hysterical fits, made animal noises, and spoke in tongues, until one nun was identified as the controlling witch. The number of such cases increased after the Reformation. Interestingly, many Calvinists refused to exorcise witches, because they saw demonic possession as a punishment by God.

Roman Catholics, however, saw exorcism as a way to highlight the mediating power of their Church and its ministers in the struggle against Satan. For them, exorcism displayed the miraculous authority of ordained celibate priests and the sanctifying power of their religious accoutrements and sacramentals, such as the Blessed Host, holy water, and relics. Some of these Roman Catholic practices validated behaviors that earlier reformers had tried to label as superstitious, such as the overuse of relics. The Counter-Reformation mood, though, embraced whatever might differentiate Roman Catholicism from Protestantism.

Victims of possession often exhibited penitential ascetic behavior, self-induced suffering of the body that was usually used as an act of spiritual devotion. Spiritual guides, who offered religious counsel to believers, praised acts such as fasting, whipping, or confining oneself in isolation. Similar torments brought on by demons paralleled these religious acts. Too much consorting with demons, though, might bring an accusation of witchcraft, allowing some criticism of the victim as voluntarily opening herself to the possession. Many skeptics have suspected that demonic possession actually arose from repressing the sex drive. Often sexual temptation played a key role in the manifestation of possession, with demonic activity in the form of succubi or incubi.

Although possession followed from the actions of demons, demonologists and strixologists often implicated witches as mediators who brought the demons to their victims. This view might have made it simpler to free a possessed person, because execution of the guilty witch, instead of an elaborate exorcism, supposedly sufficed to break a demon's hold on an innocent. The hunt for witches and the labors of exorcists thus linked together to reinforce the unusual religious moments that demonic possessions came to represent.

People who were allegedly possessed showed various symptoms, which exorcists were supposed to note as proof of genuine possession. Common markers of possession included speaking in tongues, foreign languages, or strange voices and revealing secret knowledge such as distant or future events or examples of other people's sins. The body underwent fits, contortions and ecstasy, rigidity and catatonia, bouts of unusual strength, and loose sexual behavior. The possessed might be insensible to pain (tested by pricking) or twisted with agony. Some even claimed to observe the possessed levitating. The possessed usually shrank back at displays of sacred objects, prayers, and biblical readings.

Those who claimed to be possessed and their exorcists probably believed that what they experienced was truly demonic in nature. Modern physicians would diagnose some form of mental illness; epilepsy; or psychosomatically induced stress and fantasy based on guilt, a desire for notoriety, or the need to escape an uncomfortable situation. Once begun, it was hard to escape an escalation of symptoms.

Of the many possessions that took place in early modern France, a few examples amply illustrate the circumstances. In 1565–1566, the case of Nicole Obry (Aubrey or Obrey) in Picardy seemed to launch a wave of possessions. Just after All Saints Day in 1565, Nicole, a young sixteen-year-old bride, claimed to be possessed by her dead grandfather. Although she claimed the spirit wanted only good, especially Masses to be said or a pilgrimage undertaken to St. James of Compestella, the possession left her frequently unable to move, see, or hear. A local Dominican priest, Pierre la Motte, came to exorcise the ghost but determined her possession to be demonic, not spectral. The priest made the demon admit to being the biblical Beezelbub, or Lord of the Flies.

Nicole then became the center of an amazing public spectacle of exorcism, on a scaffold in front of the church at Vervins. The Bishop of Laon moved the show to his cathedral, where thousands saw him try to drive out the demons through the Real Presence of Christ in the blessed Host. Beelzebub finally left Nicole on February 8, which was long after celebrated as the "Miracle of Laon." Efforts by Huguenots to discredit the miracle, which even included holding Nicole prisoner for a few weeks, came to naught. Modern scholars explain her claims in various ways: desire for adventure; being married too young; agonizing over her sins; or confusion at the onset of menstruation and her sexual initiation in an arranged marriage. Although this case did not lead to a hunt for witches, the cases that followed soon did.

THE URSULINES IN AIX

A notorious possession case began in 1609 in Aix-en-Provence in an Ursuline religious house. The Ursulines were a modern religious order, rejecting the isolation of the cloister in order to educate young lay women. Ironically, this openness seemed to make them vulnerable to becoming the center of spectacular possession cases. Many young girls were entrusted to their care, without the vocation to become celibate nuns. Two of them in Aix, the twenty-year-old Madeleine de Demandolx de la Palud and the year-younger Louise Capeau, began to show the signs of possession. They shook, had cramps, fell in fits, had spurts of anger, spoke in a strange voices, and publicly smashed a crucifix. The demons even forced them to make lewd gestures. A Jesuit priest failed for months to exorcize the demons. As more and more nuns started to exhibit symptoms of possession, he sought help from the Grand Inquisitor of Avignon, the Dominican Sébastien Michaëlis.

Michaëlis had already been involved with demons and witches, having written about the trials he conducted at Avignon in 1582. Michaëlis' investigation convinced Louise (or, rather, her demon "Verrine") to accuse Madeleine of witchcraft and in the process revealed the girl's lurid past. Madeleine, who had been often confined to a sick bed, probably had fallen in love with her confessor, the priest Louis Gaufridi (or Gauffridy). He was twenty years older than she and enjoyed a bit of a reputation as a rogue. Michaëlis expanded the exorcism of the confused young women into a hunt for witches.

Michaëlis' investigation of Gaufridi convinced the *parlement* of Aix to charge him with witchcraft in February 1611. They arrested Gaufridi and put him in prison, kept in chains. The court accepted evidence from Madeleine, still possessed by hundreds of demons, although down from a high of 6,666. The authorities shaved Gaufridi of all hair and found three Devil's Marks. Two doctors pierced him with a needle on blemishes on his right thigh, lower back, and near the heart to the depth of two or three fingers' widths, noting no pain, swelling, or bleeding from the wounds. They tortured him until he wrote down a confession based on Madeleine's (or her demons') stories, on April 11, 1611. He confessed to having sold his soul to the Devil. As a "Prince of Synagogue," he confessed that he had regularly convened a sabbat, where he and his followers cannibalized children. He had also seduced more than a thousand women. Gaufridi had bewitched Madeleine to take her to the sabbat and have sex with her, among the other blasphemies conducted there.

Gaufridi, however, refused to admit blasphemy against the sacraments or to name other accomplices. Even worse, he tried to withdraw his confession in court on April 15. Authorities continued to torture Gaufridi for two more weeks. They used squassation, which meant jerking his body on the strappado, hoisting him close to the ceiling, and then letting him fall to just above hitting the floor. Weights tied to his ankles added to the bodily torment. On the day of his execution, April 30, they had him dragged through the streets of Aix for five hours, until they strangled him and burned his body.

The other parties endured various fates. After Gaufridi's death, the demons slowly left the possessed nuns, Madeleine and Louise. On the latter's testimony, though, the inquisition burned a young blind girl, Honorée, for contributing to the possessions. In 1652, Madeleine served a sentence of ten years for witchcraft, after the Devil's Marks were found on her. Michaëlis wrote his own account of the possession, boasting of his success.

The case provoked different reactions in France. A physician of King Louis XIII wrote a pamphlet in 1611, *Des marques des sorciers* ("Witches' Marks") in support of the idea that such marks showed the Devil at work. He offered his expert medical opinion on distinguishing true Devil's Marks from fake. Others protested the treatment of Gaufridi and tried to restrain the exorcising activities of Michaëlis. The whole case raised serious questions among Roman Catholics about how to discipline their own. Scholars at the University of Paris, at least, sensibly declared in 1620 that testimony by demons, even under exorcism, should never be accepted, since the Devil was, of course, a liar.

Possessions continued to attract attention, though. In 1620, Elizabeth de Ranfaing in Lorraine accused her doctor of witchcraft. She had been married at the age of fifteen to a sixty-seven-year-old soldier, who died after nine years of marriage and fathering six children. De Ranfaing accused Dr. Charles Poirot of giving her a love potion in the form of salt pork, leading to her possession. She could converse in tongues, read closed letters, pick out a sanctified Host from among other wafers, and spout horrible curses, all while her body contorted. Theologians at the University of Paris were suspicious about her alleged demon speaking through her, because she did not faint often enough. Still, twenty-four judges convicted Dr. Poirot, along with a peasant girl implicated in the witchcraft. Both were strangled and burned at the stake. Elizabeth de Ranfaing recovered and eventually headed a convent, where many admired her piety.

THE DEVILS IN LOUDUN

Probably the most infamous case of demonic possession took place in Loudun. The rich documentation about this case has fueled a book by Aldous Huxley and a film by Ken Russel, *The Devils*. Loudun was a small, largely Huguenot town, guaranteed by the Edict of Nantes to have the right of some self-government and defense. Cardinal Richelieu, King Louis XIII's minister, disliked this nominal independence from the absolute authority of the king. Even more offensive, a local priest, Urbain Grandier, had allegedly written both a treatise against celibacy and a pamphlet insulting the cardinal. So Richelieu may have been looking for an opportunity both to intervene in the town and avenge himself on Grandier.

Grandier's sexual impropriety provided the rationale. In 1627, the newly arrived Mother Superior of an Ursuline convent, twenty-two-year-old Jeanne de Anges, blamed her attraction to Grandier on demons, perhaps prompted by her confessor, the local priest Jean Mignon. This first accusation failed, and the charges were dismissed, along with some other moral cases lodged against Grandier. In the autumn of 1632, however, Mother Jeanne and more than two dozen other nuns again began to act possessed: speaking in tongues, writhing their bodies as if in pain or ecstasy, and reacting against sacred objects and words. This time the confessor Mignon convinced several nuns to attest that Grandier had bewitched them by their smelling bouquets he had thrown over the convent's walls. Cardinal Richelieu first ordered an investigation and then the arrest of Grandier at the end of November 1633.

While the inquiry progressed, the number of possessions increased. Public exorcisms attracted great interest of "spiritual tourists." Grandier, isolated in a locked room in Loudun, refused to cooperate and maintained his innocence. In late April, a nun during exorcism produced evidence in the form of a pact with the Devil, allegedly signed by Grandier. In this fabricated pact Grandier wrote, "I promise never to do good, to do all the evil I can, and would wish not at all to be a man, but that my nature be changed into a devil the better to serve thee, thou my lord and master Lucifer.... "[6] Examiners then sought for the Devil's Mark on his body, piercing him repeatedly with needles, finally locating two marks near his anus and on his testicles. A special judicial panel was convened in July, and on August 18, 1634, it found him guilty.

Grandier's punishment that same day was exemplary in its cruelty. The guards shaved the condemned and brought him to the court to hear his sentence, clothed only in a shirt soaked in flammable sulfur and with a hangman's rope around his neck, carrying a two-pound torch. He was to be tortured (euphemistically called "put to the question ordinary and extraordinary") to reveal his accomplices and then burned alive with his book, which criticized imposing celibacy and chastity on priests. They applied the Spanish Boot to his legs for more than forty-five minutes. The Spanish Boot confined a victim's leg in a tight trough of boards, and then the torturers hammered wedges between the wood to squeeze the flesh. As the wedges crushed his legs, allegedly to the point that the bones burst, Grandier still refused to implicate anyone else. A cart carried him through the town to the place of execution, where they burned him alive, although he had been promised strangulation. They scattered his ashes to the winds.

The death of Grandier did not end the possessions. Mother Superior Jeanne slowly recovered through several exorcisms over the next three years. During that time she set an example of holiness in resisting possession, going on tour to show her hand marked with the names of Jesus, the Blessed Virgin Mary, and Francis de Sales, who, she said, had defeated the demons. Many other nuns, however, continued in their possessed behaviors. The nunnery remained a tourist attraction until Richelieu withdrew his interest.

People at the time were divided on the truth behind these events. Some saw God's allowing such tribulations to happen both as an opportunity for people to achieve grace and for the Roman Catholic Church to prove its superiority. The antics of the nuns, whom they believed were truly possessed, illustrated supernatural powers affecting the world. Others, however, asserted that Richelieu had manipulated a situation to buttress royal centralization and absolutism. Grandier's conviction had removed an enemy of the state and had weakened the independence of Loudun. For those who saw political maneuvers, the nuns had suffered from sexual hysteria, not possession. Similar cases at Louviers in 1646 and Auxonne in 1660 evoked similar conclusions.

By the middle of the sixteenth century, however, these outrageous cases seemed to mock the ideas of demonic possession and witchcraft to many, believers and skeptics alike. Intellectuals and critics began to realize how easily the behaviors of possession could be both simulated and manipulated. Some noted how cases of possession caused scandal to the Church, tarnishing belief in the power of Christ and miracles. Profiteering from a tourist trade in viewing the possessed drew forth additional criticism. At the same time, medical professionals were making more progress in diagnosis and treatment of mental illness. Physicians dismissed supernatural demonic possession as a cause for fits and strange behavior, instead offering natural disease to explain symptoms. Others just began to apply simple common sense to the situation.

CYRANO DE BERGERAC

One such critic was Cyrano de Bergerac, famous as the fictionalized hero of the late nineteenth-century play by Rostand. In the play, the large-nosed chevalier romances Roxanne, the woman he loves, on behalf of another man. The real Cyrano was a poet and social critic of mid-seventeenth-century France. In his letter *Contre les sorciers* ("Against Witches") of 1654, he asserted that "one ought to believe about a man only what is human, i.e., possible and ordinary. Therefore I admit no Witches until someone proves it to me."[7] Anecdotal stories of old peasant women in far-away places remained unconvincing. He allowed some sincerity to belief in the Devil, but felt that holding the Devil's power to be the equal of God's was to honor that demon too highly.

TOWARD THE END OF THE FRENCH HUNTS

Cyrano was a precursor of the Enlightenment. Intellectuals, called *philosophes*, from all over Europe were soon flocking to Paris. They joined salons where they would converse about the important topics of the era. Drawing on empiricism and science, they attacked superstition and religious abuses. Since religious passion so easily slipped into superstitious beliefs, *philosophes* commonly attacked both. The Enlightenment attacked belief in magic even more strongly. Witches did not fit into the sensible world of agnosticism and deism. The world was becoming less enchanted with magic and more scientific.

The *Chambre Ardente* Affair

The last serious incident in France involving witches, though, indicated the enduring hold of superstition on imagination. The *Chambre Ardente* (Burning Room) Affair, also called the Affair of the Poisons, illuminates the mixture of popular attitudes toward magic with naive beliefs. The name, *Chambre Ardente*, comes from the room draped in black where the investigators met. The affair started on two levels, around petty fortune tellers and in the royal court itself. In 1673, priests in the confessionals began hearing about a ring of poisoners who killed off husbands with arsenic. The commissioner of the Paris police, Nicolas de la Reynie, investigated and confirmed the rumors, focusing on the fortune teller Marie Bosse. A sting operation caught Bosse selling poison to a police informant. Others were drawn in, including members of her family and another fortune-teller, Le Dame Vigoreux.

Reynie had her tortured by the witch's chair or *sellette*. This was an iron chair to which the torturer strapped the victim and then set a fire underneath. The heat would first cause discomfort and then burns of increasing intensity. Torturers applied "Spanish Boots" to smash her legs as they did Grandier's at Loudun. Confessions led police to focus on Catherine Deshayes Monvoison, known as "La Voison."

Catherine Deshayes had a public aspect to her work, which involved crafting beauty treatments and plotting astrological charts. In secret, though, she allegedly kept dead fetuses from an abortion ring to use in magic. She also entertained powerful people with Black Masses, perversions of the Church's Eucharistic service. A priest would tie a naked girl across an altar and conduct a Mass with the name of "Satan" and with the names of other devils substituted for mentions of God, Christ, and the Holy Spirit. Holy elements would be rubbed against parts of the girl's body. The service ended with an orgy, perhaps with sex on the altar. Allegedly babies would also be sacrificed on the altar, their throats cut to honor the demons Ashtaroth and Asmodeus. Participants then concocted weird potions from the blood, consecrated wine, menstrual blood, urine, semen, powdered bats, and flour. Several priests admitted to scandalous behavior at such Masses and in the woods at night.

Reynie's investigation next stumbled onto the astounding second level of the magical plot, namely its connection to the royal court. Madame de Montespan (Françoise Arthenias de Mortmart) was the mistress of King Louis XIV (r. 1643–1715). De Montespan had been fearing, correctly, that the king's affections had drifted to a new favorite, Mademoiselle de Fontanges. She also wanted to prevent the queen from becoming pregnant, and she wanted the king to repudiate the queen and marry her instead. De Montespan slipped La Voison's love potions into the king's food, without, however, achieving her intended result. In service to her plan, De Montespan had even served three times as the naked girl on the altar.

Because of the highly placed personages involved, King Louis XIV kept this investigation under wraps as much as possible. He had many of the official records destroyed in 1709, and so exact details will never be known. Historians do know that Reynie arrested more than 300 people. About a third wound up convicted of some crime. Some of De Montespan's friends were among the thirty-five hanged and five sent to the galleys. Bosse and Vigoreux both burned in 1678, and La Voison went to the stake on February 22, 1680. Another twenty-three were exiled, and others were imprisoned. Madame de Montespan herself returned briefly to court only later to be completely replaced in Louis' affections by Madame de Maintenon, whom he did eventually marry. De Montespan soon retired comfortably to a country manor.

Despite this close brush with magic, Louis XIV favored the reduction of hunting. Another king might have launched a massive hunt, based on reasonable evidence of magical practices targeted against him. Louis and his advisors, however, knew that magic had no real harmful power. He demonstrated this opinion in 1669–1670, when a hunt in lower Normandy allowed nine witnesses to implicate more than 500 people. Torture produced confessions to condemn forty-six of them to death. The families of the condemned appealed to the *parlement* of Rouen, but that court still confirmed the validity of the death penalty for thirty-four. The families then appealed to King Louis XIV himself. Louis converted the death penalty to banishment, and even prevented the confiscation of property. He had his famous minister Colbert increase the pressure to stop hunts.

The Decree of 1682

These efforts culminated in a royal decree in July 1682 that reformed the laws of France concerning witch hunting. It declared that "those who call themselves diviners, magicians, and enchanters ... by means of the illusion of the workings of pretended magic and other similar illusions ... have deceived numerous ignorant or gullible individuals."[8] Thus, the belief of people acting on magic was found to be only superstition. The law did not deny the reality of witches, but shifted the focus toward fortune-telling, superstitious abuse of the Bible or prayers, sacrilege, and poisoning (as per the *Chambre Ardente* Affair). The death penalty became reserved only for these last two crimes: poisoning since it involved murder and sacrilege as an insult to God in the Counter-Reformation beliefs that prevailed. In 1687, the king also decreed that pretending to be able to use sorcery was against the law. This act further pushed magical thinking into the realm of imaginary fears, not real dangers. Despite the *Chambre Ardente* Affair, Louis recognized that while poison, a dagger, or a bomb were the real threats that might kill a king or a peasant, magic could not. Louis ordained that magic could harm no one; only laws against murder continued to be enforced.

Some witch trials did occur after Louis's prohibition, because local courts were slow to obey the central government and rural people refused to give up their fears. In 1691, authorities burned some shepherds at Brie for using witchcraft to kill sheep. But French intellectuals of the Enlightenment increasingly adopted the skepticism of Montaigne and Cyrano de Bergerac. One sign of the end of witch thinking is found in Malebranche's *Recherche de la Vérité* ("Researches on Truth") from 1674. Malebranche built on Weyer's opinion that most witches were delusional, either through drugs or overactive imaginations.

He still agreed that real witches deserved to be killed, but found that such were few and far between.

The last significant witch case in France took place in the port town of Toulon in 1731. As a sickly teenager, Marie-Catherine Cadière began a quest to develop a holy, even saintly, life through acts of charity and by following the precepts of the Carmelite order. Along the way, her Jesuit confessor, Jean-Baptiste Girard, apparently seduced her. After tiring of her, he tucked her into a nunnery, where she soon began experiencing strange visions, then fits, and then bleeding stigmata. Her worried family had her exorcised, including rituals performed by her own brother, a Dominican, at midnight, in public. Girard's friends, though, arranged for an indictment against Cadière in November 1730, charging her with demonstrating the witchcraft of divination during her rants.

The nine-month-long trial produced many lurid details of sexual behavior. Cadière published her own account, to implicate her confessor further. She alleged his sexual abuse of her, magical practices, and procuring of an abortion. He admitted some improper behavior, but tried to expose her claimed sanctity as a fraud, labeling her a seductress. The public from all over France followed the scandalous tales, taking her side or his. Eventually, the court acquitted both. Girard escaped from the town and further ecclesiastical censure, dying two years later. Cadière's fate is unknown. The whole sordid mess further plunged belief in possession and witchcraft into ill-repute.

The last execution for witchcraft in France took place in 1745. In 1742, authorities had charged Father Bertrand Guillaudot with perverting the Holy Mass to divine a treasure's location. Although neither a diabolic pact nor *maleficia* against people or property were involved, the court found him guilty and had him burned. His testimony implicated dozens of others, some of whom were sent to the galleys as punishment. One, Father Luis Debaraz, holds the honor of being the last witch executed in France, burned at the stake three years after Guillaudot.

The intellectual movement of the Enlightenment ensured that the fear of witches would not rise again. Common people would continue to believe in and suspect magical wickedness, but they lacked control of the courts. Intellectuals could occasionally still be fooled by charlatans who boasted of magical powers. Frauds like Cagliostro, the Count de St.-Germain, or even Anton Mesmer drew in the gullible and their money, but no one in France hunted and killed such frauds for crimes of magic they could not possibly commit. The witch hunts ended in France, as elsewhere, because the political rulers no longer accepted the belief in a dangerous conspiracy of witches.

NOTES

1. Johan Huizinga, *The Autumn of the Middle Ages*, trans. Rodney J. Payton and Ulrich Mammitzsch (Chicago: University of Chicago Press, 1996), 291.

2. Nicolas Remy, *Demonolatry: An Account of the Historical Practice of Witchcraft*, trans. E. A. Ashwin, ed. Montague Summers (1930; reprinted, Mineola, NY: Dover Publications, 2008), 56.

3. Henry Boguet, *An Examen of Witches*, trans. E. Allen Ashwin, ed. Montague Summers. (London: John Rodker, 1929; reprint ed., New York: Kessinger Publishing, n.d.), 234.

4. Montaigne, *The Autobiography of Michel de Montaigne*, trans., selected and ed. Marvin Lowenthal (1935; new printing, Jaffrey, NH: Nonpareil Books, 1999), 199.

5. *On the Inconstancy of Witches: Pierre De Lancre's Tableau De L'inconstance; Des Mauvais Anges Et Daemons 1612*, ed. Gerhild Scholz Williams, trans. Harriet Stone and Gerhild Scholz Williams, Arizona Studies in the Middle Ages and the Renaissance 16 (Turnhout, Belgium: Brepols, 2006), 218—19.

6. Michel de Certeau, *The Possession at Loudun*, trans. Michael B. Smith (Chicago: The University of Chicago Press, 2000), 98.

7. Cyrano de Bergerac, "A Letter Against Witches (1654)," in *European Witchcraft*, ed. E. William Monter, Major Issues in History (New York: John Wiley & Sons, 1969), 115.

8. Brian P. Levack, ed. *The Witchcraft Sourcebook* (New York and London: Routledge, 2004), 164.

Illustration 1. This illumination comes from the margin of a manuscript of Martin le Franc's *Le Champion des Dames* ("The Defender of Ladies") from 1451, which generally argues against misogynist and witch stereotypes. This picture portrays "Waldensian" witches as women dressed in simple peasant's clothing riding on brooms—the first drawing of witches flying on broomsticks. Photo credit: Snark/Art Resource, NY.

Illustration 2. This early woodcut comes from an edition of Ulrich Müller or Molitor's *De Lamiis et Phitonicis Mulieribus* ("On Witches and Female Oracles") printed in Cologne in 1489. Two women dressed in clothing typical for the lower urban and peasant classes are conjuring a hailstorm by adding a rooster and a snake to a flaming cauldron. This and other drawings from the text were highly influential for later witchcraft imagery. Molitor, Ulrich. *De Laniis* [sic] *et phitonicis* [sic] *mulieribus*/On Witches/Von den Unholden und Hexen, 1489; facsimile ed. Paris: Emile Noury, 1926.

Illustration 3. The woodcut heads a collection of sermons by Johannes Geiler von Kaysersberg, *Die Emeis* ("The Ant Colony") published in 1516–1517. It illustrates a story from Nider's *Formicarius* about a woman (right) who took part in the Wild Ride on a bench, holding a banner. The man in the tree is identified as Satan or the god Saturn. The powerful imagery develops from Molitor's witches in Illustration 2, especially the sexualized portrayal of nude witches with cauldrons in the center. Courtesy of the University of Pennsylvania.

Illustration 4. This famous woodcut of Hans Baldung Grien's "A Group of Witches" from 1510, brings the witch into high art, further developing the images in the woodcut in *Die Emeis*. Three witches do magic around a magically streaming jar while a fourth flies on a goat with another jar. The nudity and jars also make it highly sexualized, while the bones and hat littered on the ground add a macabre touch. Photo credit: Reunion des Musees Nationauz/Art Resource, NY.

Illustration 5. This page by Hans Schäuffelin for a legal handbook by Ulrich Tengler, *Der Neü Layenspiegel* ("The New Mirror for Laymen") of 1568, illustrates typical concerns with black magic, sorcery, and demons. The magistrate in the center wields a sword and holds a book of justice, magically protected from a demon within a circle and candles. Around him are supernatural dangers, from the top right clockwise: a witch riding to the sabbat; a witch and a demon having sex; a witch milking a post; two magistrates (possibly the author and his son) and a lame person frame the burning punishment of witches; a witch shooting a poisoned arrow; a witch brewing a hailstorm; another witch flying on a ram to a sabbat; and a demon bargaining with a man over eggs. Courtesy of the University of Pennsylvania.

Illustration 6. This portrayal of the sabbat is one of many illustrations from Francesco Maria Guazzo's *Compendium Maleficarum* ("Compilation of Witches") of 1626. This picture shows witches, both male and female dressed in fine clothing of the upper classes, eating with and being served by demons. They are probably consuming dead babies, shown being cooked in another illustration from the book. Courtesy of the University of Pennsylvania.

Illustration 7. The broadsheet woodcut by Erhard Schön depicts a witch being burned at Oberndorf in 1533. The scene lacks the court officials and crowd from the city who would normally be present. The witch allegedly committed arson at the Devil's request, burning down the town of Schiltach in the background. Photo credit: Foto Marburg/ Art Resource, NY.

Illustration 8. This depiction of the ordeal of "cold water," swimming, or dunking the witch comes from Eberhard David Hauber, *Bibliotheca sive acta et scripta magica*, ("Library of Magical Acts and Writings") of 1738–1745. The guilty party improbably rests on top of the water as if on ice. In the lower right, only the hands and feet of an accused who has proven her innocence remain above the water's surface. Courtesy of the University of Pennsylvania.

Illustration 9. The title page of Joseph Glanvill's *Saducismus Triumphatus* ("Sadducism Triumphed Over") from 1689 includes six pictures from witch and ghost stories in the collection. Most important is the story of the Drummer of Tedworth, with demons playing the drums, in the top left. Courtesy of the University of Pennsylvania.

Illustration 10. The title page of Christian Thomasius' *Kürze Lehrsätze* ("Short Lessons") from 1703 shows the skeptical author thinking in the foreground. Above him witches fly on brooms, rakes, and a goat toward a goat-demon preparing a sabbat on a mountaintop, from which a man falls. The original caption warns the reader that the witches may seem real, but they are actually just a drawing on paper. Courtesy of the University of Pennsylvania.

Illustration 11. This illustration is linked to the Witches of Warboys, included by Richard Boulton in his book, *A Compleat History of Magick, Sorcery, and Witchcraft*, published in 1715–1716. It shows a witch using a wand and a book to conjure various demons, while protected by a magic circle and candles. Although the scene typifies what people imagined witches did, the actual history of the Witches of Warboys included no such moment. Courtesy of the University of Pennsylvania.

Illustration 12. This plate from the legal collection *Constitutio Criminalis Theresiana* of 1769, the law code that outlawed witch hunts, depicts a man hoisting a victim into the air using the strappado. Victims were left to hang for set times, determined by the investigators, while the weights below the victim could be tied to his feet to increase the pain—as would jerking the wheel of the pulley to bounce him. Courtesy of the University of Pennsylvania.

Illustration 13. This selection from a larger engraving by Jan Ziarnkov for Pierre de Lancre's *Tableau de l'inconstance des mauvais anges et démons* ("Description of the Fickleness of the Evil Angels and Demons") of 1613. De Lancre focused on dancing as a particularly dangerous practice of witches because of its sexual nature. At the sabbat illustrated here, a musical group plays in the background while nude women and girls dance a ronde. Courtesy of Cornell University.

Illustration 14. This illustration from Christian Scriver's *Curieuse Gespräche im Reiche derer Todten* ("Curious Conversations in the Realm of the Dead") from 1731 still argues at this late date against the logical skepticism of Balthasar Bekker's *De Betoverde Weereld* ("The World Bewitched"). It portrays Bekker as blindfolded or ignorant while demons are all around him. Bekker, talking to the author in the center, says he sees no devils, yet he is obviously blinded by one. Courtesy of Cornell University.

Illustration 15. This title page of a 1726 German translation of Francis Hutchinson's *An Historical Essay Concerning Witchcraft* (1718), called *Historischer Versuch von der Hexereÿ*, shows the nude figure of "Understanding in Knowledge" triumphing over and dispelling superstition. To either side flee witches and demons in darkness. Under her feet are a demon and a figure of corrupt justice, while the all-seeing eye helps dispel ignorance. Courtesy of Cornell University.

Illustration 16. This selection comes from the title page of Nathaniel Crouch's *The Kingdom of Darkness* of 1688. In the foreground a witch's burning, being observed by numerous officials and soldiers, is shown, while in the background one lone lamenter attends the hanging from a gallows of two witches at once. Courtesy of Cornell University.

CHAPTER 5

Witch-Hunting in the British Realms

Witch-hunting in the British Isles varied according to region. By 1400, England politically dominated both Wales and Ireland. Neither of these areas experienced much witch-hunting, perhaps because the tensions around English supremacy provided enough outlets for local fears and complaints. The Welsh and the Irish could always blame the English for their misfortunes. In contrast, Scotland retained its hard-fought independence until 1603, when its king, James VI (r. 1567–1625), also became James I of England (r. 1603–1625). Both before and after that unification, Scotland experienced the most frequent and vicious witch-hunting in the British Isles, with three times as many victims as in England. Given the comparatively small and scattered population of Scotland, the witch hunts also had a greater impact on the people than in neighboring England. The different regions within England, meanwhile, experienced varying levels of witch-hunting. Some counties, like Essex and Lancashire, saw far more than most, while many areas suffered almost none. In all areas, though, the fear of witches wove itself into British culture.

IRISH WITCHES

Ireland's infrequent hunting might seem surprising, given the notoriety of the early witch trial of Lady Kyteler (see Chapter 2). Later strixologists continued to cite the hunt. The case remained, though, nearly unique in Ireland and its century. During the age of the witch hunts, only a handful of trials occurred in Ireland, and no panics. In 1660, the servant Mary Longdon allegedly suffered possession because of Florence Newton, the Witch of Yougal, yet whether Newton was convicted or not is unknown. In 1711, at Carrickfergus, eighteen-year-old Mary Dunbar accused seven women of tormenting her with fits, making her vomit feathers, pins, and buttons, and causing poltergeist activity.

The authorities put the seven women on trial. Fortunately for them, they were only sentenced to four times in the stocks and a year in prison.

The stocks or pillory were a frequent penalty for crimes in both Scotland and England, including first-time or mild offenses of witchcraft. Familiar today from media and recreations, the stocks were wooden devices that imprisoned the legs, arms, and/or neck, while displaying the guilty for public scrutiny and humiliation. The mocking by the local population formed an essential part of the punishment, confirming to the community the criminal's antisocial behavior. The hope was that humiliation would lead to a reform of behavior so that the punishment would not have to be repeated. The stocks were, of course, also used for many different kinds of offenses, both moral and criminal. They have been closely associated with Puritan zealotry.

SCOTTISH PERSECUTIONS

Scholars have suggested a number of reasons for the greater intensity of witch-hunting in Scotland. One reasonable explanation is that Scotland had a more primitive structure of government than France or England. The Scottish royal government's inability to supervise investigations properly allowed local officials to get carried away on a wave of paranoia and suspicion. This royal weakness also affected the application of torture in Scotland. According to law, torture could only be permitted by the king's Privy Council of advisors or by the Scottish parliament. Nevertheless, local judges often sanctioned torture, citing a need to protect the state from the imminent evil of witchcraft.

Scottish tortures offered a number of creative options. Sleep deprivation, called "walking" or "watching," may have been a Scottish contribution to the torturer's repertoire. Screws for the legs changed into mere "bootes," while those for thumbs were charmingly nicknamed "pilliwinks." The caspiclaw device was probably binding iron, whose effectiveness increased by heating it. Pincers used to pull out fingernails were called "Turcas," named after their reputed use by the vicious Ottoman Turks. Another common method was the cords. They were tied around the head and then jerked about to rattle the brain. Hairshirts soaked in vinegar irritated the skin. Filthy jails providing insufficient clothing, food, and heat were also quite common and killed many. Some accused victims managed to hang themselves, although officials would sometimes blame the Devil or other witches for abetting such suicides. To add insult to injury, accused persons, found innocent or not, had to pay for the costs of their imprisonment, examinations, and even executions. In 1596 Janet Wishart and Isabel Crocker received bills for the peat, coal, tar, and barrels to burn them in, as well as the cost of the stake. Usually, the executioners strangled witches before burning them, but not always.

Execution followed only after a trial by one's peers, but Scotland's strong jury system allowed ambivalent consequences for hunting. A Scottish jury only needed a majority to convict, not unanimity. The Scots also used the verdict "not proved," in addition to "innocent" or "guilty." "Not proven" might free an accused from the stake, but it left a whiff of guilt to linger over an unconvicted person.

In addition to political considerations, Calvinist religious ideology and a heightened religious fanaticism in Scotland may have led to increased witch-hunting. The Reformation encouraged hostility to royal control, especially during the reign of the Roman Catholic Mary, Queen of Scots (r. 1542–1567), a period when the most intense period of persecution began. Tensions about faith and power may have been channeled into concerns about witches. Some historians suggest that Protestant dismissals of charms and traditional counter-magic rituals left people feeling defenseless against magic. Fearful of evil, people were more willing to blame witches for misfortunes. The occasional use of the term "covenant" for the pact with the Devil especially resonated with Calvinist theology, mocking the Calvinist concept of God's bond with humanity. Attitudes about the sabbat and the diabolic pact consequently provoked extreme measures. Scottish sabbats, however, were characterized by feasting and sexual activity; charges of cannibalism were rare.

Certainly the socioeconomic situation in Scotland proved conducive to hunting. Compared with England, Scotland was a very poor country. The many people living in marginal economic conditions probably found some attraction in the fantasy of a Devil's Pact that promised that they would "never want." Some historians have also suggested that Scottish men were more patriarchal than Englishmen and therefore more inclined to persecute "uppity" women who disturbed the proper order of things in a time troubled with much change.

Accusations of *maleficia*, called malefice in Scotland, either by neighbors against alleged witches or by witches against one another, prompted most hunts. As elsewhere, some people were targeted for being scolds, cranks, troublemakers, or generally antisocial. Reputations would be passed down in families, with a child of an alleged witch being called a "witch's get." The marginalized might accept these labels, only intensifying their positions as social outcasts and targets.

FAIRIES

For Scots, the supernatural world included not just demons, but also elves and fairies. More than in other nations, the Scots entangled the idea of such creatures with witchcraft. Two cases illustrate the Scottish fascination with fairy folk. In 1576, authorities in Ayrshire accused Elizabeth Dunlop of sorcery. Elizabeth had been a local midwife and wise-woman, handing out advice about useful herbs, healing animals, and finding stolen goods. Her confession, made under torture, told of how the ghost of Thom Reid, who had been killed in battle in 1547, had assisted her in her cunning work. She had neither known him when he was alive, nor met him through the Devil. Instead, he came recommended by the Queen of Fairies, coming from Elfame, the land of Elves. Thom acted as an odd sort of familiar, teaching her to find objects, such as a stolen cloak or plough irons, and to heal, usually by brewing mixtures of spices such as cloves, ginger, and sugar. The ghost did, however, tempt her to deny her baptism and come away with him to the court of Elfame, accompanied by eight women in plaid and four men in gentlemen's clothing. On the basis of this temptation, the authorities considered the connection to Thom to be satanic. They convicted and burned Elizabeth on the Castle Hill in Edinburgh.

In May 1588, a court charged Alison Pearson with witchcraft because of her associating with fairies. Her cousin William Simpson had allegedly learned magical arts in Egypt and brought them back to Scotland. First, William cured Alison of a laming illness; then he took her to Elfame. The fairies treated her poorly, but taught her to heal. Her proposed cure for the ailing bishop of St. Andrew's made her suspect of witchcraft. The court found her guilty and sentenced her to be burned, although they allowed her to be strangled with a wire first. In 1623, consorting with Alison's ghost led to Isabel Haldane's execution in Perth.

EARLY HUNTS IN SCOTLAND

Well before these elvish and spectral incidents, the hunts had started quite modestly in Scotland, around 1500. Most hunting took place in the South and in coastal areas influenced by English culture, rather than in the Gaelic-speaking Highlands. A witchcraft law was passed under Mary Stuart, Queen of Scots, in 1563. Calvinist reformers promoted this as one of many laws necessary to regulate moral and sexual behavior. The law had the Privy Council (the central government) appoint commissions of judges with power to investigate and punish witchcraft. Along with treason, witch-hunting was one of the few crimes the Edinburgh government pursued nationally; local magistrates supervised most other crimes. The witchcraft judges usually carried out limited, isolated trials on the estates of the great landowners. Although witchcraft was still a minor issue at the time, this criminalization of witches enabled cases to coalesce into a larger, nationwide hunt.

A case in 1594, however, briefly slowed official enthusiasm for hunting. Authorities in Edinburgh tortured Alison Balfour with the caspiclaw for forty-eight hours, without a legal warrant. This device seems to have been a heated iron cage that surrounded the victim. They also afflicted her eighty-one-year-old husband by pressing him with hundreds of pounds of iron bars; her servant with caspiclaw for 264 hours; her son with "bootes" and lashes; and a seven-year-old daughter with thumbscrews. Balfour recanted after torture, but they burned her anyway. Partly in reaction to this cruelty, in 1597 the royal Privy Council reduced the witch-hunting commissions and tried to restrict the number of sanctioned hunts.

JAMES VI AND THE NORTH BERWICK WITCHES

Mary's son and successor, King James VI, would revive a fear of witches. He had come to the throne quite young, after his mother had fled from Scotland for being implicated in the murder of her husband by explosion. Once he came of age, James thwarted the Privy Council's attempt to rein in hunting. James, at first, believed in the reality of witches and thought their danger to the state to be comparable to that of rebellious nobles and English invasions. He even wrote his own book, *Dæmonologie* (*Demonology*, 1597), about the phenomenon.

The book relates the dialogue of two characters who argue against the formidable John Weyer (see Chapter 3) and Reginald Scot (see page 123). In the first part, they discuss the reality and power of magic and of the Devil. In the second part, they review details of sorcery and witchcraft. Women are, of course, more vulnerable to his deceptions, ever since Eve's being fooled by the serpent in Eden. Against the reasonable argument that "if Witches had such power of Witching of folkes to death, (as they say they have) there had [been] none left alive long [since] in the world," he answers that God had limited the Devil's powers since the beginning so that witches can only do certain harm.[1] The third part deals with spirits, including incubi and succubi, although the characters dismiss the most extreme tales of women giving birth to monsters. James accepts demonic possession, which can be cured through simple exorcism of fasting and prayer. He adopted the views popular on the Continent, drawing on arguments by Jean Bodin (see Chapter 4), that Satan initiated a diabolic conspiracy with those witches to whom he granted powers of witchcraft. Scholars today debate whether his arguments reflected a paranoia about witches or a desire to understand a confusing situation.

The notorious case of the North Berwick Witches captured the attention of this royal strixologist and helped inspire him to write his book. A servant girl's mysterious behavior sparked the hunt that soon burst into a plot against the king himself. In 1590, a local magistrate suspected Geillis (or Gilly) Duncan, who had earned a local reputation as a healer. He arrested her for witchcraft and tortured her with "pilliwinks" and with the cords around her head that he rattled violently. Gilly eventually confessed and accused others, who were themselves then tortured.

An old woman, Agnes Sampson (or Simpson), was implicated in the next wave of confessions. Her previously honored position as a cunning-woman had led people to call her Grace Wyff or the Wise Wife of [the district of] Keith. King James himself examined her in his palace of Holyrood, after officials had already found the Devil's Mark on her nude, shaved body. They tortured Sampson with the witch's bridle, a device that kept the mouth open with four prongs. They also used the cords, twisted tightly around her limbs. From pain, prodding, and sleeplessness, she finally confessed.

Agnes Sampson's confession reached upward to accuse Francis Hepburn, the Earl of Bothwell, of trying to enchant the king. The earl allegedly had an ointment to smear on the king to arouse James's affection. Authorities arrested this important personage, but he managed to escape and flee the country. Bothwell's friend, Euphemia Macalzean (or Maclean), the wealthy daughter of a lord, suffered the rare extremity of being burned alive, on July 25, 1591. Another significant accused was John Fian (or Feane), the schoolmaster of Berwick.

Fian became something of a legendary figure with his alleged witch exploits. One story, which was actually a variant on a story from the ancient writer Apuleius's *Metamorphoses*, was that he wanted to make a love charm to woo a local girl. Fian convinced her brother to provide him with some of her pubic hairs, but the girl's mother discovered the plot and instead had her son give Fian some hairs from a cow. As a result, the moonstruck cow began chasing Fian around the town. This story is charming, but complete fiction. In reality, Fian managed to escape, but wound up captured again, personally examined by King James, and then tortured. The examiners applied several methods: the cords, "bootes" applied until his bones burst, pins stuck in his tongue, the "Turcas" thrust into the exposed wounds, and "pilliwinks."

All these confessions of witchcraft culminated in the "exposure" of an elaborate magical plot to kill the king. The Devil had allegedly targeted the king because James was his greatest enemy. The witches supposedly met in North Berwick, dancing "widdershins" (going counterclockwise) around the church. Fian opened the locked building by blowing into the lock. Once in the church, the Devil took the form of a tall black man, with a goat's beard, a rabbit nose, a hawk's beak, and a long tail, clad in a black gown and skullcap. When the Devil accidentally named one of their number by his Christian name, which was forbidden, the witches ran about "hurdy gurdy." They divided up a corpse and danced to music played on a Jew's harp by Geilly Duncan. One method for the proposed regicide was to sink the royal ship with James on board, using a spell cast by throwing a cat into the sea and shouting "Hola!" Another proposal was to spread poison from a black toad onto the king's bed clothing.

The trial convicted the accused witches. A jury did try to acquit Barbara Napier, the wife of a burgess of Edinburgh, but James threatened them with his royal displeasure, as expressed in his Tollbooth speech of June 7, 1591. Unlike the jury, he considered the fantastic testimony sufficient to prove the charge of *lèse-majesté*. Under pressure, the jury changed the verdict to guilty. Napier only escaped the hangman because of pregnancy. Unfortunately, the same excuse could not save Agnes Sampson, John Fian, and others, who were strangled and then burned at Edinburgh castle at the end of January 1591. The plot seems impossible to the rational mind today. In all probability, none of these persons plotted against the king's life. His personal involvement in the case, however, convinced King James of the real danger of witchcraft.

The legacy of the Berwick witches and their emphasis on diabolic intervention resulted in decades of more witch-hunting in Scotland. Although James' attitudes and interests changed after he became King of England in 1603, the

Scots had begun a habit of hunting that they did not give up easily. In 1629, a new wave peaked, largely because officials dealt with a backlog of accumulated cases.

The crises of the English Civil War (1642–1651) between the parliamentarians and the king may have contributed to another major series of hunts in 1649, with additional bouts of hunting continuing regularly for the next dozen years. Rivalries over moral issues erupted among Calvinists, between leaders of the official Scottish Kirk (Church) and laymen parliamentarians. The ruling Covenanting party, nervous about war and position, wanted to show their independence from the clergy, while the clergy wanted to prove their zeal for morality. Witches provided a convenient enemy on whom both sides could agree. The Presbyterian Calvinism of the Scots did not necessarily align with the Puritan Calvinism of the English, however. During the domination of Scotland by Cromwell's English Calvinist regime, commissioners from England actually dismissed dozens of witch cases for lack of sound evidence in 1652.

THE LAST GREAT SCOTTISH PANIC

In the early 1660s, the Stuart dynasty came back to power over Scotland and England in the Restoration. During this time of readjustment, a major witch hunt broke out, sometimes called The Great Scottish Witch Hunt. The Scottish Kirk took seriously its duties of upholding moral behavior according to its Calvinist beliefs. Worrisome moral failures ranged from sleeping in church, doing chores on Sunday, dancing, gossiping, and fornicating, to practicing magic and witchcraft. Many preachers sermonized on how Scotland was under spiritual attack by Satan.

The "magical" roots of the great hunt extended back into the final few years before the Restoration. During this time, neighbors had reported each other to the authorities, a practice called "delation." The charges were typical "malefices": causing illness, spoiling ale or butter, or killing livestock and people. Although the use of torture remained limited, some accused people confessed to dancing and having sex with the Devil. The hunt soon spread to cover much of southern Scotland during 1662.

The most remarkable case is probably that of the young Isabel Gowdie of Auldearne, Morayshire. Isabel freely confessed to her witchcraft activities in April and May of 1662. That she made four slightly different confessions and seemed rather mentally confused did not concern the authorities. She told how she had renounced Christianity to serve the Devil fifteen years earlier. The Devil made his mark on her shoulder by biting her and then sprinkling her own blood on her head and rebaptizing her as "Janet." The Devil assigned to other witches in her coven of thirteen members new names such as "Throw-the-corn-yard," "Pickle-nearest-the-wind," or "Over-the-Dyke-with-it." Each witch likewise had a familiar, each assigned names like "Red Reaver," "Thief of Hell," or "Hendrie Craig." The witches stole wealth from a local farmer in an unusual fashion. The Devil directed a plow made of a ram's horn and pulled by frogs over other people's lands, while the Devil promised that his followers would receive the crops themselves. The coven stopped cows from giving milk by plaiting a rope between the cow's hooves and calling on the Devil. In animal forms, such as a cat or a bird, Isabel said that she stole the best food and drink from her neighbors' homes. Once, dogs attacked and nearly caught her when she was in the form of a hare. She also worked with her coven to change other people into animals and cause storms.

Isabel offered interesting details about her meetings with witches. She claimed to have attended a witch's meeting in 1659 where witches adopted the forms of different animals. If suspicious husbands should awaken in the night and look for their missing wives, they were deceived by three-legged stools that appeared to be the women. Isabel herself had ridden to her meetings on a straw between her feet, which had been made into a horse, while others flew about on bean stalks and reeds. They entered a mountain that housed a great feasting hall, where the Devil would entertain them, but also scourge them. Isabel admitted to killing several people who had not blessed themselves, as the witches had flown past them in the form of straws blowing in the wind. Isabel also mixed in ideas of fairies. She said that the Queen of Fairies had regularly fed her, while other elves supplied the witches with elf-shot arrows. Despite this lurid and often-cited set of confessions, no record remains of the end faced by Isabel Gowdie or for many others of the accused.

Isabel Gowdie's confessions illustrate the popular folk superstitions that long endured interwoven with diabolic fears. Her confession was the first and possibly the only usage of the term *coven* (or *covine*) as a way to organize witches. The coven was seen as a weird perversion of Christ and his disciples, thirteen witches who regularly met together. The coven, both the word and the idea behind it, remained rather limited to Scotland until the revival of Paganism and modern Wicca in the twentieth century, when the concept became popular.

"Prickers" who stuck pins in alleged witches to find the Devil's Mark, provided a great deal of proof against witches in this last great hunt. The most famous, John Kincaid, found much demand for his services. Many started as amateurs and became "professionals" because of the good money: they earned several pounds per test and examined hundreds. Sticking people with pins could cause great pain and loss of blood, but the Scottish prickers did not overly obsess with seeking the Devil's Marks on the genitalia. As the hunt slowed, complaints about unauthorized pricking curtailed the activities of prickers, bringing them under investigation. One of them, John Dick[son], turned out to be a woman who had disguised herself as a man so she could identify witches and bring them to "justice." This fraud and others, such as using pins with retractable points, helped to end their practices. Nevertheless, prickers' alleged power to find the mark had already convinced many to believe that they themselves were witches, even without knowing it.

More than 200 accused witches died between 1661 and 1662, many burned with charcoal and tar. By the end of that panic, the worst of the hunting was over in Scotland. The clergy of the General Assembly repeatedly preached reminders to the Scots of the dangers of witches for decades afterward, but the government no longer responded by authorizing hunts.

WITCH HUNTS IN ENGLAND UNDER THE TUDORS

England and its laws had long differed from those of the other countries on the European Continent, well before the witch hunts started around 1400. Although some of the revived Roman legal methods had found their way into English jurisprudence, England relied heavily on its own tradition of Common Law, which derived from ancient Germanic customs. Some elements of this unique English system helped protect the innocent caught up in the criminal justice system. The central government carefully supervised the network of circuit courts, so legal abuses through ignorance were prevented. The English developed a jury system, where people similar to the accused ("peers") made key decisions. Grand juries, as in the United States of America today, served to limit the power of prosecutors by requiring that jurors decide whether enough evidence existed to make a court case worthwhile. Trial juries possessed the key responsibility to decide guilt or innocence, although judges enjoyed great influence in swaying juror's opinions. In comparison, juries in countries on the Continent often merely served to ratify the judge's findings rather than to decide guilt or innocence themselves.

Officially, the English legal system also did not allow torture, except with royal permission. With less torture, suspects named fewer accomplices and the circle of accused usually stayed comparatively small. Even when torture did take place, it rarely matched the excesses committed in France and the Holy Roman Empire. Of course, court officials could extort false confessions through threats, trickery, leading questions, and unrelenting pressure, even where actual violence was not applied. However, in general, lack of torture meant fewer confessions that could be twisted into diabolic fantasies.

ENGLISH EXECUTIONS

Witches also were not normally burned to death in England, as on the Continent. The most common and usual method of execution was hanging. Hanging could be quite unpleasant, since before the nineteenth century it involved slow strangulation. The "drop" method of hanging, which killed with a sudden fall and breaking of the neck, was not invented until long after the witch hunts were over. The strangulation method could take several minutes of struggling by the victim, depending on how efficient the hangman was with knots. Such "dancing" amused the large crowds that attended public executions. The dying also usually groaned, urinated, and defecated before they ceased moving. After a hanging, the dead body frequently remained hanging on the gibbet as a display. Several executed corpses hanging in various states of decomposition decorated the gallows, as an object lesson in the power of the law.

Antiwitch zealots did manage to overrule some English legal protections. While English law accepted the reality of witches, legal theorists recognized that their crimes might be hard to expose, just like the secretive crime of poisoning. Thus, a few legal experts leaned toward considering witchcraft a *crimen exceptum* that suspended normal rules of legal procedure. Some courts, then, allowed greater leeway in arresting and convicting witches than murderers or thieves. Rules of evidence were bent and even broken. On the one hand, the poor character and reputation of a person as a witch might get her arrested, whereas on the other hand the poor character and reputation of a witness against witchcraft was overlooked. Witnesses against witches often included persons usually considered otherwise unreliable, like the very old, the very young, or the mentally unstable. Spouses were even allowed to testify against their husband or wife, and children could give evidence against parents.

Comparatively minor "proofes" sufficed to gain convictions. A reputation for witchcraft, the habit of cursing, or the mere association of the accused with the illness of another person through a look, gesture, or brief physical contact was enough to establish reasonable suspicion. Finding images or pictures of an alleged victim in the possession or home of the accused also served to establish guilt. A corpse that bled when touched by the witch accused of killing the dead person provided convincing proof. The most common accusations involved actual physical harm to property or persons, blamed on supernatural means.

Many popular contemporary pamphlets reveal some understanding of the methods, causes, and results of witch hunts. Although sensationalized, these pamphlets expose the fears and attractions of seeing the world as full of witches. People connected misfortune with the malice of a witch. If illness or accident struck, they did not blame bad luck or divine justice, but saw their pain and suffering as the evil intention of a witch. An accusation often followed from an act of unkindness or lack of charity. Over time, gossip and innuendo could grow into certainty that a person was a witch. Only a minor incident then led to arrest, trial, and death. The more serious charge of a diabolic pact only later became a part of the witch-hunting mentality in England.

People could protect themselves from witches through several means, according to popular notions. Avoiding witches was perhaps the easiest way. One could either move from a neighborhood that had witches or just ignore such persons. A simpler method may have been to accumulate charms and amulets, or sacred objects such as relics or a consecrated Host, to ward off witches. Making the sign of the cross also allegedly worked. The most challenging method may have been to live a life a moral rectitude and religious devotion. It seemed that witches could not attack the righteous and godly. Such Christian behavior, though, also included generosity toward one's neighbors and the poor, who might wear one down with requests for cups of sugar or for alms.

Cunning folk may have provided some advice and protection against witches. People wanted to know the future, how to regain lost or stolen property, and how to restore health. They probably believed that wise-men and wise-women had genuine supernatural powers. Cunning folk probably provided services similar to modern-day psychics, convincing people of their abilities through clever questioning and good guesswork and impressing the gullible with small magical devices, most commonly a basin of water that reflected the client. Reputations were made after a few successes; the many failures were conveniently forgotten or blamed on bad timing, mistakes, the client herself, or, of course, the intervention of witches. Through leading suggestions, cunning folk sometimes helped victims of misfortune identify witches as the source of their troubles. Although wise-women claimed their powers to be from spirits of nature or angels, many political and religious authorities saw them as little better than witches. Thus, they sometimes wound up accused of witchcraft themselves, although not as often as their numbers might suggest.

THE WITCH'S MARK

English witch lore emphasized the use of witches' imps or familiars. These magical beings represented the Devil or helped witches cast spells through their magical agency. They might help witches fly or do things like sink ships (although actual evidence that any specific ship had been sunk was not necessary). The English consequently obsessed about finding the witch's teat or Witch's Mark. The Devil's Mark of the Continent was seen as a spot left by the Devil claiming his own. A Witch's Mark, in contrast, was a place on the body where witches could nourish their familiars, who suckled on it and drew milk, blood, or some magical substance from the witch's body. Just as with the Devil's Mark, though, any odd blemish could serve as a Witch's Mark, and many English examiners looked for them among women's genitalia. This feminine aspect of nursing the imp may have been a factor in the English's targeting women as witches much more frequently than men, who were not seen as providers of nourishment from the body. To expose the guilty, the witch would be placed under watch or kept isolated until a familiar showed up looking for nourishment. Of course, that meant any living creature appearing in a jail cell, from a rat to a moth, might be labeled as the evil spirit familiar.

EARLY HUNTING IN ENGLAND

The first witch trials in England involved political plots and important personages. In 1375, the mistress of King Edward III, Alice Perrers, was banished on the charge of using image magic to bewitch the king. The Witch of Eye, Margery Jourdain (or Jourdemayne), burned in 1441 for allegedly helping Eleanor Cobham, the Duchess of Gloucester, try to kill King Henry VI. The lady Eleanor herself did public penance by processing to a shrine through the streets

of London, bareheaded with a two-pound wax candle; then she spent the rest
of her life in confinement. In 1470, the Duchess of Bedford was accused of
making images of King Edward IV and his future bride Elizabeth Grey.
Although the court found the Duchess innocent, Richard III (r. 1483–1485)
later used this case to support his own claim to the throne, blaming Edward
and Elizabeth's marriage on the sorcery and witchcraft of his mistress, Jane
Shore.

The case of Henry VIII's second wife, Ann Boleyn, was one of the last cases
of witchcraft against the powerful. The original charges against her included
using magic to make the king fall in love with her. The court only convicted
her, though, on the charges of treason and adultery with her brother. Henry
VIII's experience with Ann Boleyn perhaps convinced him to issue a law
against witchcraft in 1542, but few cases arose from the law and it was repealed
under his successor, Edward VI.

HUNTING UNDER ELIZABETH I

The ascension of Elizabeth to the throne coincided with a growing concern
about witches by her clergy of the newly established Church of England. The
clergy themselves ranged in religious attitudes from inclining to Roman Catholic, leaning to Lutheran, embracing the Anglican compromise, or being forth-
right Calvinists. Parliament passed a witchcraft law in 1563, institutionalizing
the growing fear of witches. The motives behind the law were to some extent
based on a paranoid association of witches with Roman Catholics. The crimes
that involved magic and witchcraft included finding treasure, making love
potions, and attempting divination (especially predicting the sovereign's death
date). First offenses of harming an animal or person carried minor penalties,
such as a year in prison or being publicly locked in the stocks. Torture might
be applied to stubborn suspects who refused to enter a plea, either guilty or
not guilty. The death penalty only followed for witchcraft that involved murder. Still, any invocation of spirits became a felony. The last decades of Elizabeth's reign saw hundreds of indictments made against alleged witches.

FIRST HUNTS AT CHELMSFORD

The court based in Chelmsford in the county of Essex became an important
center of witch hunts. An early string of cases centered around the beer brewer
John Samond (or Smyth or Smith or Salmon; Elizabethans often spelled names
in various ways), who had gained reputation as a witch. In 1560 he had been
accused of murdering John Graunte and Bridget Pecocke by witchcraft, but
was acquitted in Chelmsford the next year. Another accusation followed in
1570, for stealing sheep. In 1572 he had allegedly cursed and killed two cows
belonging to one of the accusers of his sheep stealing, while his wife, Joan, had
allegedly hurt two other men. He was found innocent again, although two

other women, Agnes Francys and Agnes Steademan, were convicted of similar crimes. In 1587, a court charged Samond again, for using witchcraft to murder Henry Hove and kill a cow. This time, they convicted and hanged him (although two other women tried at the same time were acquitted).

The first widespread hunt began in 1566 as authorities accused Elizabeth Frances of bewitching a child, William Augur, until he became physically incapacitated. Under questioning, Elizabeth began to admit to witchcraft. She declared that her grandmother, called Mother Eve, had first led her to renounce Christ and ally with the Devil. Satan had provided her with a cat familiar named Sathan, who constantly promised that she would gain wealth, although somehow she never did. She did once have some sheep, but they wasted away. As a result, Frances sent the cat to destroy the goods of others and even kill some people. One victim was Andrew Byles, with whom Elizabeth had had sexual intercourse outside of marriage. The cat did provide her a husband, Francis, with whom she had a child, but the cat soon killed the baby. The cat also lamed her husband and gave her instructions on how to make a potion that produced abortions. After sixteen years, she tired of the cat, partly because she fed it on her own blood from pricked wounds. At that time, she gave Sathan to Agnes Waterhouse and her eighteen-year-old daughter Joan in exchange for a cake.

The Waterhouses consequently found themselves accused of witchcraft. Agnes allegedly used the familiar Sathan, now in the form of a toad, to kill a neighbor's three geese and to bewitch and kill another neighbor, William Fynee, because of a quarrel she had with his wife. Joan caught blame for a large black dog that harassed their neighbor of twelve years, Agnes Brown. Joan allegedly held a grudge against Brown because the latter had refused her bread and cheese. Agnes Brown testified against the large black dog as an agent of witchcraft, who also stole butter and could be only driven away when Brown threatened the dog with a knife and called on Jesus.

In July 1566, Sir John Fortescue presided over the trial of the three accused witches. The court found Agnes Waterhouse guilty and had her hanged and the corpse burned. Joan Waterhouse was found innocent. He sentenced Elizabeth Francis to a year in prison and several appearances in the pillory. In the public pillory, she publically admitted her guilt four times and had thus established to her neighbors that she had used witchcraft. Unfortunately for Elizabeth, she found herself accused again in 1579 and blamed, and hanged, for the death of the local women Mary Cooke and Alice Poole.

MORE HUNTS AT CHELMSFORD

Chelmsford again presented itself as a witch nexus in trials adjudicated at St. Osyth by Justice of the Peace Brian Darcy in 1582. Darcy had been taught about witch hunts elsewhere in Europe and favored harsher Continental methods over English ones. He was able to start the hunt by picking on Ursula (or Ursley) Kemp, a wet nurse and woman of ill repute, as attested by an eight-year-old illegitimate son, Thomas Rabbet. She had allegedly charmed young Davy Thurlowe, caused another Thurlowe infant to fall out of the cradle and break its neck, and lamed the mother, Grace Thurlowe. The magistrate had Ursula's own son testify to the regular appearance of familiars: a lamb, a toad, and two cats, named Tiffin, Piggin, Titty, and Jack. She fed them milk and bread or allowed them to suck on her Witch's Mark. Her case seems to be the first time the court had women search for a Witch's Mark on the accused.

At first, Kempe would only admit to having learned a useful charm for curing illnesses, which she had regularly put to good use. She admitted to the above crimes and more, following Judge Darcy's promise of leniency if she confessed. She implicated more than a dozen other people, leading to fourteen arrests. Of those, one won acquittal, a few confessed to damaging some property, and others won suspended sentences or imprisonment. Only two, including Ursula Kemp, were hanged. Judge Brian Darcy afterwards published "A true and just Recorde of the Information, Examination, and Confession of all the Witches.... Wherein all men may see what a pestilent people Witches are, and how unworthy to lyve in a Christian Commonwealth."[2]

Just a few years later, in 1589, yet a third major hunt took place in Chelmsford. A woman of the village of Sible Hedingham, Joan Prentice, was accused of forming a pact with Satan at the cost of her soul. He had appeared as a ferret named "Bidd" with fiery eyes, who sealed the deal by sucking blood from her left cheek. She asked Bidd to nip Sara Glascock, in revenge for her family refusing alms to Prentice. The ferret went too far, however, and "had nipped Sara Glascock that she should die thereof."[3] At her anger, the ferret never returned. This hunt also used evidence from children to an unusual degree to gain convictions. A woman named Joan Cunny stood convicted on the evidence of her eleven- and nine-year-old illegitimate grandsons.

REGINALD SCOT

The Chelmsford hunts helped to provoke the most important English book criticizing the hunts. Reginald Scot, an English gentlemen who believed in witches but saw the terrible affects of hunts, published *The Discoverie of Witchcraft* in 1584. He had seen the trials in St. Osyth and Chelmsford in 1582. He begins his book by claiming that everyone would experience the same kind of weather, for good or ill, whether all old women were witches and all priests were sorcerers, or if all devils were dead and all witches hanged. He asks, since such "mischeefes as are imputed to witches, happen where no witches are; yea and continue when witches are hanged and burnt; [why] then should we attribute such effect to that cause, which being taken awaie, happeneth neverthelesse?"[4] Scot especially doubted the incredible charges made against witches, such as boiling babies and cannibalizing them. Women who did believe themselves to be witches, he thought, citing Weyer, were suffering from delusion, melancholy, or depression. Those who might actually practice harm did so through natural means, such as poisoning. A large portion of his text explains conjuring or magic tricks that could seem to be real magic. He also imputes some of the excess fear of witches to the false magic tricks of papists, by which he meant rituals of Roman Catholicism. Although cunning-folk should be prosecuted for their superstitious practices, thought Scot, no one should be executed for magical crimes that did not happen.

While some responded positively to Scot's book, negative reaction predominated. King James VI of Scotland and England classified Scot with the ancient Sadducees, ancient Jewish contemporaries of Jesus who denied both the afterlife and spiritual beings such as demons or angels. The king ordered all copies of Scot's book burnt. He wrote his own book, *Demonology* (see page 113), partly as a response to Scot.

THE WITCHES OF WARBOYS

Scot's opinions did not slow down hunting. A hunt began in August 1589, in Warboys, Huntingdonshire, because nine-year-old Jane Throckmorton fell ill. Her Cambridge-educated physician actually helped initiate a suspicion of witchery as the cause, and the charge fell on an old, poor neighbor, Alice Samuel. "Mother" Samuel had allegedly sent spirits named Pluck, Hardname, Catch, Blue, and the three Smacks to harm the children. Jane's sisters soon succumbed to fits, then the servants. The poor victims to varying degrees and at various times sneezed, slept, convulsed, shook, laughed, cried, became catatonic, and often refused food or drink. The father of the girls forced Mother Samuel into his home, where the girls scratched her, in an attempt to break the spell. Lady Cromwell, the noble landlord of both Mother Samuel and the Throckmortons, advised the latter to break the spell by burning a snippet of hair that the landlady had clipped from the old woman. That very night, Lady Cromwell had a nightmare about Mother Samuel and her cat. The next day she, too, fell ill. The Throckmortons continued to harass Mother Samuel and try to force her and her daughter Agnes into making a confession. Alice did do public penance in an attempt to end the accusations. After Lady Cromwell died in mid-1592, the possessed girls accused the Samuels of bewitching her. The bishop of Lincoln examined Mother Alice and Agnes in December, and then turned them over to the justice of the peace who jailed Alice to await trial. At the trial, the evidence provided by Joan Throckmorton's sister Jane convinced the judge of the guilt of Alice, her husband, and Agnes. When any of the three admitted to have bewitched Jane, she came out of her trance. All three were hanged on April 5, 1593, after Mother Alice confessed again on the scaffold, while her husband and daughter refused to admit guilt. Judge Fenner used the anonymously authored pamphlet, *The Most Strange and Admirable Discoverie of the Three Witches of Warboys* (1593), to bolster his reputation.

Such pamphlets multiplied the notorious cases of possession, to edify or horrify the reading public. The official English clergy after the Reformation discouraged the idea of demonic possession. They considered exorcism either too Calvinist or too Roman Catholic or too magical, being thus both heretical and treasonous. The official exorcism ritual was a twisted version of the conjuration of demons (or vice versa). Some Protestants saw Satan luring good Anglicans back toward popery through such possession. Likewise, under Roman Catholic exorcism, the demons professed to be in league with the Protestants. Nevertheless, some English people, whether Anglican or Roman Catholic, continued to claim to suffer possession by demons, and exorcists continued to claim to be able to cast the demons out. Extreme cases involved pinching, striking, and binding the possessed to force the demon to leave.

THE "BOY OF BURTON"

Illness provoked another notorious witch trial a few years later. In 1597, a physician diagnosed a case of worms in thirteen-year-old Thomas Darling of Stapenhill near Burton-upon-Trent. When the "Boy of Burton" had been about to go to a prayer meeting one day, he felt himself struck down. As the boy's symptoms of pain in the stomach and vomiting increased, together with unusually pious behavior, the physician, family, and friends blamed witchcraft. They suspected sixty-year-old Alice Goodridge (or Alse Goodenridge) and her eighty-year-old mother Elizabeth Wright, notorious locally as the Witch of Stapenhill. The Justice of the Peace brought in Wright, Goodridge and her husband and daughter for questioning. They tested Alice by scratching around her mouth or "scoring above the breath," believing shedding blood there would break the spell. She also had to recite the Lord's Prayer, in which she made a mistake. Some upstanding women searched both women and uncovered warts and scars suspected of being Witch's Marks. Authorities got Alice to confess through illegal torture, allegedly by putting her feet to the fire. She died in jail before they could hang her.

The Puritan exorcist John Darrel intervened in the Boy of Burton case. He was trying to make a career of fighting the Devil and claimed success with exorcisms. He advocated prayer, fasting, and reading a tract that made the Devil cry out. His first attempt to establish a reputation came in 1587, when he accused Margaret Roper with the possession of Katherine Green, a charge that was tossed out by the judge. Darrel's apparently successful exorcism of the Boy of Burton in 1597 at first won him renown. A year later, however, the Darling boy admitted to fraud, although only after physical and verbal abuse in jail for seven weeks. A court held by Bishop Bancroft of London convicted his exorcist, John Darrel, of imposture. Darrel lost his clerical orders and spent a year in prison. Later, he had his ears cut for insulting the rector of Cambridge.

Bishop Bancroft's chaplain, Samuel Harsnett, initiated a pamphlet war with his *A Discovery of the Fraudulent Practises of John Darrel* of 1599. While Darrel and other supporters of exorcisms countered the criticisms, Harsnett summed up the attitude of many Anglican clergy with *A Declaration of Egregious Popish*

Impostures (1603), whose title obviously indicates where he placed the blame for the false possessions. Tensions between Anglicanism, Calvinism, and Roman Catholicism provided fodder for arguments and accusations that embroiled witches.

MARY GLOVER

Meanwhile, in 1602 and 1603, fourteen-year-old Mary Glover of London provoked another notorious exorcism. This merchant's daughter experienced hysterical fits, especially whenever she came near a local charwoman, Elizabeth Jackson. Elizabeth was put on trial for witchcraft. When a woman disguised in Elizabeth's clothing failed to provoke fits from Mary, the court increasingly sided with the possessed girl. Mary's seeming immunity to pain, inflicted by holding fire near her hand to cause blisters or sticking a hot pin up her nose, and Elizabeth's failure to recite the Lord's Prayer properly added to convincing evidence. Examiners also found Witch's Marks on Elizabeth's body.

At trial, one testifying physician, Dr. Edward Jorden, diagnosed hysteria as the cause of the possession. Under the judge's questioning, however, Jorden could neither be sure nor offer a cure. Worse, other physicians from the Royal College of Physicians of London disagreed. Medical testimony admitted that much was unknown about whether Mary's symptoms were natural or not. The formative medical science of the age had not sufficiently developed its ability to diagnose. So Judge Anderson disparaged the vague physicians and declared the fits to be supernatural in origin.

The judge's declaration of the reality of witches encouraged the jury to find Elizabeth Jackson guilty. Because the possession did not involve murder, she suffered only a year in Newgate prison and regular stays in the pillory, where she announced her guilt. Meanwhile, some Puritans prayed over Mary Glover and ended her seizures, discrediting the institutional Anglican clergy and arousing the anger of Bishop Bancroft. In contrast, Dr. Jorden bolstered his views of Mary Glover's fraudulence with a pamphlet of 1603, *A briefe discourse of a disease called the Suffocation of the Mother, Written uppon occasion which hath beene of late taken thereby to suspect possession of an evill*. His diagnosis, "Suffocation of the Mother," would later be called hysteria, a feminine illness caused by an imbalance in the uterus. Although modern medicine would in turn reject hysteria as an actual disease, Dr. Jorden's efforts aimed at a natural explanation for possession-related phenomena. Such efforts remained insufficient to deter witch-hunting at the time.

Bishop Bancroft of London was elevated to become Archbishop of Canterbury in 1604. He and his chaplain, Samuel Harsnett, who became Archbishop of York in 1628, guided the reforms of canon laws in 1604. Article 72 of these new laws prohibited exorcisms without the bishop's permission. In the official Church of England, exorcism vanished for three and a half centuries. Although Dissenters and Roman Catholics still believed in, and acted to remove, diabolic possession, the Anglican religious authority stepped in to halt one phenomenon that led to witch-hunting.

WITCH-HUNTING IN ENGLAND DURING THE SEVENTEENTH CENTURY

King James VI of Scotland surprisingly joined in to slow witch-hunting once he became King James I of England. At first, James Stuart still worried about witches. At the beginning of his reign, his English Witchcraft Act of 1604 facilitated easier convictions and executions for witchcraft than Elizabeth's law. Like the 1563 law it replaced, the Act of 1604 still prohibited consulting evil spirits and increased the penalties for harming animals, people, or goods. Judges were allowed broad leeway to interpret the law, and the death penalty might be invoked even when an intended murder victim did not die. The law did not connect every act of witchcraft to a diabolic pact, however. This rationality kept the English trials from going as far as those elsewhere. The Act did specifically mention the Witch's Mark, anchoring that peculiar evidence in English jurisprudence.

Barely after the law had passed, though, James began to moderate his personal views. The case of Anne Gunter in 1606 marked a turning point. Anne claimed possession, demonstrating it by refusing food, falling into fits, proclaiming visions, and spitting up pins (technically called allotriophagy). The Star Chamber, a special royal court with extraordinary legal powers, looked into her case. The Bishop of Salisbury helped to expose Anne when he placed specially marked pins in places where she would be sure to find them. When she later coughed up those pins, the implication was that she had swallowed them, not that some demon had magically placed them in her stomach. King James's own interview with her convinced him of her fraud. Under examination by the trained experts of the Star Chamber, Anne Gunter soon admitted she had been faking, put up to it by her father. A pamphlet about the Warboys/Throckmorton case of 1589–1593 had provided many of the inspiring details. This example may have encouraged a more skeptical attitude in the monarch. The harsh 1604 law still remained, however, at the ready for zealous prosecutors throughout the realm.

In the same year, Shakespeare presented his play *Macbeth* before King James and the court during a visit with the King of Denmark. The play *Macbeth* famously opens with the three "Weird Sisters," witches who set the plot in motion by foretelling Macbeth's future. Yet Shakespeare's literary representation of witches does not necessarily illustrate widespread fears of the supernatural. The fairies and magical creatures of his *A Midsummer Night's Dream* or *The Tempest* are played for humor and surely worried few people, especially in Shakespeare's urban audience. To what extent Shakespeare drew on actual fear of real witches, encouraged witch ideas, or was recognized as entertaining fantasy cannot be decided with any degree of confidence.

PENDLE FOREST WITCHES OF LANCASHIRE

The famous case of the Lancashire witches of the Pendle Forest in 1612 (see Chapter 1) reflected the classic views of witches that had been promoted by King James in his *Demonology* text. They demonstrated the power of local beliefs in charms and traditional magic and the influence of Continental ideas. The ideas of a sabbat ritual revealed by some conspirators made a rare appearance in English witch lore. The step from the white magic of cunning practices to an accusation of black-magic witchcraft was a short one. Local religious divisions of Anglican vs. Roman Catholic probably made the situation worse. The plan to blow up Lancaster Castle echoed the more famous Gunpowder Plot involving the Roman Catholic Guy Fawkes several years earlier. Only the confession of a coconspirator had foiled Fawkes' attempt to blow up Parliament and the king. The event is still celebrated in England every year with fireworks. The fight between Old Demdike and the Device family against Old Chattox and her family began with the refusal of begging. Some historians apply social accusation theory to this hunt. According to this theory, when people turn down requests for charity, they feel guilty and blame subsequent accidents on the malice of witches. These Lancashire hunts also showed the power of the local population to become incensed and alarmed over perceived witchcraft. Thomas Potts's selective account of the trial, *The Wonderfull Discoverie of Witches*, published the year after, helped to popularize these views of witchcraft further. This well-documented hunt has become the focus of a local tourist industry today.

The lurid reports of witchcraft in Lancashire did not divert King James from his increasingly cautious attitude. In the summer of 1616, a more cautious king overturned the conviction of witches based on evidence from children. The "Leicester Boy," thirteen-year-old John Smith, had blamed his possession on several local women. Nine were hanged and one would die in prison before King James happened to pass through the area and stopped to investigate. As with Anne Gunther, his careful personal questioning led the boy to confess fraud. James had several other women released and he harshly rebuked Judges Winch and Crewe. The lessons of this fraud helped expose those of the "Bilson Boy," William Perry, in 1620. A Roman Catholic priest had helped prep his faked possession, including the trick of passing blue urine with the aid of an ink bottle.

THE PENDLE SWINDLE

By the beginning of the reign of James I's son, Charles I (r. 1625–1648), witchcraft ideas had become even more problematic, as revealed in what became known as the Pendle Swindle of 1633–1634. Again in the Pendle Forest of Lancashire, a hunt began, launched because of ten-year-old Edmund Robinson. The boy had heard tales of the hunt of 1612 and had seen the feared

Jennet Device near his father's house. Edmund first borrowed witchcraft as an excuse to escape his father's punishment for not looking after the cattle. Edmund's success with one lie led him to make money as a witch finder. He claimed to have followed a strange greyhound through the woods and stumbled upon a sabbat meeting. In February 1633, Justices of the Peace questioned him. He led magistrates to churches so he could identify witches and they arrested more than two dozen suspects. Alone among the accused, the old woman Margaret Johnson confessed to strange crimes of witchcraft, although they did not match the descriptions of the sabbat provided by Robinson. She said she had sold her soul to the Devil, who called himself Mamilion and sported a fine suit of the latest fashion with silk points. He promised to grant her all she wished and sealed the deal with intercourse. She consulted with dozens of other witches and their familiars about how to kill and hurt others.

Conscientious examinations by authorities helped to deflate this hunt. In June, the Bishop of Chester, John Bridgeman, personally questioned those suspects who had not already died in jail. He believed that malice by the Robinsons provided a nonmagical motive for the accusations. The authorities sent the boy and his father to London to be interrogated. Four of the accused women also went to London, landing in the capable hands of William Harvey. This early scientist was the first to explain the blood's circulatory system in humans. He personally supervised midwives who examined the genitalia of women accused of witchcraft to look for the Witch's Mark. He did not find anything unnatural. His skepticism slowed the hunt, but did not entirely lead to freedom. Three of the accused died in prison as nearly twenty were convicted and imprisoned for witchcraft crimes. Later trials would also, ironically, demand additional embarrassing invasions of bodily privacy, because courts demanded Witch's Marks as physical proof of diabolic pacts.

Meanwhile, further investigation in the Pendle case revealed that Edmund Robinson's father had put him up to the false accusations, motivated by revenge and greed. The elder Robinson's target was Frances Dickinson, who had been in dispute with Robinson over payment for a cow. With the fraud exposed, the king pardoned the condemned. He did, strangely enough, keep them in prison at his "pleasure" for some time more.

HUNTS DURING THE ENGLISH CIVIL WAR

The reign of Charles I led to the conflict called the English Civil War, or the Puritan Revolution. This turmoil gave rise to a brief revival in witch-hunting, despite the notorious cases of fraud. The revolution began with James's belief in the divine right of kings and his own sovereignty. His autocratic rule offended Englishmen and led to some attacks on his courtiers and officials. His son, Charles I, further pressed the sole authority of the monarchy, driving his opponents to outright rebellion. The Civil War broke out when a majority of Parliamentarians gathered their own army to fight the king. They eventually succeeded in defeating the royal armies, capturing the king, and beheading him for treason. The leaders of the parliamentarians were Puritans, who were fervently Calvinist-minded in their religious beliefs. Both the Puritan effort to transform the Church of England into a Calvinist institution and the Parliamentarian goal to change the kingdom into a republic failed to gain total victory. The Puritan leader Oliver Cromwell established a military dictatorship instead. After Cromwell's death, the English invited Charles I's son, Charles II (r. 1660–1685), to become king. The Church of England's bishops were likewise restored to their cathedrals. Calvinist worship, however, gained significant ground, and English government became structured along more republican lines. In the Glorious Revolution of 1688, the Parliamentarians tossed out Charles II's brother and successor James II, because he was both Roman Catholic and a supporter of the divine-right theory. Thereafter, representative government through Parliament became dominant in English affairs.

HOPKINS

The political chaos and uncertainty of the war enabled the most notorious English witch hunt, led by the self-proclaimed "Witch-finder General" Matthew Hopkins. Hopkins managed to kill as many as 400 people in East Anglia from 1644 to 1646, perhaps more than twice as many as had been executed for witchcraft in the previous hundred years in all of England. Hopkins' origins and early life are largely unknown, but he was probably a gentleman in his early twenties during his witch-hunting. His self-confessional book, *The Discovery of Witches in answer to severall Queries, lately Delivered to the Judges of Aßize for the County of Norfolk*, published in 1647, describes and defends his hunting. Hopkins began to be concerned about witches in December 1644 after overhearing neighbors near his house in Manningtree talking to imps about Devil's Marks. Hopkins subscribed to the Continental ideas of the witch hunts, which included sex between a witch and the Devil and weekly meetings with readings from a demonic book. In Hopkins' concept of the criminality of witches, the diabolic pact mattered more than mere *maleficia*.

In March 1645, Hopkins and another local gentleman, John Stearne, brought some accusations to a local judge with the colorful name of Sir Harbottle Grimstone. The investigations that followed unleashed the hunts. Hopkins and Stearne offered their services to local authorities after managing to convince them that witches were to blame for much trouble in the realm. It is impossible to know now what truly motivated the two witch hunters. Some historians have suggested greed. The pair earned a lucrative fee for finding witches, as much as the enormous sums of £15 from the town of King's Lynn and £23 from Stomarket. In their own defense, though, they said that they charged a mere twenty shillings per town, and such fees did not make the hunters rich. There is also little evidence that Hopkins and his coworkers had any exaggerated religious fanaticism. Their success depended on the latent fears and resentments of the local population. Witch-hunters usually relied on a wide number of people who needed little convincing or pressure to go along with attacking alleged witches. And many of the locals eagerly supported Hopkins' hunting practices.

The first suspect, Elizabeth Clark, was an elderly, one-legged widow. Four women searched her for Witch's Marks, of which she had three. Several officials then watched Elizabeth for several nights looking for imps to appear and suck at her Witch's Marks. Several imps did appear, according to Hopkins, Stearne, and others. Elizabeth had granted them cute names, such as Vinegar Tom, Jarmara, or Sack & Sugar. She also admitted to having given her body in lust to the Devil. Upon her arrest, she implicated others, including young Rebecca West. Rebecca had imps named Pyewackett and Grizell Greediguts, and she had participated in a sabbat—again, highly unusual for English witches. Rebecca turned witness for the Crown and won immunity from prosecution.

Once locals had begun to identify suspects, Hopkins applied his own methodology. He discovered witches through the classic method of stripping and examining them for Witch's Marks. He claimed these marks could be distinguished from normal warts or hemorrhoids by keeping the witch awake for twenty-four hours without any of her spirits appearing to nurse at them. Unused, the teats would then expand, nearly to bursting, he thought. Hopkins did superficially acknowledge the legal prohibition on torture without royal sanction, but he felt the prohibition did not include the torture of "walking" or *tormentum insomniae*. A subject would be kept awake and moving as long as necessary, sometimes for several days, or they would be kept sitting for several days on a stool in a cramping cross-legged position, with the right toe tied to the left thumb and the left toe bound to the right thumb. Deprived of sleep, the accused became disoriented and hallucinatory, easily confessing to fantastic crimes. Hopkins also used pricking. Another popular "nontorture" used was the ordeal of cold water or "swimming" the witch. Accused people even requested swimming, convinced that it would prove their innocence. Hopkins and his assistants used it so much that popular sentiment turned against it. Indeed, some communities tried to ban the hunt by passing ordinances, but the weak laws did not slow Hopkins' zeal. He instigated trials though several counties in East Anglia. Setting up his headquarters in a local inn, he invited people to bring accusations and then acted on them. Long-held grudges and suspicions of neighbors found an outlet in Hopkins' investigation.

In July of 1645, trials at Chelmsford dealt with the first batch of Hopkins' accused, although several had already died from horrible prison conditions. Almost a hundred people testified against the witches. Nearly twenty were found guilty and hanged, including Elizabeth Clark. Nevertheless, several others won reprieves, although only one, Joan Rowle, was a woman.

One famous victim was a local vicar, John Lowes (or Lewis). Lowes was well known as a contentious Anglican preacher, having already been in conflict with his Puritan parishioners for insulting them. A few years earlier Lowes had tried to defend a woman, Ann Annson, from being arrested for witchcraft and had himself been accused of witchcraft. Hopkins kept the seventy-year-old priest walking for three days, badly blistering his feet, and then had a "swimming" test done in a ditch. After the harsh torture, Lowes confessed to having two imps, one allegedly nicer than the other. To appease the mean one, Lowes allowed the imp to sink a ship off Ipswich. At his execution on August 27, 1645, Lowes read his own funeral service from the Book of Common Prayer.

After a year of trials, some people began to turn against witch-hunting. Most effective was the preaching of John Gaule, a local vicar, who published his anti-Hopkins pamphlet *Select Cases of Conscience Touching Witches and Witchcrafts*. Gaule did not deny that witches were real, but saw how the hunts disturbed the public peace and challenged God's providence. He even accused the Witch-finder General of being a witch himself. By the fall of 1646, courts were acquitting accused witches more frequently than convicting them. Hopkins died a year later of consumption, although legends arose that he himself was swum and then hanged for a witch.

THE WITCH OF WAPPING

Several executions for witchcraft occurred during the time of the Cromwell's Commonwealth. In April 1652, Joan Peterson, the Witch of Wapping, was hanged at Tyburn, London's famous gallows near today's Marble Arch. Peterson had been identified as an associate of a large black cat that had frightened two old nursemaids and a baker. Authorities hanged her despite her refusal to repeat her confession, as required by law. The next year, another woman, eighty-year-old Anne Bodenham, also refused to repeat her confession. Her case can be traced back to her former master, Dr. Lamb, who was murdered by a mob in 1640 because they believed him to be a necromancer, an astrologer, and an associate of the unpopular Duke of Buckingham, favorite of King Charles I. Lamb reportedly could make a tree grow instantly in the middle of a room and then cause it to be cut down and taken away by three elves with baskets. Lamb's servant Bodenham was accused by Anne Styles, a local girl in Salisbury whom Bodenham had taken in as a maid. Styles accused Bodenham of trying to get her to sign the Devil's book, as well as conjuring through appeals to devils and concoctions of herbs listed in her Book of Charms. When Bodenham denied these accusations, Styles suffered fits and reported spectral appearances and the use of imps. Bodenham admitted using simple charms of cunning-folk and astrology, but no witchcraft. Despite her lack of confession, the jury found her guilty, and the judge had her hanged. As a clergyman tried to offer prayers for her, she became drunk en route to the gallows, getting free drinks from the crowd. Once there, she cursed the crowd and the executioner.

The Restoration regime of King Charles II also carried out some witch trials. In Chester in 1662, the quarrels of some local women escalated into a witch hunt. Anne Wright's illegitimate twelve-year-old daughter died after claiming to have been pricked by Mary Briscoe. Briscoe had a reputation for witchcraft, having even been suspected by her own husband, but this time the accused witch suffered no lethal consequences. Instead, the accuser, Anne Wright, wound up performing public penance. This case offered a useful reminder that authorities recognized how neighbors could fabricate accusations of witchcraft out of petty resentments.

Trials held at Bury St. Edmunds in Suffolk illustrated the enduring problems of finding evidence to convict people of a nonexistent crime. These trials are even more remarkable because they were conducted by Sir Matthew Hale, a famous chief Justiciar of England who wielded great influence on English law. His legal opinions and arguments would be cited for centuries. Hale believed in witches because of biblical scripture. In his writings on jurisprudence, however, Hale noted how easy it was to accuse someone of rape or of witchcraft, yet how difficult it was to prove either. This view ended up helping those accused of rape (almost always men), but hurting those indicted for witchcraft (mostly women).

TRIALS IN LOWESTOFT

Sir Matthew Hale oversaw a group of trials in Lowestoft, East Anglia, which erupted in the early 1660s. The town of Lowestoft was suffering an economic slump. Witch accusations began in October 1661 when the wealthy merchant Samuel Pacy refused to sell herring to the elderly Amy Denny (often incorrectly cited as Duny). Thereupon his nine-year-old daughter Deborah suffered pains like pin pricks in the stomach. Samuel Pacy managed to get Amy Denny punished with four weeks in the stocks. In the stocks, Denny complained about the Pacys. Soon Deborah and her sister, eleven-year-old Elizabeth, began to exhibit the full-blown symptoms of possession. They had fits, spat up pins and nails, and could not even say the name Jesus Christ. They blamed Rose Cullender and Amy Denny, who had spectrally appeared before them and threatened them.

Other neighbors joined in blaming the two women, leading to more than a dozen other charges. Anne Baldinge (or Baldwin) said she languished in illness due to a fascination by Cullender. The toddler William Durrant had supposedly fallen ill after Amy Denny, despite her age, had given him her breast to suckle while she cared for him one day. His mother, Dorothy Durrant, had consulted a cunning-man who told her to wrap the child in a blanket and to throw into the fire anything suspicious found in the house. She did indeed find a toad, which exploded in the fire, leaving no trace. Going next door, Dorothy Durrant discovered Amy Denny scorched and burned as if from a fire. Dorothy was lame afterward and was only healed upon Denny's conviction. Dorothy also blamed the death of her daughter Elizabeth in 1659 on Amy, whom she had caught visiting the child. Other acts of witchcraft ranged from possession, killing livestock, and knocking down a chimney, to getting a haycart stuck between two posts. After the last incident, Durrant reported that she had been "very much vexed with great Number of Lice of an extraordinary bigness."[5] Six women also found Witch's Marks during a search of Rose Cullender, stripped naked in her home.

The trial showed a brief inclination to apply scientific skepticism. In court, Elizabeth Pacy was allegedly unable to speak, but she angrily attacked and scratched Amy Denny when the accused was brought before the plaintiff. A renowned medical authority and author, the physician Sir Thomas Browne, testified that the girl was bewitched, although he had also diagnosed her with a natural organically based disease. On the suggestion of "an ingenious person that objected" to the evidence thus far presented, Elizabeth was blindfolded with her apron and tested for reactions when touched by one of the accused witches or by an innocent person.[6] When she gave the same startled and angry reaction to the innocent person touching her, the men conducting the test tried to get the case thrown out. Despite lack of reasonable evidence, Samuel Pacy convinced the court to disregard this test of his daughter's credibility. Against all jurisprudence, the eminent jurist Hale accepted "spectral evidence." This notion allowed witnesses to testify about what ghosts or spirits, which only they could see, allegedly did to them. Thus witnesses could invalidate an accused person's alibi, because a spirit could appear in one place while the body was in another. Hale's brief direction to the jury stressed the undoubted existence of witches, based on the Bible and parliamentary law. Hale had Cullender and Denny hanged on March 17, 1662.

This case reassured those who still clung to the fear of witches, even though those numbers were dwindling. Hale wrote a short version of his reactions to the trial directly afterwards, which was published in 1693 as part of *A Collection of Modern Relations of Matter of Fact Concerning Witches & Witchcraft ...*, reconfirming the reality of witches, but not mentioning the case. The record of the court proceedings (*A Tryal of Witches* published in 1682) would influence the most famous trials in America, those held at Salem, Massachusetts.

MAJOR WEIR

The case of seventy-year-old Major Thomas (or John) Weir of Edinburgh forced itself on the government in 1670. Weir turned himself in to the authorities, declaring he had a pact with the Devil that led to black magic; worked with a staff carved with images of satyrs; and committed incest and sodomy. It was his sister's freely given testimony that the Devil had helped her in her spinning and marked her on her forehead. The Devil had taken them both magically in a coach with horses to the town of Musselburgh and back. The authorities convicted Weir of various sex crimes: adultery, incest with his sister and stepdaughter, and bestiality, and his sister of incest and witchcraft. They strangled and burned Weir on April 11 and his sister the next day. Most historians believe their guilty consciences had produced satanic fantasies. The bizarre case probably put off more people from witch-hunting than it convinced.

JOSEPH GLANVILL

One of the last important widely read treatises still advocating witch-hunting was written by Joseph Glanvill (b. 1636–d. 1680). Glanvill recognized the validity of both faith and science. He himself was both a clergyman and a member of the Royal Society, which organized the early scientists of Britain. In the 1660s, Glanvill had written books such as *Scepsis Scientifica* ("Scientific Skepticism"), in which he praised the scientific method and hoped that it would lead humanity to a better future. Yet Glanvill also remained fascinated by witchcraft. In *A Blow of Modern Sadducism* of 1668, Glanvill told the story of the Dæmon of Tedworth. Drumming noises and other poltergeist activities began to haunt the house of a certain Mr. Mompesson after he had confiscated a drum from William Drury in 1661. A subsequent trial found William Drury innocent of witchcraft but guilty of theft, for which the government transported him to the prison colony of Australia.

Glanvill's friend, Henry More, shared his interest in the supernatural. More compiled various posthumous editions of Glanvill's writings, including material on demonology and ghost stories he himself added before his own death in 1687. The final versions, called *Saducismus Triumphatus* ("Sadducism Triumphed Over"), were published in 1688 and 1689. This collection claimed to defeat various anti-witch-hunting texts. Glanvill defined a witch as "… one that has the knowledge or skill of doing or telling things in an extraordinary way, and that in vertue of either an express or implicate sociation or confederacy with some Evil Spirit."[7] He argued for the reality of witches based on the testimony both of scripture and honest people. Glanvill advocated the possibility of the reality of magic because contemporary science was still ignorant about causes in both the natural and spirit world.

Glanvill's scientific colleagues, however, and even many among the general public, were less and less convinced that witches were real, let alone a danger. Glanvill was the last gasp of serious strixology. The high tide of the hunts in England had long passed. Most jurists and theologians had ceased to fear witches. In the final decades of the seventeenth century, the numbers of those tried declined sharply and the numbers of those found innocent or reprieved skyrocketed.

COLONIAL HUNTS

At the time the witch hunts flourished, the British Empire began its rise to world supremacy. Britons sailed across the oceans and conquered lands in Asia, Africa, and the Americas. Witch-hunting in British colonies, though, would only take place in North America. The first British settlement was in Jamestown, Virginia, in 1607. Shortly after, in 1620, the Pilgrims arrived in Massachusetts. The Pilgrims were Calvinist Separatists, so alienated from the Church of England that they felt a need to have their own, separate religious organization. After a few years in exile in Holland, they were given leave to set-tle in Virginia, but detoured instead to "New England" and founded their col-ony at Plymouth. More Calvinists soon arrived in Massachusetts Bay, officially still members of the Church of England. In practice, though, many used the freedom and distance allowed by colonial settlement to found their own Puri-tan religious regimes.

While asserting religious liberties for themselves, these Puritans refused tol-erance to others. In fact, they criminalized people of all other religious view-points. These crimes included the magical practices of cunning-folk, who used charms and spells. Preachers railed against the use of magic, even when prac-ticed as countermagic to spells. Prayers, fasting, and religious devotion were the solutions offered by the clergy and politicians. Whether the colonial gov-ernment accepted the Church of England or Calvinist Puritanism, the English colonies generally outlawed worship by other branches of Christianity. Quakers, in particular, were persecuted much as if they were witches, or, rather, heretics.

The colonists likewise worried about the religious beliefs of the Native Americans, often perceiving them to be worshipers of Satan. Colonists some-times compared Indian shamans with the witches that had been feared back in England. Nevertheless, the European immigrants rarely hunted Indians as witches per se. They killed large numbers of natives as enemies of the settlers and civilization instead. In the southern colonies, where most people belonged to the Church of England, some slave owners feared magic brought with their slaves from Africa. Their fears, however, focused on magical poisons concocted from roots and herbs, rather than invisible forces conjured by charms or demons.

The colonists imported the strixological literature that flourished in Eng-land, both for and against witch-hunting. As colonial courts began to conduct witch trials, they needed clear guidelines. The multiple viewpoints of strixolo-gists failed to provide them. Often, the courts confused issues of *maleficia* with the idea of a diabolic pact. Most colonists worried about *maleficia* that caused misfortune; educated elites cited the heretical crime of the diabolic pact. Witchcraft in colonial New England was prosecuted, but not in a constant regular effort, as popularly portrayed. Still, enough trials took place to make early American Puritan witch-hunting sufficiently notorious.

The first official witch executed in the colonies, Alice Young, was hanged on May 6, 1647, in Connecticut. Nevertheless, the conviction of witches did not automatically lead to their execution, as it might have in England. Of the doz-ens of witches convicted before 1692, more than twenty were hanged, but many others were whipped, fined, dunked with the ducking-stool, made to stand in the pillory, or exiled. When condemned to die, no witches were ever burned in the American colonies, contrary to the popular imagination. British law only allowed hanging for the death penalty.

EARLY TRIALS IN THE AMERICAN COLONIES

An early witch case entangled advocacy for religious freedom in America with witchcraft. Puritan clergy attacked Anne Hutchinson as a woman who disagreed with their theology. She also had befriended the midwife Jane Hawkins, who had been accused of contact with the Devil because of her assistance at the birth of a deformed child to Mary Dyer in October 1637. The Puritan Governor of Massachusetts, John Winthrop, ordered the fetus' corpse exhumed, so he could describe it in intimate, horrible detail. Anne Hutchinson herself soon also gave birth to a dead, deformed fetus. Hutchinson's association with Hawkins contributed to the Puritans' exiling Hawkins and Hutchinson, along with Mary Dyer, from Massachusetts Bay colony. The following year, Puritan ministers declared to Hutchinson their opinion that her unorthodox religious views came from Satan. She left to help found the new colony of Connecticut. The Puritan regime executed Mary Dyer a year after she returned to Massachusetts in 1659, for being a Quaker.

In 1648, the case against Margaret Jones, another midwife and cunning-woman in Massachusetts, created another victim. Her patients blamed her for making diverse persons and livestock sick with her malignant touch and secret medicines. Jones and her husband were watched to see if a familiar came to suck. Although none did, authorities produced other evidence. A Witch's Mark had been found, "an apparent teat in her secret parts, as fresh as if it had been newly sucked, and after it had been scanned, upon a forced search, that was withered, and another began on the opposite side."[8] A ghostly child came to her in prison and vanished again. Her hanging on June 15 in the Boston area was blamed for causing a storm in Connecticut, a connection noted by the governor, John Winthrop.

Some trials illustrate the ambivalence about the danger of witches felt by people who saw no need to kill all suspected people. A large hunt in Hartford from 1662 to 1666 began with allegations that Elizabeth Seager caused the possession of Anne Cole. Another alleged witch, the invisible Goodwife Ayres, magically choked eight-year-old Elizabeth Kelly to death. They tested two witches, probably Goodwife Ayres and her husband, by swimming, cross-bound hand and foot, who floated, while an innocent bystander who volunteered sank right away. Although courts found several people guilty and executed them, Goodwife Ayres managed to flee the state. Divided juries in three trials hesitated between innocent or guilty for Elizabeth Seager. Twice in 1663 she won freedom, but in 1665 a jury found her guilty of witchcraft. Fortunately for her, the governor, John Winthrop, Jr., overturned her conviction the next year.

Governor Winthrop, Jr., actually pushed for a more rational judiciary. His legal revision required two people to see a witch in the same demonic form at the same time before such testimony could be admitted as evidence. As a result, in 1671 and 1672, the leaders of Groton, Massachusetts, did not follow up the accusations against a local elderly woman by sixteen-year-old Elizabeth Knapp about her possession.

Some historians suspect that disputes about property and inheritance fueled hunts such as these. As the widow Katherine Harrison of Wethersfield, Connecticut, tried to hold on to the estate left her by her husband in 1666, her neighbors entangled her in accusations of witchcraft. Various trials and exile in New York dragged on for two decades. Harrison's admitted activity as a cunning-woman did not help her position with her neighbors or with juries, not to mention that widows and orphans were always among the most vulnerable of society. The availability of witchcraft as a legal weapon for adversaries only worsened their condition. Harrison, however, seems to have survived to a natural death.

COTTON MATHER

Despite this ambivalence, some clergy pounded on the pulpit and on the printing press about the danger of witches. Most famous and effective was the Puritan clergyman Cotton Mather (b. 1663–d. 1728). Mather's experience and writings provided many illustrative examples of witchcraft and theological arguments. His book *Memorable Providences Relating to Witchcraft and Possessions* in 1688 began with the warning: "Go tell Mankind, that there are Devils and Witches; and that tho those night-birds least appear where the Day-light of the Gospel comes, yet New Engl[and] has had Exemples of their Existence and Operation."[9]

Memorable Providences tells the story of the Goodwin possessions. The eldest Goodwin daughter, thirteen-year-old Martha, accused their laundress of the theft of some bed linens. The laundress's mother, Mary Glover (not to be confused with the Mary Glover of 1602 in London), was an old disreputable outsider. She only spoke Irish Gaelic; she was Roman Catholic in the very Puritan Massachusetts, and even her late husband had allegedly complained that she was a witch. The elder Glover responded to young Martha Goodwin's accusation of her daughter with insults. Martha soon fell ill with fits. Once a sister and two brothers also began to suffer possession symptoms, a consulted doctor blamed witchcraft. He noted how the children slept well at night, but during the day their mouths were contorted, their heads would flop on their necks, they lost some senses and complained of unbearable heat, barked like dogs or purred like cats, and cried as if being stabbed or struck. They shrieked when religious services were held within earshot.

Authorities arrested Mary Glover. A search of her house turned up several dolls made of rags and stuffed with goat hair. Glover actually admitted that she manipulated the dolls by stroking them with her finger wetted with her own spit. When one of the poppets was put into her hand in court, the Goodwin children who were present exploded in fits, as if the magic had hurt them.

Glover then confessed that the Devil had worked through her. Several physicians pronounced her of sound mind. She could not quite recite her Lord's Prayer correctly.

Mather himself interviewed her, through an interpreter, but failed to gain a conversion. Even though the government executed her on November 16, 1688, the children continued to succumb to fits, as the condemned witch had predicted to Mather. The clergyman took Martha Goodwin into his own home, both to test and help her. After a brief respite, her fits resumed, including a habit of looking oddly up the chimney. He believed her to ride an invisible horse. Eventually the possessions stopped. All these experiences absolutely convinced Cotton Mather of the reality of demons and witches.

THE SALEM HUNTS

The most famous, most deadly, and most studied witch trial in the British colonies took place at Salem, Massachusetts, in 1692. Its unique course and intensity also make it stand out from other hunts in America. To try to explain the bizarre events at Salem, historians have offered a variety of competing theories that echo many of those offered for other hunts. The persecutors, in their excess of religiosity of Puritanism, truly believed that the Devil wanted people's souls and that women were more easily ensnared than men. Political fears had been raised by the Civil War in England, by the suspension of Massachusetts's governing charter, and by recent fighting with Indians. Groups of accusers and victims reflected social tensions between different factions in Salem Village and Salem Town over property and prestige. Some women seem to have been targeted because of an attitude that women should not be allowed to own property. Awkward girls coping with adolescence and sexuality enjoyed receiving attention. Less plausibly, some historians believe the panic may have arisen from a disease. Encephalitis spread by migratory birds, ergot eaten in moldy rye bread, or convulsions and hallucinations leeched from the Jimson weed used to treat the fits have all been used to explain some symptoms, but can hardly cover all the victims and perpetrators of the hunt. In any case, the growing fears led normally circumspect and calm citizens to ignore common sense and proper criminal procedure. Panic led to the deaths of innocents.

Before 1692, witch-hunting had not been common in New England. Only about a hundred cases had taken place in the previous fifty years, and probably only a quarter of those cases had led to executions. Most of these trials involved accusing a witch who was already the focus of local resentments and troubles. At Salem, anyone was liable to be accused. Thus, the hunt in Salem was exceptional, by any standard in the colonies. Hunts got out of control in Germany, or France, and even in England, but outside Salem, such panics simply did not happen in America.

The Salem hunt began during the winter of 1691–1692 in the household of Samuel Parris, a Puritan minister. His nine-year-old daughter Elizabeth and his eleven-year-old niece Abigail Williams began to display some odd behavior. They had fits of violence alternating with frozen catatonia, and they uttered strange languages. The local doctor, William Griggs, suggested that witchcraft lay at the root of their illness. He recommended prayer and fasting as a cure, although the Parrises had already been doing so. Griggs's own niece, seventeen-year-old Elizabeth Hubbard, and her friend, twelve-year-old Ann Putnam, then also began to show similar symptoms.

The girls' possessed behavior began to spread among other local teenagers. Mary Sibley, a parishioner of Parris and the aunt of one of those girls, Mary Walcott, tried another solution: fighting witchcraft with witchcraft. She went to the Parrises' household servant, possibly slave, Tituba and her husband, Indian John. Mary Sibley asked them to make a witch's cake. This odd bakery item, which included urine from the hexed children, was fed to the Parrises' dog, who was then supposed to sniff out the witch who had cast a spell on the girls. The girls' fits only worsened after this attempt at countermagic. A few days later, an outraged Samuel Parris filed formal legal charges, and the arrests began on February 29, 1692.

The first three witches of the Salem hunt were Tituba, Sarah Good, and Sarah Osborne. Tituba and her husband are mysterious and fascinating figures. She and Indian John seem to have been of mixed Caribbean and African heritage. They probably brought magical beliefs from their tropical West Indies cultures. Tituba had served in the Parris household, often watching the children. Many historians have suggested that her exotic tales, perhaps tinged with Voodoo, had helped plant fantasies of possession in the impressionable minds of Elizabeth Parris and Abigail Williams. How much Tituba and Indian John were involved in influencing any of the girls, however, remains unclear and disputed. Under pressure from the Salem authorities, though, Tituba confessed to dealings with the Devil and immediately named other witches. The Devil, a white man in black, had her sign his book. She also said that she saw other witches change into animals and she herself flew about on a pole.

Tituba accused two social outcasts, Sarah Good and Sarah Osborne, as fellow witches who hurt children. Forty-year-old Sarah Good originally came from a prosperous family, but her poor choices in marriage and investments had driven her deep into debt. By 1692, she and her family wandered homeless, outcasts of the community, dependent on charity. Her own husband, William, and daughter, Dorcas, would testify against her, although her pregnancy, possibly with an illegitimate child, delayed her sentence. Although Sarah Good denied being a witch herself at first, she also accused the third woman, Sarah Osborne, of pinching the girls. Sarah Osborne was an elderly widow of some property, but her behavior had shocked her neighbors. She had lived openly with a lower-class lover, an Irish indentured servant, Alexander Osborne. She had also tried to disinherit her own legitimate children by her late husband. All three of this first group of accused witches were marginal members of the community, isolated from "decent" society. Their low status lent credibility to their alleged dealings with the Devil.

At a public hearing in the village meeting house the day after the initial arrests, the possessed girls testified against the three women. The most damning testimony was through spectral evidence. As seen in the Lowestoft trials, the court accepted as fact what the girls said they saw and experienced due to spirits sent by the witches. The evidence might be given through echomania, the careful imitation of the alleged witch's movements; overlooking, the falling into fits if the witch looked at the victim; and touching, the fits ending upon the witch's touch of the victim. The girls told of being tortured by the spirits of the accused witches, who poked them or twisted their bodies in the night. The witches forced the girls to sign the Devil's book. They observed the witches suckling familiars from the Witch's Marks. The girls' shrieks and fits convinced both court authorities and spectators.

More people fell under investigation, as the hunt soon spread to other, more respectable figures. The former minister Rev. George Burroughs, who was in Maine, was accused of appearing in spirit and admitting to have murdered his first two wives. Evidence used to convict him included testimony about his unusual strength in lifting molasses barrels and holding heavy guns. John Proctor came under arrest for accompanying his wife to court, where the girls focused on him. Rebecca Nurse, a well-respected seventy-year-old wife of a wealthy farmer, stood mystified as various accusers shrieked, moaned, and fell into fits while questioners accused her of afflicting them. Even the thirty-year-old mother of young Ann Putnam claimed that Nurse appeared to her with the suspect Martha Corey on March 19, "and they did both torture me a great many times this day with such tortures as not tongue can express, because I would not yield to their hellish temptations, that, had I not been upheld by the Almighty arm, I could not have lived [the] night."[10] Perhaps because of conflicting testimony and her good reputation, the jury at first found Nurse not guilty, but the judge bullied the jury into reconsidering. Even an attempted reprieve by the governor failed to save her, because of protests from ministers who excommunicated her.

Some women, other than Tituba, did confess, for instance Abigail Hobbs and her stepmother, Deliverance Hobbs. The latter testified to attending a meeting where the Proctors, the Coreys, Goody Nurse, and the innkeeper Bridget Bishop plotted to bewitch the whole village. The Rev. Burroughs allegedly sealed the plot with a sharing of blasphemous sacraments of red bread and red wine tasting like blood. Free, and false, confessions probably came from two causes. First, people internalized what was being said to them. They knew that they had certainly sinned in some way. Few could withstand the rigorous and imposing pressure by authorities and neighbors. Second, some thought that if they did confess, they would be lightly punished, at least in Salem, where more than fifty of the confessed won freedom. Only those who refused to confess wound up in jail or at the end of a noose.

Eventually, the number of accused reached 165, although serious charges were only placed against thirty-nine people, most of whom were women under the age of twenty-three. Governor William Phips convened a special Court of Oyer and Terminer ("hear and determine") in May to hear the cases. Whenever someone accused tried to give testimony, the afflicted girl accusers in the courtroom would wail, shriek, and shout about appearances and attacks by specters. A search for Witch's Marks on Bishop, Nurse, and Proctor during the morning of June 2 found a "preternathurall Excresence of flesh between the pudendum and Anus much like to Tetts & not usuall in women ..." but by the afternoon a second examination found but dry skin.[11] One judge resigned in June, refusing to go along with the improper, even bizarre, proceedings. Astoundingly, a prosecuting attorney immediately replaced him. Convictions proceeded easily, given the acceptance of spectral evidence and a meager legal defense allowed the accused. Testimony of and petitions by neighbors to someone's good character were ignored, while gossip and claims of the teenage girls about spirit attacks convinced the court and many spectators.

The first hanging, of Bridget Bishop, took place on June 10. Rebecca Nurse and Sarah Good, whose baby had died in prison shortly after birth, followed on July 19. Another daughter of Good, four-year-old Dorcas, gained her freedom, but was never quite right again after being chained for seven months in a cold jail. Sarah Osborne died in prison. None had confessed to witchcraft.

The most famous death was that of Giles Corey, who refused to say anything, much less confess. Corey's notoriety was that his third wife, Martha Corey, had born an illegitimate son, obvious by his non-English skin color and hair color. Nonetheless, Corey had accepted the boy as his own. Once authorities accused him of witchcraft, Corey refused to enter a plea, either guilty or not guilty. He declined to participate with the court in any fashion, perhaps to protect his property from confiscation and certainly to avoid any implication in witchcraft. So, on September 16, the authorities decided to torture him with pressing. They laid him on a wooden platform while another wooden frame was put on his chest. Authorities then added stones, which weighed down on him, slowly preventing him from breathing. The legend goes that when the magistrate asked him one last time to plead, all Corey asked for was "more weight." By the second day he had been suffocated. His wife and daughter were hanged on September 22 with six others.

A few who refused to confess survived. Elizabeth Proctor survived because she was pregnant. Her husband, John, described in a letter the torture of their son William, who was hung upside-down for twenty-four hours until blood ran out of his nose. Proctor himself died with dignity at the scaffold, after disinheriting his wife, perhaps in an attempt to keep the property from being confiscated since he would have expected her to be executed after the birth of the child. The Rev. George Burroughs defended his innocence with a speech and prayers, including flawlessly reciting the Lord's Prayer at the gallows on August 19, by the side of John Proctor and several others. Cotton Mather attended and approved of the executions that day to the crowd, although his reported shouting down of Burroughs is a later embellishment to the tale.

By September 22, twenty people had been officially executed, and the circle of accused was growing. The governor's wife was implicated, as was the Rev. Samuel Willard, who had documented the 1671 possession of Elizabeth Knapp. Fortunately for the victims, forces began to align to shut down the hunt. Increase Mather, the president of Harvard University and Cotton Mather's father, had already weighed in with *Cases of Conscience concerning Evil Spirits Persecuting Men* (1692). He thought it better that ten suspect witches should go free rather than one innocent person be falsely found guilty. Meanwhile he talked with important officials in the capital, including Governor Phips.

On October 12 the governor issued a moratorium on further hunting. He shut down the Court of Oyer and Terminer on October 26, released those under investigation, and reprieved most of those who had been convicted. Those who had spent time in jail, or their relatives, still had to pay the costs for their upkeep, though. One poor woman, Margaret Jacobs, languished in prison until a citizen paid her fees. The slave Tituba attempted to recant. Her life was spared, but she was sold to another master, to pay the jail costs. Indian John seems to have escaped prosecution, but nothing else is known of his life after these events. The couple's daughter, Violet, remained in the Parris household. In 1693, the governor issued a general pardon. The tally for the hunt was four dead in prison, one pressed to death, and nineteen hanged, in addition to the ongoing trauma to the accusers, officials, friends, family, and general public.

Under influence of the panic, the Massachusetts legislature passed a law in December 1692 strengthening the prosecution for witchcraft, but three years later the royal regime in London vetoed it. In 1696, the legislature called for a day of praying and fasting to apologize for mistakes. Judge Samuel Sewall, who anguished over his role, led the fasting on January 14, 1697. In the first few years of the 1700s, court jurors and many of the accusing girls also recanted, apologized, and expressed their regret about the witch hunt in Salem. In 1706, Ann Putnam blamed Satan, not for causing the bewitching, but for deluding her into thinking she had been bewitched and leading her to accuse people falsely. By 1711, the government had paid restitution to the families of victims, officially compensating them for the miscarriage of justice. All these apologies and admissions of error helped to prevent any further hunts.

Another participant in the Salem trial, the Rev. John Hale, tried to sort out its consequences in his *Modest Enquiry into the Nature of Witchcraft* published posthumously in 1702. Hale had been present at some of the examinations and trials and had given evidence against accused witches. Within a few years, though, he had converted into a critic of the conduct of the trials, if not their purpose. He admitted mistakes had been made in convicting or acquitting people on the basis of similar, and insufficient, evidence: "... such was the darkness of that day, the tortures and lamentations of the afflicted, and the power of former [precedents], that we walked in the clouds, and could not see our way."[12] He offered the suggestion of more strict and complicated rules of evidence, which might prevent any future mistaken convictions of innocent people for witchcraft. Nevertheless, Hale still warned of the dangers of diviners, malefic witches, and the torments of Satan.

MERCY SHORT

Cotton Mather disagreed with the abandonment of witch-hunting. His *The Wonders of the Invisible World* appeared in October 1692, just as the Salem hunt was being shut down. Mather defended the conduct of the judges and continued to warn of the danger of witches. He thought that the apocalypse predicted by the Book of Revelation seemed about to take place. For him, the Devil still plotted to pull down all the churches of New England through witchcraft.

Cotton Mather entangled himself in the possession case of Mercy Short in the summer of 1692, even as the famous witch hunt raged in Salem. In 1690, Indians kidnapped seventeen-year-old Mercy Short after they had murdered her family. The governor had ransomed her and returned her to Boston, where she worked as a servant. On an errand to a jail where some of the accused Salem witches were locked up, Mercy exchanged insults with Sarah Good over some tobacco.

Mercy then began to have fits, which Mather was convinced were genuine evidence of demonic possession. Mather worked to exorcise the demon who possessed her. Mercy described the demon as a short dark-skinned man with a tall hat, straight hair and a cloven hoof. Mather's slow methods of patience and prayer seemed to heal her. His accounts of this case and of the Salem hunts, though, found more criticism than credibility.

Despite the increasingly obvious absurdity of witch-hunting, Salem was not the last witch hunt in the colonies. It was the last time, however, that authorities executed a witch. In September 1692, in Stamford, Connecticut, Elizabeth Clawson and Mercy Disborough went on trial for bewitching a servant, seventeen-year-old Katherine Branch. The girl suffered fits of pain and believed that cats spoke to her, hurt her, and tempted her to go to a better place. Both women were swum as a test, and both failed. The judges, though, used a delay caused by a hung jury to gather opinions from a higher court and local ministers. These latter convinced the judges that there was insufficient evidence. A reconvened jury found Mercy Disborough guilty and Elizabeth Clawson innocent, but a technicality allowed Mercy's verdict to be overturned the following year. The handful of remaining trials in New England also ended either in acquittals or reversed verdicts.

The last notable trial in the colonies took place not in New England, but in Virginia, which had previously experienced very few hunts for witches. In 1705 Luke Hill and his wife went to court with an accusation of witchcraft against Grace Sherwood. In March 1706, a deputized panel of women found two teat-like spots on Grace but refused to perform the search again in June. The court then resorted to the ducking or swimming test. The swimming did not go well and another search found two black teats on Grace's genitals. The court remanded her for trial, but she seems to have lived until 1740. Three hundred years after the trial, the Commonwealth of Virginia apologized for this miscarriage of justice.

THE END OF WITCH-HUNTING IN THE BRITISH REALMS

In both the American colonies or in the home isles, the turn of the seventeenth to eighteenth century saw the last of the witch hunts. Books disbelieving in witchcraft and discouraging witch-hunting had been adding up throughout the century. Among the most prominent authors, Sir Robert Filmer, Thomas Ady, James Wagstaffe, and John Webster wrote to oppose the hunts.

Another major figure in ending the hunts was the judge Sir George Mackenzie, nicknamed "Bluidy" (bloody) because he was so willing to punish and execute religious dissenters. Mackenzie was a lawyer for Parliament, the Lord Advocate, from 1677 to 1686. As a lawyer, he had grown concerned about flaws in court procedures during the Scottish hunt of 1661–1662. Later, he even represented an accused witch, Maevia, as described in his *Pleadings in Remarkable Cases* of 1672. Maevia had allegedly flown in the shape of a dove, cursed an innocent woman with a disease, and then cured it by binding to the woman's head a plantain and to her wrist a paper with the word "Jesus."

Another of Mackenzie's books, his *Laws and Customs of Scotland in Matters Criminal* of 1678, helped to explain the legal system of the realm. In doing so, he addressed the situation of witches. Mackenzie believed that witches were real, because they were mentioned in the Bible. True witches deserved punishment, but so did those judges who recklessly and unjustly killed thousands for the crime. He accepted the traditional sense of witches as foolish people deceived by illusion, according to the *Canon Episcopi*. Mackenzie doubted that the Devil would offer riches to people, noting that most people accused of being witches remained poor and hungry. He also refused to consider witchcraft a *crimen exceptum*, which removed legal safeguards for the innocent. He thought those accused of witchcraft were too often ignorant or abused by prison to comprehend the seriousness of the charges, which in turn produced false confessions.

As Lord Advocate of Scotland, or chief judge, Mackenzie acted on his views and freed many accused witches. In his investigations of witch hunts, he defended some accused witches and dismissed proceedings against others, especially if the legal procedure had been carried out in an unprofessional manner. His perceptive rulings exposed cases motivated by jealousy and confessions made under duress. In turn, some leading clerics attacked Mackenzie for his alleged atheism and betrayal of the Christian faith. This criticism notwithstanding, Mackenzie's influence helped discourage the British government from pursuing additional witch cases.

Another Lord Chief Justice, Sir John Holt, who served from 1689 to 1710, acquitted almost a dozen witches through his serious questioning and skepticism of supernatural events and evidence. Spitting up pins, having a Witch's Mark, or accepting the word of a bitter neighbor were insufficient for Holt to condemn a person to death, much less convict them of any real crime. Holt even exposed fraud. Richard Hathaway of Southwark, for example, had long accused Sara Morduck of making him suffer pains and fits; spit up pins, pieces of metal, and stones; foam at the mouth; and bark like a dog. His accusations had led to her arrest in 1700 and an expected trial for witchcraft. Instead, Holt put Hathaway himself on trial, exposed his fakery, and sentenced him to a year in prison and three sessions in the pillory. In Sir John Holt's court, juries found witches not guilty. Even some clergy recognized the basic problem of evidence in witch trials, realizing that the "Prince of Lies" could scarcely be relied upon to provide reliable information useful for conviction in a court of law.

THE LAST EXECUTIONS

The witch hunts eventually ended in Britain, once and for all. In 1682, England killed its last witch, Alice Molland of Exeter, convicted of murdering three people. In America, the last witches hanged were at Salem in 1692. Seven men and three women were hanged and burned at Paisley, Scotland, in 1697, for causing the possession of eleven-year-old Christine Shaw. One final Scottish execution was Janet Horne in 1727, who was convicted of using her daughter as a flying horse to travel. The Devil's sloppy shodding of Janet's daughter as a pony accidentally made the daughter lame, too. They burned the senile mother in a tar barrel. By that time, the total of British citizens executed as witches numbered at least fifteen hundred.

THE LAST TRIALS

In 1712, Matthew Gilson accused Jane Wenham, the reputed Witch of Walkerne, of witchcraft because he had refused to give her some straw. Gilson had then begun to act strangely, stuffing straw and dirt into his shirt. Wenham responded with a charge of slander. The local minister admonished both for bad behavior, but then his own servant, Anne Thorne, added yet another accusation of witchcraft: first that her knee had been hurt, then that something had compelled her to pick up sticks, and finally that many cats with the face and voice of Jane Wenham had haunted her. Soon all kinds of charges were filed against Wenham, from harming livestock to the evil eye. The sensible judge tried to dismiss all the most absurd charges, flippantly remarking at one point that flying was not against the law. On the only surviving charge, that Wenham had turned herself into a cat, the jury found her guilty. The judge, however, refused to condemn her and gained her a reprieve. Finally, a kind man from another town housed her for the rest of her days.

Wenham's case helped inspire Francis Hutchinson to write *An Historical Essay Concerning Witchcraft* (1718). Hutchinson was from Bury St. Edmunds, which had seen its share of hunting, and he met Wenham after her trial. Hutchinson did assert that the spiritual world was real and should be believed in by Christians, but he categorized those who clung to the worst fantasies as being "in one of these five Ranks: Children, Fools, Women, Cowards, sick or black melancholick discompos'd Wits."[13]

A court in Leicester rejected one last attempt at a witch trial in England in 1717. In 1736, the government repealed the Witchcraft Laws of England and Scotland, over the objections of many clergy, especially Scots who defended their local custom of witch-hunting from English cultural domination. Officially declaring magic and witchcraft not real, the law instead aimed at "preventing and punishing of any Pretences to such Arts or Powers as are before mentioned, whereby ignorant Persons are frequently deluded and defrauded...."[14] The 1736 reformed law remained in force until 1951, when all prohibitions or criminalization of magic was removed. The government recognized the lack of any credible evidence for either the existence of a diabolic conspiracy of witches or the efficacy of *maleficia*.

Although official courts and government renounced the fear of witches, common people did not. Belief in witchcraft and folk magic lingered. Accusations sometimes surfaced, but went nowhere. In 1773, the Presbyterian clergy reavowed their belief in the reality of witchcraft. Among the common folk, suspicion of neighbors continue to result in spontaneous violence against alleged witches. From the end of the seventeenth and into even the nineteenth century, crowds periodically formed to accuse and test a witch, usually by swimming. In one notorious case from 1751, a mob in Long Marston attacked John and Ruth Osborne for allegedly making cows and people sick. The mob tracked down the couple from their sanctuary in a church, dragged them to a local pond, and threw them in. Ruth Osborne drowned, while members of the mob kicked and beat John Osborne to death. The government, by this time, feared the disorder of the mob more than the *maleficia* of witches. Authorities hanged the mob's ringleader for the crime of murder. Bridget Cleary in Clonmel, Ireland, died from burns in 1894 after her family and friends tried to force a possessing fairy out of her by holding her over a turf fire. Authorities sentenced most of those involved to hard labor.

Increasingly, witchcraft became a matter of fiction and fantasy. The rake Francis Dashwood (b. 1708–d. 1781) and his Hellfire Club stirred up notoriety with their mock witch ceremonies and pagan rituals, along with licentious carousing. Although many good citizens were morally offended, no respectable authority actually feared the powers of magic or thought the rituals worthy of punishing by law. Stories of witches and fairy tales multiplied, but only for entertainment. Few magistrates found anything fearful in magic anymore.

NOTES

1. King James the First, *Dæmonologie (1597), Newes from Scotland*, Elizabethan and Jacobean Quartos (1922/1926; reprint ed., New York: Barnes & Noble, 1966), 28.

2. Barbara Rosen, ed., *Witchcraft in England, 1558–1618* (Amherst: University of Massachusetts Press, 1969), 187.

3. Ibid.

4. Reginald Scot, *The Discoverie of Witchcraft*, intro. Montague Summers (1930; reprint ed., New York: Dover, 1972), 8.

5. Gilbert Geis and Ivan Bunn, *A Trial of Witches: A Seventeenth-Century Witchcraft Prosecution* (London and New York: Routledge, 1998), 226.

6. Ibid.

7. Joseph Glanvill, *Saducismus Triumphatus: or, Full and Plain Evidence concerning Witches and Apparitions*, trans. and intro Coleman O. Parsons (1689; facsimile ed., Gainesville, FL: Scholar's Facsimiles & Reprints, 1966), 29.

8. David D. Hall, ed., *Witch-Hunting in Seventeenth-Century New England* (Boston: Northeastern University Press, 1991), 22.

9. George Lincoln Burr, ed., *Narratives of the Witchcraft Cases, 1648–1706*, Original Narratives of Early American History (reprint; New York: Barnes & Noble, 1972), 99.

10. Paul Boyer and Stephen Nissenbaum, eds., *Salem-Village Witchcraft: A Documentary Record of Local Conflict in Colonial New England* (Boston: Northeastern University Press, 1993), 19.

11. K. David Goss, *The Salem Witch Trials: A Reference Guide* (Westport, CT: Greenwood Press, 2008), 167.

12. John Hale, *A Modest Enquiry Into the Nature of Witchcraft*, p. 167, *Salem Witch Trials: Documentary Archive and Transcription Project* (2002) available at http://etext.lib. virginia.edu/salem/witchcraft/archives/ModestEnquiry/images.07/source/17.html (accessed 4 December 2008).

13. Francis Hutchinson, *An historical essay concerning witchcraft …*, p. 14, *Cornell University Library Witchcraft Collection* (2007) available at http://dlxs2.library.cornell. edu:80/w/witch (accessed 4 December 2008).

14. Marion Gibson, ed., *Witchcraft and Society in England and America, 1550–1750*, Documents in Early Modern Social History (London: Continuum, 2003), 8.

CHAPTER 6

Witch-Hunting in Southern Europe

Southern Europe includes those countries and regions running along the northern coast of the Mediterranean Sea. This chapter focuses on the Iberian peninsula, with the modern-day countries of Portugal and Spain, as well as on territories in the Italian peninsula (bearing in mind that the modern state of Italy did not appear until long after the witch hunts). The Mediterranean territories of the Balkans, comprising modern-day Albania, Greece, Bulgaria, Montenegro, Serbia, Macedonia, and Bosnia-Herzegovina are not considered here. They were ruled by the Ottoman Empire, and witch hunts did not take place there.

In the Iberian and Italian peninsulas, however, witch-hunting did occur, often connected with the ominous name of the Inquisition. The inquisitions of early modern Europe differed from those of the late Middle Ages that persecuted Cathar and Waldensian heretics. In Spain and Portugal, inquisitors allied with the royal governments to monitor converted Jews, Muslims, and their descendents. They also persecuted Protestants and witches, but more as a sideline. In comparison, the Italian Inquisition, supervised by the popes in Rome, focused largely on what was considered the "Protestant heresy." It attended less to converted Jews and more to alleged witches. Measured against the numbers of witches killed in the Holy Roman Empire, France, and Great Britain, however, far fewer victims suffered in southern Europe. Scholars in Spain also produced fewer texts on demons or witches compared to treatises in Germany, France, England, or Italy. Nonetheless, notable strixological ideas were published, and witches were hunted around the Mediterranean.

SPANISH AND PORTUGUESE INQUISITIONS AND WITCH-HUNTING

As the inquisitors in the Iberian kingdoms of Portugal, Aragon, Castille, and Navarre pursued religious heretics in the fourteenth century, they also began to take an interest in witchcraft. At one early trial during 1424 in Valencia,

Anthoni de Balcebre, judge of Pallars, executed women who paid homage to the Devil and allegedly killed infants by putting them into a sack. At their executions, the guilty were tied to the tail of an animal and dragged to the place of execution, where they were burned. In 1466, the people of Navarre petitioned the king to hunt witches who were harming them. The king, however, apparently did not respond to their request, perhaps because the new concept of witch-hunting remained undefined.

THEOLOGICAL DEBATES

Several theologians offered their opinions both for and against witch-hunting in the fifteenth century. A professor in Pamplona, Martin of Arles, doubted the reality of witches in his *Tractatus de superstitionibus contra malefica seu sortilegia* ("Tract about Superstitions against Witches or Diviners") of 1410. By contrast, the Franciscan Alphonso/Alonso de Espina in his *Fortalitium Fidei* ("Fortress of Faith") from 1460 linked together his perceived evils of religious heretics, unbelievers, Jews, and Muslims, with witches. Another Spanish theologian, Alphonso/Alonso Tostado (b. ca.1400–d. 1455) had been at the Council of Basel (see Chapter 3) and may have lost some of his skepticism because of the theological debates about witches conducted there. In a commentary on the Book of Genesis from the 1430s, he links witch activity to drug-induced fantasy. Like his contemporary, Juan de Torquemada, Tostado at first doubted a witch's ability to fly. He did consider how flying could be real, instead of imaginary or a dream, by conducting a test. Tostado attempted to force a witch to fly by beating and burning her, but she would not take off. A few years later, though, in his commentary on the Gospel of Matthew, Tostado accepted the ability of demons to transport witches, comparing the action with Satan's transportation of Jesus to the pinnacle of the temple, as told in the Gospel of Matthew. Regardless of these theological debates, the first few scattered witch trials were reorganized into an unexpected new kind of inquisition by the end of the century.

THE SPANISH INQUISITION

The Spanish Inquisition is notorious as one of the most cruel efforts ever carried out by Christians. It is also often misunderstood. The Spanish Inquisition was unique to Spain. It was not medieval; indeed, it had nothing to do with the Middle Ages but rather lasted through much of the early modern period. Although it did carry out much of the witch-hunting, its main effort was to guarantee that every subject in the kingdom was a faithful Roman Catholic. The Spanish Inquisition acted on behalf of the rulers in Spain, not the pope in Rome.

The rulers who initiated the Spanish Inquisition were also the couple who founded the Kingdom of Spain itself. In 1479, Ferdinand became the king of Aragon. Through marriage, he united Aragon with the kingdom of Castille, already ruled by his wife, Isabella (r. 1474–1504). Before their marriage, these kingdoms were two separate states, each with its own history, traditions, and even language. Ferdinand (r. 1479–1516) and Isabella, though, produced off-spring who inherited the united realms, creating the kingdom of Spain. The kingdom of Spain gained an additional province in 1492, when the monarchs conquered the final Muslim stronghold of Granada in a last crusade.

Both Ferdinand and Isabella were fervent Roman Catholics and both wanted to increase their control over their subjects. For centuries Christians, Jews, and Muslims had lived together in the Iberian peninsula, but as Christian rulers, Ferdinand and Isabella believed that all their people should likewise be Christians. So they issued an ultimatum that all Jews and Muslims were to covert to Catholicism or leave the country. Hundreds of thousands of Jews and Muslims left; many other thousands converted and stayed. Converted Muslims were known as Morriscos, converted Jews as Marranos.

The monarchs then created the Spanish Inquisition, or, formally "Tribunal of the Holy Office of the Inquisition against Heretical Perversity and Apostasy," to supervise these new Christian subjects. Its first leader, Tomás de Torquemada (b. ca.1420–d. 1498), had risen to be confessor to Queen Isabella. Appointed by the king as Inquisitor-General, Torquemada could boast of thousands of burnt heretics. Under his leadership, a central bureaucracy, called the *Supremo de la Santa Inquisición*, or Suprema, was set up. It supervised twenty-one regional tribunals throughout Spain. Portugal imitated the Spanish and developed a similar inquisition. The new organization for imposing religious conformity was a model of how to apply modern political power.

The Inquisition's greatest weapon was secrecy. Only inquisitors knew who might be a suspect, an informer, or an innocent bystander. The Inquisition operated equally through preaching, spying, and arresting. Priests of the tribunals preached about and called for information regarding secretly practicing Jews and Muslims. They relied on neighbors to inform on each other. Because slaves of convicted heretics won freedom, they had great incentive to testify against their masters. Children of heretics could win mercy for their own crimes by turning in their parents.

The accusation of two witnesses might lead to an arrest, often in the middle of the night. The accused was brought to a dark room, facing judges in hoods. The judges tried to encourage the accused to confess, both in the sense of admitting the crime and of practicing the sacrament of confession, unburdening one's soul from sin. Although all the evidence and procedures were dutifully and carefully recorded, the accused had no access to legal defense. If the judges were not satisfied, they imprisoned the accused. Prison visitors would be encouraged to convince the accused to confess, while an inquisitor listened in on all conversations for possible evidence.

If further interrogation failed, torture, called "being put to the question," usually followed. The five degrees of torture were as follows: first, threatening with torture; second, entering the torture chamber; third, prepping the victim by stripping and binding; fourth, presenting the instrument of torture; and fifth, inflicting pain. At each stage the victim was encouraged to confess. Common tortures were the rack (*potro*), ropes (*garrotes*), water torture, and the strappado (*garrucha*). Edgar Allan Poe in his famous story of "The Pit and the Pendulum" confused the idea of the *garrucha* with a vast slicing pendulum mechanism, which he created entirely out of fantasy. As described in previous chapters, the strappado meant hoisting a person up by arms tied behind the back. Swinging the victim, perhaps with weights tied to the feet, may have given this torture its resemblance to a pendulum. The water torture was highly popular during the Spanish Inquisition. It produced a high level of anxiety with little applied violence or actual physical harm. A version called the *toca* was similar to today's waterboarding, recently used by American agents on terrorist suspects. Examiners poured eight large jars of water over the accused's face, which made the victim think he was drowning. Another version forced the victim to drink large volumes of water. The torture of the *garrotes* twisted eight ropes on various limbs. Other tortures were unauthorized, but sometimes were used, especially at the local level outside of the inquisition's jurisdiction. Torturers might cut off toes or carry out flogging. The Spanish Chair was a version of the witch's chair that bound a victim to a chair under which a fire burned. Roasting or putting feet to the fire were common also. Although most tortures were done in secret chambers, in one public ritual, the torturers bound several victims together between the rungs of a ladder, and then forced all of them to walk together, only periodically to shove the victims down to the ground and force them to struggle to get up again.

Once the confession was made, it was repeated in public a day later in formal court. Then the sentence could be carried out. Because the actual purpose of the Spanish Inquisition was to maintain the orthodox Roman Catholic faith, not to kill heretics, the inquisitors offered opportunities for repentance. If the inquisitors believed that true conversion was possible, punishments could be quite light, such as saying prayers or eating only bread and water for forty days. Still, anyone found guilty lost all legal and social status, and the stigma was passed on to both children and grandchildren. The royal regime also confiscated property, another incentive that made the operation self-sustaining, although not necessarily profitable. For physical punishments, the convicted were "abandoned" to the royal government. Punishments ranged from fines, slavery in the galleys, and banishment, to burning, known in Latin as the infamous *actus fidei* or *auto-de-fé* in Spanish (*auto-da-fé* in Portuguese and the preferred English spelling), or "act of faith." The auto-da-fé was the most elaborate and ritualized way of burning heretics. The pomp and ceremony included chanting, singing hymns, processions, and public recitation of the crimes in the vernacular language so that the audience clearly understood the horrible acts. Inquisitors found enough obstinate heretics to burn to establish a notorious reputation called the Black Legend, which painted the Spanish as vicious, intolerant zealots with little care for the humanity of heretics or Indians.

Although the Black Legend exaggerates Spanish atrocities, historians still put the death tolls for their definition of heresy at a few thousand spread over the course of several centuries.

In addition to religious heretics, the Spanish Inquisition also became interested in witch-hunting, although it usually applied relatively moderate procedures. The process evolved slowly. The Spanish Inquisition burned its first witch, Gracia la Valle, in 1498 at Zaragoza. A few more hunts brought sentences of death to a handful of witches in the next two decades. A turning point came with a larger hunt in Navarre that raged between 1526 and 1528. Two young girls led the hunt as witch-finders, perhaps the first of their kind in Spain. The girls claimed to be able to see the Devil's Mark in the left eye of their fellow witches. One hundred fifty people were investigated during this hunt. The sentence for the guilty was to have property confiscated to pay for Masses. The hunt drew the attention of the Suprema, which had about thirty prisoners transferred to its jurisdiction. The Suprema then had to determine the reality of the charges.

A meeting of inquisitors in December of 1526 in Granada debated whether witches "really and truly commit the crimes they have confessed, or whether they are in fact fooled."[1] The delegates were split in their decisions. A bare majority decided that witches actually attended the sabbat rather than imagined it, as in the traditional teaching. The remedies they proposed, though, emphasized preaching according to the *Canon Episcopi*; close attention to Catholic worship and sacramentals; and building churches on sites of alleged Devil worship, rather than torture and death.

Thus, although the Suprema came to accept witchcraft as both real and under its authority, it considered the crime to be much less serious than the heresy of Jews and Muslims. In cases of witchcraft, inquisitors often restricted the confiscations of property from the condemned, thus reducing the motive of greed; reviewed cases more carefully for second convictions; and demanded more than the testimony of another accused witch for arresting, much less convicting, a person. Of the perhaps 100,000 people caught by the Inquisition, only around 3,500 were found guilty of witchcraft, and of those, only a few dozen were executed.

The divided opinion on the traditional position of witchcraft as self-delusion led the Spanish Inquisition to promulgate more policies emphasizing education rather than punishment. New regulations required a sound basis for evidence. They banned persecution of witches based only on the testimony of other witches. Eventually, the Spanish Inquisition stopped witch-hunting altogether in the areas under its control. Only a handful of burnings took place in the sixteenth century. The regional inquisition in Barcelona had already permanently banned hunting witches by 1530. The Suprema turned down requests from Navarre for trials around 1550 and only allowed whipping and banishment of some male witches tried in 1577.

The skeptical Martín de Castañega, who published his *Tratado ... de las superstitiones y hechicerías* ("Tract ... on Superstition and Witchcraft") in 1529, added to the resistance. After witnessing some trials of witches in Pamplona, he claimed that the wild tales about witches were based on deception. There was no pact with the Devil, he wrote, and people were only allowing themselves to be fooled. De Castañega did believe it was possible that God allowed flight through the air or that the Devil could appear in various forms to people, but in his opinion, the more fantastic allegations of magic and conspiracy just did not happen. To stop any problems, he recommended regular confession and attendance at Mass, praying the Lord's Prayer, and obeying the Commandments.

In sum, the Spanish Inquisition concluded that witches were much less dangerous than the usual targets of suspicion, namely converted Jews and Muslims. Limited resources meant the Spanish Inquisition could investigate few cases. If society needed a group of people to serve as an outlet for fears and tensions, the Morriscos and Marranos were already at hand. Outside of northern Spain, the Inquisition hunted hardly any witches at all. Neighboring Portugal, which had imitated Spain in setting up its own inquisition, executed hundreds of "Judaisers," but not a single witch.

THE BASQUE HUNT

Despite this restraint, a major episode of witch-hunting broke out during 1608 in the Basque region of northeastern Spain. As mentioned in Chapter 4, the Basques seem to be one of the earliest surviving ethnic groups of Europe. Their unique language and their determination to maintain their cultural differences often brought them into conflict with more powerful neighboring regimes that dominated them. The accused witches involved were simple peasants and laborers, mostly from the villages of Zugarramurdi and Urdax. The hunt began in December 1608, because twenty-year-old Maria de Ximildegui admitted to having attended a sabbat while she had lived in the Pays de Labourd in France. Maria claimed to have been converted back to Christianity, but she accused other girls in Zugarramurdi of having attended sabbats. Local authorities pressured others to confess to witchcraft. Soon ten people admitted to attacking children and sucking blood like vampires, to murdering adults, and to damaging crops with magical powders (the crops probably actually suffered from plant diseases called blight). The inquisitors called in to investigate in January 1609 were confused by the claims of witchcraft, never having dealt with such a charge before. Their research into court records, though, quickly provided them both with ideology and precedents.

Their questioning of the accused, two of whom were tortured by the *garottes*, fleshed out the information of witch confessions. At a sabbat (*aquelarre*), the guilty worshiped the Devil, who appeared to some as dark-complexioned, with three horns on his head, claws for hands, goose-feet, and wearing a fine black suit. The Devil rewarded his followers with gifts of clothes-wearing toads.

He gave them these imps at sabbats in a nearby meadow on Mondays, Wednesday, Fridays, and holidays. Witches flew there after anointing themselves with an unguent made from the toad excrement and then passing through cracks in their homes. They kissed the Devil in various rude places, danced, had sex, ate corpses, and buried the bones to use later in making poisonous powders.

Thirteen men and eighteen women were put to trial, but many of them died in prison before judgment. The Inquisition sentenced a monk and a priest to the galleys. On Sunday, November 7, 1610, at an auto-da-fé in Logroño attended by tens of thousands of onlookers, it burned six witches alive along with the corpses of five others who had died in prison. The next day, the chief inquisitor forgave eleven repentant witches. He welcomed them back to the Holy Catholic Church with sentences of imprisonment or exile for life (although, with good behavior, that might mean only a few years). He also forgave an additional seven who had already died.

The hunt had three consequences. First, French authorities across the border launched their own hunts, leading to the activity of Pierre de Lancre (see Chapter 4). Second, almost 2000 witches, including many children, came under suspicion as a result of preaching about the auto-da-fé in Logroño the following year. Third, the high numbers of accused shocked the Suprema into further investigation, which would eventually curtail witch-hunting in Spain. The turning point can be credited largely to the inquisitor Alonso Salazar y Frias (b. 1564–d. 1635).

ALONSO SALAZAR Y FRIAS

Forty-four-year-old Alonso Salazar y Frias joined the Inquisition investigating witches in Logroño in June 1609. Salazar showed some early skepticism, but the other inquisitors ignored him. By the spring of 1611, however, Salazar was in charge of his own investigation and was armed with the Suprema's Edict of Grace, which absolved anyone who confessed. Salazar soon challenged all the premises of witch-hunting. For eight months, he zealously investigated with a cool rationality, personally hearing the testimony of almost 2,000 people, including many young teenagers. He noted the contradictory information about specific details: where, when, and with whom the eating, dancing, sex, etc., took place. He realized that some of the pressure he himself had put on witnesses had forced inconceivable confessions. Salazar also exposed perjured accusations. He tested twenty-two alleged ointments used by witches on animals; none caused any effects. He had doctors and midwives confirm the physical virginity of women who had claimed to have had intercourse with the Devil. His inspection of places where sabbats were reported to have been held found no sign of any alleged activities.

Salazar informed the Suprema that he had "not found a single proof nor even the slightest indication from which to infer that one act of witchcraft has actually taken place, whether it comes to sabbat journeys, participation in the sabbat itself, damages or any other of the referred effects."[2] Instead, Salazar y Frias concluded that mass suggestion swelled panic about witches. Even granting that the Devil was at work, Salazar could only find credible the traditional opinion that the Devil worked through deception, making people believe magic was at work, when, in reality, the fantastic was nothing but illusion. In a report running to thousands of pages, he asked that the Suprema in Madrid review all the guilty sentences.

The Suprema soon supported Salazar's conclusions and stopped the hunting of witches altogether in 1614. It even returned the property of witches confiscated in 1610. Unfortunately for accused witches outside Spanish power, the inquisition's emphasis on secrecy, including ordering absolute silence about this report, meant that the abandonment of witch-hunting was not publicized. Furthermore, some inquisitors resisted these conclusions. Inquisitor Gaspar Navarro's *Tribunal de la supersticion ladina* ("Tribunal on the [Ladina] Superstition") in 1631 still argued for the danger of diabolical witches. The centralized religious authorities of the Spanish Inquisition, however, paid little attention. A few more trials took place after the 1620s, but no more executions. About 1,600 cases were heard by the regional inquisition at Toledo over the course of the next century, but they mostly involved minor matters like love spells and amulets. Of course, the Spanish Inquisition did continue to persecute families of converted Jews and Muslims until Napoleon briefly suspended it between 1808 and 1814 when he controlled Spain. Only in 1834 did the Spanish government end the authority of the Inquisition for good.

SECULAR COURTS

Although the inquisition turned away from hunting witches, persecutions continued in a small way in Aragon's secular courts. In Catalonia from 1618 to 1620 about a hundred people were executed until the authorities grew tired of the hunt and sentenced the responsible witch-finder himself to the galleys. Probably the last trial was of Ana Barbero of Seville, convicted in October 1818 for making a pact with the Devil. The court first sentenced her to being flogged with 200 lashes and banished for six years and then changed the punishment to eight years in a special prison for convicted prostitutes.

WITCH-HUNTING IN TERRITORIAL POSSESSIONS

As the most powerful state in Europe from 1500 to 1648, Spain controlled many territories in western Europe outside the Iberian peninsula. In the Italian peninsula, it held Milan in the north and Naples and Sicily in the south. The Spanish Inquisition, however, never took root in Milan or Naples. Only in the very south of Italy and Sicily did the Inquisition make some efforts against heretics, while witch-hunting remained practically nonexistent. One Grand Inquisitor in Sicily, Ludovico a Paramo, is often quoted as writing in 1598 that the inquisition had served humanity by burning at least 30,000 witches over the previous century and a half. Such a claim seems more boast than sober reporting, considering that documents reveal very few hunts and none at all from his own term in office. Even in the few trials recorded, inquisitors did not burn any of the few witches found guilty. Instead, they condemned men to the galleys and women to flogging.

THE SPANISH NETHERLANDS

Only in the Spanish Netherlands, today the countries of Belgium and Luxembourg, were alleged witches in serious danger from the Spanish Inquisition. In 1542, Emperor Charles V brought in inquisitors to fight Protestant heretics. His son and heir, the extreme Roman Catholic King Philip II of Spain, saw heresy in Lutheranism and Calvinism, yet lost control of the Dutch Netherlands (see Chapter 3). Philip's own law of 1592 linked witchcraft to heresy and allowed the mechanisms of the Spanish Inquisition to operate in his Belgian territories. The County of Namur tried several hundred witches and executed a few hundred over the course of the fifteenth and sixteenth centuries. The most intense period of hunting in Belgium was 1610–1635. This period witnessed dozens of trials, although victims for those years totaled fewer than 200. In neighboring Luxembourg, more than 300 people died in the first half of the seventeenth century. Officials there had been influenced first by Boguet's text and then by the hunts in neighboring Cologne, Mainz, and Trier during the late 1620s and early 1630s. Still, inquisitors imposed the punishment of exile more frequently than that of execution. The hunts were over by the end of the seventeenth century.

MARTIN DEL RIO

Perhaps the greatest strixologist to come out of these hunts was Martin Del Rio (or Delrio; b. 1558–d. 1608). Del Rio was born in Antwerp. His academic brilliance brought him success at a number of universities and schools, from Salamanca in Spain, through Paris and Louvain, to Mainz and Graz in the Holy Roman Empire. Del Rio became convinced of the reality of witches, an opinion he expounded upon in his book *Disquisitiones magicarum libri sex* ("Six Books of Magical Discourses") first published in 1599 and 1600. The book was very popular, going through dozens of editions in the next centuries. He wrote the text for lawyers, judges, physicians, and confessors who would be dealing with witchcraft matters. In his judgment, witchcraft was an "extraordinary and exceptional crime … of great enormity, great seriousness, and great wickedness because in it are combined the particular circumstances of outrageous crimes—apostasy, heresy, sacrilege, blasphemy, murder, and not infrequently parricide, unnatural sexual intercourse with a spiritual creature, and hatred of God; and there can be no offenses more dreadful than these."[3] The first four books discuss issues of magic and witchcraft. Del Rio criticized those who supported the traditional interpretation that magic was not real. He felt this interpretation, dating from the *Canon Episcopi*, endangered the Church and society, while it also contradicted truth. As proof, he pointed to the popes who were condemning modern witches. Del Rio pushed confessional conformity, insisting everyone should be obedient to Roman Catholicism and blaming Lutheranism as a heretical cause of witches. He dismissed Weyer's work and argued for punishing Dietrich Flade and Cornelius Loos, learned men who fell victim to the contemporary hunts in Trier. The fifth book gives advice for judges, recommending that torture be limited to only three sessions and requiring a free confession to be obtained within a day. Any judge who did not condemn witches to death, Del Rio maintained, would himself commit a deadly sin. Confessors should also use that sacrament to combat evil. Still, Del Rio refused to generalize against all accused, and he did find ways for some accused to be declared innocent. Overall, though, his detailed explications of the various arguments about witches convinced many of their reality and their danger.

WITCHES IN LATIN AMERICA

At the beginning of the modern age, Spain and Portugal established vast colonial empires through conquest. The so-called Voyages of Discovery brought Spanish and Portuguese power into Africa, Asia, and the newly discovered Americas. In the Americas, confronted with religions that were interpreted as demonic, some witch-hunting took place, although both the Portuguese and Spanish colonialists nevertheless were comparatively restrained. Some colonizers wanted to exploit the natives as animals, claiming they lacked divine souls. Appeals by clergymen like Bartholomew de Las Casas, however, managed to make the regimes recognize the basic humanity of the native Indians, although the natives were still exposed to much exploitation.

Since the Indians were found to have souls, part of colonialist motivation was to bring them the salvation of Christianity. While many Roman Catholics interpreted native religions as demonic, most religious systems of the native Americans lacked a powerful evil figure like the Devil of Christianity. Pagan deities of the New World, like those of ancient Greece and Rome, often incorporated both good and evil characteristics. These deities were kept appeased by offering worship and sacrifice. The Spanish viewed the religions of the native Americans as evil, comparing them to ancient paganism and contemporary Islam. The theologians also brought with them a demonological mindset that saw demons lurking behind the "false" beliefs of the native Americans. These demonological thinkers did not always insist on strixological conclusions, however. Demons might promote rejection of Christianity, worship of false gods, and even forming demonic pacts, but the demons "discovered" in the Americas seem to have rarely granted their followers magical powers of witch-craft that could inflict *maleficia* on their neighbors, as they allegedly were doing back in Europe.

In many parts of Latin America, the conquistadors and missionaries quickly wiped out much of the organized native systems of worship. Still, many local beliefs and practices lingered among the "converted." Some practiced simple, traditional magic like the cunning-folk of Europe, while a few tried to maintain their status by preserving the old claims of the gods. Some even went so far as trying to continue pre-Columbian practices of human sacrifice. The European civil and ecclesiastical hierarchies reasonably worried whether the conversion to Roman Catholicism was authentic and permanent. They wanted to avoid syn-cretism, combining elements of Christianity and paganism, whether by natives or European colonizers, or by the mixed ethnic populations (creole, mestizo, black, and mulatto) that followed.

The Spanish Inquisition arrived in the Americas in 1519, led by Franciscan inquisitors. Just as it had authority over converted Jews and Muslims in Spain, the Inquisition controlled converted native Americans. Yet in this early period, the inquisition lacked effectiveness. During the most intense period, between 1536 and 1543, the inquisition under Archbishop Juan de Zumárraga perse-cuted fewer than one hundred natives or *caciques*. The quick trial and execu-tion of Don Carlos de Texcoco in 1539 led authorities to remove all cases concerning native converts from the inquisition's jurisdiction and shift their trials to the civil courts instead. Despite this attempt, Friar Diego de Landa led another outburst of hunting in the Yucatan peninsula between 1559 and 1562. The death toll of more than 150, including more than a dozen suicides, evoked some criticism back in Spain. De Landa's superiors barely reprimanded the friar, however; instead they reconfirmed him as bishop.

These trials exposed cultural conflicts. Natives accused their Roman Catholic colonial masters, while trying to preserve their own pre-Columbian magical, medical, and religious concepts. Catholic authorities also recognized that the Indians had not been fully converted to Christianity and did not truly under-stand Christian faith, so the Inquisition was not a feasible means for enforcing faithfulness.

As a result, King Philip II began reorganizing the Inquisition in 1569. The main organization of the Latin American Spanish Inquisition was to focus on the heresy of Europeans, including the infiltration of Protestant writings and ideas. A secondary body, the Tribunal of the Faith of Indians, or the Secular Inquisition, replaced the religious inquisition for the natives of the Americas. Although the Spanish Inquisition continued to send some materials to bishops about the Catholicism of Indians, administrative lines of authority slowly sepa-rated. By the 1600s, the Inquisition only allowed arrests to be made from its central office and discouraged investigation of possession, because it no longer found possession to be a credible charge. The most common charge against natives became the crime of idolatry, the continuing false worship of their old gods. This crime lacked the elements of diabolic, conspiratorial witchcraft. Cases often dealt with the remnants of native beliefs, typically the use by cunning-folk of techniques such as herbal treatments and love spells. Painful questioning did not radically implicate others or expand the circle of witchcraft, since torture was only occasionally applied.

Once convicted, the sentences of the Spanish Inquisition in the Americas were likewise relatively mild. Public penance was the norm, not death in an auto-da-fé. The guilty would be paraded in public, wearing gags, simple tunics, and a noose around the neck, with signs that described their crimes. Officials also announced the crimes aloud. Religious leaders acted with relative mercy and leniency to ensure conversion, rather than with condemnation and harshness.

One of the last cases the Spanish Inquisition addressed in the Americas came in late 1691. In the Franciscan mission of Querétaro, women began to show signs of demonic possession. Several young women claimed to be possessed by witches. They appeared to spit up objects, such as rocks, needles, and toads, or emitted them from bodily orifices; reacted to religious symbols and ceremonies with fits and curses; and showed demons' bite marks on their arms. Exorcisms by the local Franciscans were powerless. Juana de los Reyes's possession culminated in her giving birth to a child in January 1692. Believers saw the birth as evidence of demonic planting of semen in the innocent girl. Skeptics, however, became convinced that the girls were faking. The Inquisition charged the girls with fraud and reprimanded their exorcists for foolishly disturbing the public peace. After the Querétaro incident, the Inquisition rarely took possession or witchcraft cases seriously again. It should be noted, that at the same time, several hundred miles to the north, the Salem Witch Hunts were just getting underway.

THE ABIQUIU HUNT

One notable exception to the decline in witchcraft cases occurred between 1756 and 1766 in Mexican territories. Governor Tomás Vélez Cachupín had recently arranged land grants for the Genízaro Indians in Abiquiu, trying to impose order and stability on the nomadic native tribe. He hoped these Indians would provide a buffer with other more hostile tribes like the Apaches and Commanches, whose raids caused widespread fear and destruction. In 1760, the newly arrived Franciscan priest, Juan José Toledo, brought with him witch ideas and a worry about the depth of local Christianization. He considered the Genízaros' religious rituals to be Devil worship. He then complained about being attacked with witchcraft, including image magic, fascination, and *maleficia*, causing his own illness, that of a round mass forming in his belly.

Local officials began to investigate in 1763 and succeeded in getting many people to accuse each other of witchcraft. Officials destroyed local rock paintings and carvings as adornments of sites of Devil worship. Next, local women began to complain of demonic possession. The more Father Toledo exorcised, the more possessed women came forward. His attitudes fed a panic rather than relieved tensions. Governor Cachupín finally held proceedings to end the crisis. The governor referred the entire fiasco to the central government and to the Inquisition in Mexico City. Authorities there punished one alleged female witch with flogging and forced labor. Another, La Come Gallinas, was made to stand for four hours covered with honey and feathers. Most of the others were released, although several died in jail. Thus ended all significant concern for witch-hunting in the Americas.

WITCH-HUNTING IN THE ITALIAN STATES

As the Italian peninsula entered the age of witch hunts, the region also embarked on the cultural flowering known as the Renaissance. Just as some scholars revived the philosophical writings of Plato and Aristotle, others investigated classical works dealing with the occult. Some of the new interest in magic and witchcraft arose from the interests of Renaissance scholars in reading materials from Greece and Rome. Early modern philosophical systems wove knowledge of the occult together with classical philosophy and the Christian faith. Leaders of the Church, of course, were not as enthusiastic about this endeavor. The magic described by the ancients naturally raised suspicions about its evil uses. And so, amidst contemporary interest in war and art, Italy became an early center of witch hunts. Italian hunts started out strong, but became more moderate over time.

NEOPLATONIC MAGIC

Philosophical thoughts about magic during the Renaissance played a small role in the European witch hunts. One of the most important philosophical schools of the Renaissance was Neoplatonism, founded on the writings of Plato, which had been rediscovered. The Neoplatonists opposed the more scholastically minded Aristotelian philosophers, who had promoted attitudes of witch-hunting. Neoplatonists instead embraced the occult as one more way to understand the universe. Just as Plato had emphasized the ultimate reality of ideas vs. our material existence, the Neoplatonists tried to unlock the true workings of nature through magic.

Neoplatonic schools established in Florence combined magic and Christianity. Marsilio Ficino (b. 1433–d. 1499) thought he could use the occult and astrology in medical applications while avoiding demonic participation. His ideas were widely influential. His younger colleague, Giovanni Pico della

Mirandola (b. 1463–d. 1494), proposed to publicly debate hundreds of philosophical theses inspired by classical thought. Unfortunately for him, the Church forbade debate on a number of his theses, considering them heretical. As a result, Pico withdrew into quiet scholarship. His system of "natural magic" explicitly opposed Satanic influences, he maintained. The inquisition did not see his dabblings the same way, however, and pursued him from Rome to Vincennes, near Paris. Eventually he was allowed to settle in Florence. Pope Alexander VI Borgia (r. 1492–1503) later absolved him of any suspicious activity.

Renaissance philosophers pursued these inquiries as one more way to comprehend the divine. As in Pico della Mirandola's case, the Church usually viewed these efforts as threatening. Some ecclesiastics, however, remained open to the exploration of the supernatural by intellectuals, just as they had previously accepted the efforts of Aquinas to adapt Aristotle to Church dogmas. Magical dealings were technically against the law, but were in fact rarely prosecuted. Thus the Church distinguished learned pursuits of "High Magic" from the wicked deeds of witches, or "Low Magic." The former were forbidden, but rarely prosecuted, while the latter were earnestly prohibited and prosecuted. Learned scholars claimed to control the demon, in contrast to the ignorant witch controlled by the demon.

THE SKEPTICAL RENAISSANCE STRIXOLOGISTS

A prolific debate about witches took place in Renaissance thought among Italian clergy and scholars, which influenced strixology in other countries. Some writers were skeptics. For example, the Milanese Franciscan Samuel de Cassinis in 1505 reasoned that a witch's flight and the sabbat could only occur by miracle, and only God allowed miracles to happen, so such evil acts were clearly impossible. To believe otherwise was heresy. Within a few years, treatises by the jurists Andreas Alciati and Giovanni Francesco Poncinibio also argued against the new ideas, suggesting that witches were real. In 1515, Alciati's horror at what he called a "new holocaust" led him to advise treating witches with the medicinal herb hellebore rather than with pyres leading to hell fire.

One of the leading skeptics was Pietro Pomponazzi (b. 1462–d. 1525), a professor at Padua and Bologna. In his *De naturalium effectuum causis, sive de incantationibus* ("On the Causes of Natural Effects, or on Incantations") from 1556, Pomponazzi dismissed magic and focused on "natural" causes of events. He argued in favor of magic without demons. Events that seemed magical were actually due to unknown natural causes. Indeed, demons did not cause possession and witchcraft, but rather illness did, possibly insanity or an unbalance of humors. He went so far as to assert that spiritual things, including angels, did not exist. He did allow, though, that the stars, as studied in astrology, had control over natural events, since they were themselves part of nature. These views led some, like Thomas Erastus, to label Pomponazzi as an atheist.

THE WITCH-HUNTING RENAISSANCE STRIXOLOGISTS

Others offered opposing viewpoints, redefining the role of Christian faith. Girolamo Visconti asserted after 1450 that to disbelieve in witches was to deny God. Giordano or Jordanes da Bergamo in 1470 declared it a matter of true faith that devils transported witches to secret meeting places. He also seems to have been more fascinated with succubi and their sex with men than other writers about witchcraft, who usually focused on incubi and women. He believed sex at the sabbat was with demons, not the Devil himself. In 1521, Silvester Mazzolino (or Mozzolini) agreed. Mazzolino was a Dominican theologian and an inquisitor in several towns in Northern Italy between 1508 and 1511. He believed demons used witches as agents to harm creation, especially when demons conveyed men's semen to witches' vaginas.

Paulus Grillandus, who supervised witch trials near Rome, wrote the *Tractatus de hereticis et sortilegiis* ("Tract on Heretics and Diviners") in 1534. This influential text helped to describe and define the sabbat. Although demons did not quite have natural bodies, Grillandus wrote, their actions could affect people. Another book he wrote, *De quaestionibus et tortura* ("Concerning Interrogation and Torture"), systematized methods for examining witches.

The most famous Renaissance advocate for witch-hunting was, perhaps, Giovanni Pico della Mirandola's nephew, Gianfrancesco Pico della Mirandola, who had himself earned a modest reputation as a philosopher. He reacted against his uncle's and Ficino's neoplatonic attempts to wed natural magic, Greco-Roman thought, and Christianity. Gianfrancesco had been directly involved in witch trials in Bologna and in his own little territory of Mirandola, where he attended inquisitorial examinations and interrogated accused witches himself. He had at least ten male and female witches burned. His book derived from these events, *Strix, sive de ludificatione daemonum* ("The Witch, or on the Illusions of Demons") of 1523 was immediately translated into Italian and spread its influence in the peninsula among those who lacked clerical or university educations.

Gianfrancesco's work essentially repudiated those who complained that witches did not deserve cruel deaths. In one dialogue, three characters, Dicaste the inquisitor, Phronimus/Fronino the wise humanist (who voiced the opinions of the author), and a witch named Strix/Strega debate with a skeptical fourth character, Apistius/Apistio. The doubter is eventually convinced of the reality of witches and their connection with diabolic heretics. Giving a witch a published voice, even if done only to prove the points the inquisitor wanted to make, was rare in theological works on witchcraft.

Bartolomeo Spina read Gianfrancesco Pico della Mirandola's book and agreed with it. He based his own *Questio de strigibus* ("The Question of Witches") of 1523 on his own inquisitorial practices in Modena and the teachings of his master, Prierio. He argues for the reality of witches and their flying, even after recounting a test of a witch, who, anointed with magical ointment, failed to be carried by a demon to the sabbat. Like modern-day psychics who continue to believe in their abilities even after they fail scientific tests, Spina argued that the Devil allowed his witches to fly only when it suited him. That Satan did not allow magic during a test, in such skeptical circumstances, only reconfirmed his diabolical nature. It was more important, for Spina, to believe in the incredible evidence presented by tortured witnesses than in objective experimentation. His faith in the rightness of his cause justified the burning of more than a hundred people a year in Como alone.

These intellectual exchanges show that many proposed the real danger of witches, but others equally argued against. No unanimity existed. Some Neoplatonists wanted to try to understand and use magic; others condemned it all as demonic. Some saw witches as an imminent threat; others viewed the claims about witches to be unfounded. The great diversity among the pool of writings may have been one more factor that helped moderate the Italian hunts. No strong voices hostile to witches dominated the discussion.

PAPAL PROMOTING OF HUNTS

As the period of the witch hunts opened, the popes were lavishing wealth and patronage on Renaissance artists such as Leonardo da Vinci, Michelangelo, and Raphael. They encouraged philosophy and classical learning. The popes fought to hold on to their political power in the Papal States, those territories in central Italy that they ruled directly as princes. However, they also feared the actions of witches. The popes attempted to intensify witch-hunting by regularly issuing bulls against witches. Already in 1409 Pope Alexander V (r. 1409–1410) went after these "new sects" who sought to harm the human race. Pope Eugene IV (r. 1431–1447) had addressed concerns in Bohemia and Germany about people bewitched by the Prince of Darkness. He worried about witches who profaned the sacraments, magically transported themselves, and could cure disease or cause bad weather with a few motions. In 1445, Pope Eugene commissioned inquisitors in Carcassonne to act against those who worshiped the Devil, carried out *maleficia*, and abused the sacraments. He also attacked his opponent, Duke Amadeus of Savoy, who became the anti-pope Felix V elected by the Council of Basel as it became more radical in its later years. He accused Felix of being a rebel of the church who has turned to Satan and allied with small witches, sorcerers, and Waldensians.

Other Renaissance popes regularly reinforced and supported witch-hunting in Italy. Innocent VIII (r. 1448–1492), who had encouraged the witch hunts in Germany with his *Summis desiderantes*, did likewise in the Papal States. When the *Podesta*, or governing political magistrate, in Brescia refused to enforce punishments for witches, Pope Innocent protested. Consequently, by 1510 seventy men and seventy women had been burned at the stake. Pope Innocent's successor, Pope Alexander VI Borgia, tried to expand the witch hunts into

Verona and Lombardy, territories outside direct papal rule. He gave inquisitors full power to bring destructive witches to justice. Protests from locals about the abuses of inquisitors only prompted the popes to reinforce the harshness. Pope Leo X d'Medici in his bull *Honestis* ("Of Honesty") in 1521 ordered inquisitors to use excommunication and interdict against those who hindered the hunts for witches. In 1523, Pope Hadrian VI published "On Diabolic Witchcraft" to rebuff protests about witch hunts at Como. Although he originally came from the Dutch Netherlands, Hadrian lacked his fellow countrymen's skepticism about witches.

BERNARDINO OF SIENA

All these papal proclamations translated into numerous hunts. One of the great promoters of early hunts was the famous preacher Bernardino of Siena (b. 1380–d. 1444), who was made a saint only six years after his death. During the 1420s, though, the Roman Curia suspected him of heresy because of his fanatical encouragement of venerating the Eucharist and crucifixes. Perhaps to distract from his own suspicious practices, Bernadino started to preach against witches. He convinced his listeners to accuse, investigate, and burn witches at the stake. Called to account in Rome in 1427, Bernardino managed to avoid being punished and turned the situation to his advantage by sparking a witch hunt there.

The most notable victim was a woman named Finicella. Her husband accused her of killing their children with the Devil's help. He exposed her magical complicity when he fought off and wounded a cat that had been attacking their child. Authorities later found a wound on her arm in the same place—thus proving she had transformed herself into the cat. They burned her at the stake for the murder of her own and more than thirty other children, for making powders from their corpses, and for sacrificing to the Devil.

The next year Bernardino also helped expose Matteuccia Francesco, a local cunning-woman of Todi. During the previous years, Matteuccia had given people advice, healed wounds, applied countermagic, and provided love potions and remedies fashioned from herbs. The preaching of Bernardino, combined with a scandal involving embezzlement from repairs to the local fort and her closeness to a local condottiere, or professional mercenary, Braccione Fortebracci de Montone, led the city government to try this woman for witchcraft on March 20, 1428. Accusations focused on use of a diabolical spirit. The Devil had allegedly appeared in the form of a goat, which she rode at night to suck the blood of babies. She used babies' and vulture's fat, with bat's blood, to concoct her potions. Matteuccia admitted to the accusations. They sentenced her to ride as a heretic, on a donkey with a paper hat on her head, to a place of public execution where she was burned to death.

Other witch trials are recounted by the anonymous author of the *Errores Gazariorum* ("Errors of the Cathars") from the 1430s. This author probably based his treatise on information gleaned from the Council of Basel and on hunts in the Val d'Aosta, Lausanne, and Savoy. The work goes into great detail on how witches make poisons and potions from murdered men, babies, and cats. Savoy in particular seemed to swarm with witches, against which Duke Amadeus acted forcefully, contrary to Eugene IV's accusations. Martin Le Franc, who wrote *Les Champion des Dames* (see Chapter 4), counted thousands of witches attending the sabbat, including hundreds of women in sexual liaison with the Devil. The Duke's investigations led to dozens of executions.

After this, hunts declined for a few decades, until the end of the century. Krämer's *Hammer of Witches* cited the numerous witches hunted in Brescia in the 1480s. One of them, Maria "la Medica," allegedly attended something called a "coventcile," where she worshiped the Devil during Masses dedicated to "Lucibel" or "Lucibello," had orgies, and killed more than a dozen children. Some historians see this "conveticile" meeting as an early form of the Black Mass, whereas others think it was a typical sabbat. In any case, she allegedly gained from the Devil the power to heal people of illness, as indicated by her nickname. After she confessed and repented in 1489, the authorities sentenced her to life in prison for witchcraft.

Italian bishops led the hunts in the early sixteenth century, sometimes encouraging executions despite a sometimes skeptical population. The inquisitor Bernard Ratengo experienced an interesting protest against the hunts at Como in 1510. Ratengo took seriously the concepts of witch's flight and the sabbat attended by tens of thousands of witches. He and his fellow inquisitors burned hundreds of witches over several years. In reaction, some peasants reportedly took up arms, whereas others tried to poison the inquisitors for their inhuman pursuit of alleged witches. Complaints reached the ears of popes, who nonetheless supported more hunting. Despite the Pope's encouragement, witch-hunting rarely took place in Italy, especially south of the Po River, before the mid-sixteenth century.

HUNTING WITH THE ROMAN INQUISITION

In 1542 Pope Paul III (r. 1534–1549) initiated a new direction for the papacy when he established the Congregation of the Holy Office of the Inquisition with his bull *Licet ab initio* ("It Is Permitted from the Beginning"). This new Roman Inquisition targeted neither the theological heretics of old nor the new witches, but rather Protestants. Nevertheless, old manuals against heretics, such as Nicholas Eymerich's *Directorium inquisitorum* of 1376, were brought up to date with new commentary, reprinted, and applied. The new Roman Inquisition also learned from the Spanish Inquisition to maintain strict control and supervision of the system, which carefully and diligently followed clear legal guidelines, even allowing some defense by the accused and carefully restricting the application of torture. As part of the Roman Curial bureaucracy,

this office actually lasted until 1966, when it was reorganized as the Sacred Congregation for the Doctrine of the Faith, headed by Cardinal Ratzinger, who became Pope Benedict XVI. In general terms, the body was to try to improve the priesthood, especially by encouraging celibacy. The new Counter-Reformation order of the Jesuits also became increasingly predominant in the inquisition, replacing the Dominicans.

Two of the next few popes were intimately connected with the revived inquisition. As Cardinal Giovanni Pietro Caraffa, Pope Paul IV (r. 1555–1559) had originally convinced Paul III to revive the inquisition based on his observance of the Spanish Inquisition. As the first Inquisitor General in the new system, Caraffa had himself been an eager inquisitor and torturer. As Paul IV, he pursued a hard line during his short pontificate, allowing broad authority to and intervention by the Inquisition. For example, Paul IV condemned four women to be burned in Bologna for sabbat activity in 1559. Upon Paul's death, resentful Romans sacked the offices of the Inquisition, burning records and releasing prisoners. Pope Pius V (r. 1566–1572) had likewise been a Grand Inquisitor in Como and as such had built new headquarters for the Holy Office. For the three decades from 1542 to 1572, Counter-Reformation zealotry burned bright.

Despite this fanatical attitude at the top, the Roman Inquisition turned out to be relatively mild in persecuting witches. Of the hundreds of people executed annually in Rome during this period only a tiny percentage came from charges brought by the Inquisition. The ruling popes mostly imposed the death penalty on murderers and thieves. The inquisition had only a few men burned in the 1540s, mostly for abuse of the sacred Host. The Holy Office regularly warned inquisitors to follow proper procedures in proving guilt, stipulations that offered some protection to the innocent. Even the papacy under former inquisitor Pius V seems to have discouraged the witch-hunting by seeming fanatics as Cardinal Charles Borromeo, the Archbishop of Milan (r. 1563–1584). Borromeo is best known for his reforms in the spirit of the Counter-Reformation, which led to his canonization in 1610. He also diligently hunted witches. Of about a hundred accused witches, torture and pastoral ministry brought many to repentance, allowing Borromeo to burn only about a dozen stubborn sinners.

VENICE

The branch of the Roman Inquisition in Venice focused much more on ritual magic than common *maleficia*, probably because inquisitors there relied on Nicolau Eymerich's traditional views of witches. Felice Peretti, the later Pope Sixtus V (r. 1585–1590), had been an inquisitor in Venice, in the early 1580s. His papal bull *Cœli et terræ* ("Of Heaven and Earth") restrained the hunt for witches while it reaffirmed opposition to magic. He condemned divination, whether through astrology, mirrors, or birds, and dealing with demons, especially questioning them to find treasure. Pope Sixtus focused on both the learned ritual magic of sorcery and the Low Magic of cunning-folk, rather than the sabbat fantasies of witchcraft.

By the end of the century, the Inquisition was shifting its direction. The shift brought more legal safeguards to the accused. In 1588, the Roman Inquisition limited accusations based on the testimony of other witches, thus limiting rapid expansion of a hunt. The number of witch trials briefly spiked during that time, coinciding with a decline in hunting Protestants, but the numbers of cases then dropped off again after the 1620s, as the Inquisition shifted its focus to merely supervising the practices of Catholicism.

THE INSTRUCTION

In the next century, Pope Gregory XV (r. 1621–1623) nearly inflamed the hunts again. His bull *Omnipotentis dei* ("Of Omnipotent God") in 1623 reinvigorated the death penalty for *maleficia* and diabolic pacts. At the same time, though, his own inquisitors limited the hunting with revised instructions. The *Instructio pro formandis processibus in causis strigum, sortilegiorum et maleficorum* ("Instruction on Conducting Trials against Witches, Diviners, and Sorcerers") was first written in 1620. It began to be sent informally to inquisitors over the next few years and was officially published in 1651. Although not ruling out the reality of witchcraft, the *Instructio* called for judicious care in requiring good evidence and a fair trial. It restated the classic Church teaching that people who believed themselves to have attended sabbats were fooled by dreams and illusions. These new rules for trials actually limited torture. The strappado could not be carried out for longer than an hour and no squassation, or jerking or adding of weights, was permitted. Pope Gregory XV also turned witches and sorcerers over to secular courts for trial, rather than allow church courts to be involved. Pope Urban VIII Barbarini (r. 1623–1644) further reined in the witch hunts in 1635, feeling that the zealots had become too radical.

Even the practice of exorcism retreated from extremes. The *Thesaurus exorcismorum* ("Treasury of Exorcism Practices") published in 1608 collected in one huge volume the writings on exorcism by Girolamo Menghi, Valerio Polidori, and others from the two previous decades. These writings mostly warned of the dangers of demonic possession and the necessity of preparation to defend against them. Menghi's exorcism lists what devilish harms he sought to relieve: "Do not perturb his inner or external senses, from the soles of his feet to the ends of his hair; do not dry up his bones or move his humors, do not torment him with any malady and do not impede his rest in the hour of night or in the hours of the day."[4] Shortly afterward, however, the Church published a revision of ceremonies, the *Rituale Romanum* of 1614, which sought to curb abuses. Its guidelines set established practice for the next few centuries.

Nevertheless, the exorcist ritual still went on for more than two dozen pages of formal prayers and commands, to be repeated as necessary.

In sum, the Roman Inquisition was less harsh than the notorious Spanish Inquisition. It was not panicked by fear of a grand Satanic conspiracy promoting witchcraft. Neither did it use much torture, encourage wide-reaching hunts, or condemn many to death—perhaps only a hundred between 1550 and 1750. Authorities preferred milder punishments, such as the pillory, whipping, and public humiliation, to burning at the stake. Inquisitors soon busied themselves with keeping the faith of regular Roman Catholics within proper bounds. Beyond this, the Roman Inquisition's main aim became trying to reduce superstitious attachment to folk magic, such as astrology, divination, magical healing, and misuses of sacraments. The Inquisition's secretive operations, however, continued to create fear among the people, worried about being arrested for sin.

FRANCESCO MARIA GUAZZO

Even though witch fears were slowing down, a few individuals still tried to warn about their danger. The Ambrosian monk Francesco Maria Guazzo (also known as R. P. Guaccius) published the most important Italian book about witches, the *Compendium Maleficarum* ("Compilation of Witches") in 1626. Guazzo describes the powers of witches and remedies against them, illustrated with many credulous anecdotes and with citations both from ancient authors and from contemporary strixologists such as Rémy, Grillandus, and Del Rio. Guazzo listed eleven stages to the sealing of the bond between the Devil and a witch, moving from denial of the Christian faith, through mock baptism, and writing the witch's name in the book of death, to offering gifts and sacrifices to the Devil, suffocating children, defiling relics, and recruiting new members to attend the sabbat. The Devil placed his mark, sometimes appearing "like the footprint of a hare, sometimes like that of a toad or a spider or a dog or a dormouse.... [O]n men it is generally found on the eye-lids, or the arm-pit or lips or shoulder or posterior; whereas on women it is found on the breasts or private parts...."[5] The book's simple line-drawing images became enormously popular and influential in portraying the issues of witches (see Illustration 6).

The witch events of the seventeenth century are more interesting for the personalities involved than for the fearsomeness of a widespread hunt. In 1619 Benedetta Carlini, an abbess in the Theatine Order of a convent in Pescia, Tuscany, gained initial notoriety as a saint. She showed the stigmata, the wounds of Jesus from his crucifixion appearing on the body, and claimed to be married to Jesus in a more literal way than most nuns did. Her fame spread as she allegedly prevented a plague in her town. At first the Church authorities accepted her actions as divinely inspired, but then a nun came forward who claimed Benedetta had had sex with her while possessed by an angel in male form. The investigation led the bewildered authorities to squelch Carlini's activities, although they did not go so far as to condemn her of witchcraft. Carlini wound up imprisoned for life.

TOMMASO CAMPANELLA

More infamous was the case of Tommaso Campanella (b. 1568–d. 1639). Campanella had been a Dominican friar, but had begun to use spells and amulets for protection. In the years after 1590, he read various magical and forbidden books. He also got himself briefly imprisoned for adopting Copernicus' heretical heliocentric theory of the earth moving around the sun. Next he began preaching against Spanish rule in southern Italy, using apocalyptic language. Church authorities arrested and tortured Campanella as a heretic and then in 1603 imprisoned him for life. Pope Urban VIII Barbarini, however, released Campanella in 1626, because of his alleged skills with astrology. The pope suspected that magicians, perhaps working for the Spanish ambassador, were threatening his life. So Urban and Campanella worked in secret to devise some form of countermagic, as suggested by Ficino. Campanella's support and defense of Galileo soon led to a brief prison sentence of several months. He left Rome for exile in France in 1634, fearing further implication in heresy, sorcery, and conspiracy accusations. Meanwhile, Pope Urban issued a bull prohibiting astrology, especially when it was used to predict the death of popes.

THE *BENANDANTI*

The strangest, and perhaps best-examined hunt in Italy was that of the *benandanti* ("those who would do good") in Friuli from about 1575 to 1650. These people believed themselves to be special because they had been born with the caul, or amniotic sac, around their head. As adults, they wore it preserved around their necks as a charm. This gave them the power, they believed, to fly at night in spirit form and to fight witches, thus protecting the harvest of their people. The *benandanti* also defended against witches who would enter people's cellars and pollute the wine if they failed to find a pail of water in front of a house to drink. A spirit battle would be waged with the spirit-witches wielding sorghum stalks and the *benandanti* counterattacking with fennel.

Some scholars have seen this group of people as evidence of surviving folk beliefs of fertility rites, if not actual paganism. The *benandanti* were convinced they were helping defend the Roman Catholic Church and its people. Inquisitors naturally became suspicious of any activity dealing with witches, but at least in this case found it more a matter of foolish superstition than diabolic conspiracy. Most of the *benandanti* were sentenced only to brief imprisonment or penance.

THE LAST ITALIAN HUNTS

Witch persecutions of the classic type could still take place, however. In October 1646, authorities in Castelnuovo arrested Maria Salvatori, known as

La Mercuria. Allegedly, she had left the church with the Host from the Eucharist still in her mouth and would use it in Satanic ceremonies. At first, she did admit the crime of abusing the Host and then even claimed to have caused a miscarriage in the Marchesa Bevilacqua. Under torture, La Mercuria implicated others who worked with her as witches, accomplices whom authorities soon arrested. Under questioning and torture, all their stories expanded into a conspiracy of witches who met at sabbats, used magic unguents from dead babies, and had copulation with the Devil, who appeared as a handsome young man dressed in red. La Mercuria died in prison, but a number of others implicated by her were burned in April 1647. The case gained notoriety, partly because by that time witch trials had become unusual.

The eighteenth century saw the last gasps of witch ideology. In the early 1700s Prince Vittorio, son of King Vittorio Amedeo II of the Piedmont, died under mysterious circumstances. Elites believed witchcraft had caused his death. A small hunt, involving at least nine trials and three executions, followed. The Franciscan priest Ludovico Maria Sinistrari published *De Demonialitate* ("Of Sex with Demons") in 1700 asserting that "intercourse of witches with Demons, from its accompanying circumstances, apostasy from the Faith, worshipping of the Devil, and so many other ungodly things ... is the greatest of all sins which can be committed by man."[6] Another writer, Girolamo Tartarotti and his *Del Congresso Notturno delle Mammie* ("On the Nocturnal Meeting of Witches") of 1749, offered a last effort to encourage a debate connecting demonology and strixology. He argued that demons and their aid to neoplatonic sorcery existed, but not witchcraft. Few really cared by that point.

The example of the magician Cagliostro shows how witchcraft and magic were increasingly identified by sensible people with fraud, not fear. Cagliostro was born as Giuseppe Balasmo (b. 1745–d. 1795), the son of a tradesman. He claimed, however, to be a nobleman and, more importantly, a mystical worker with the supernatural. He toured the capitals of Europe, leaving them when suspicions mounted about his claims. Cagliostro's arrival in Rome in 1789 resulted in the inquisition arresting, convicting, and imprisoning him for sorcery.

END OF THE HUNTS IN SOUTHERN EUROPE

The witch hunts had slowly withered away, influenced by the Renaissance, the Scientific Revolution, and the Enlightenment. Although Renaissance humanists at first almost unquestioningly accepted the insights of the Greeks and Romans, they slowly began to test them more carefully. Much had been learned about the world since the Greeks and Romans flourished more than a thousand years before. Textual criticism by the humanists developed habits of careful reading and fine distinctions. Recognition that the ancients disagreed with one another, teacher Plato and student Aristotle not the least, encouraged new perspectives.

Science also grew out of these inquiries, and magical ideas were part of the early formation of scientific attitudes. Renaissance men had not yet tested whether ancient opinions had any verifiable validity. The scientific mindset required solid evidence based on careful observation and experimentation. Science therefore promoted skepticism about the reality of demonic actions. While Galileo's punishment might have intimidated some scientific inquiry into areas defined by the Church, the attitude that witchcraft was imaginary simply returned the Church to its own position before 1400.

The Enlightenment, even in an Italy dominated by the conservative papacy, further helped to end the hunts. The Enlightenment carried humanitarian reforms into public conversation, as witch-hunting became even more untenable. Cesar Beccaria and his enormously influential *De Delitti e dell Pene* ("On Crime and Punishment") of 1763 further tried to put the criminal justice system on a rational basis. That, of course, meant eliminating witch-hunting. Napoleon's brief conquest of Spain and the unification of the Kingdom of Italy with his legal reforms only assured that witch-hunting became an oddity of the past.

NOTES

1. Lu Ann Homza, ed. and trans., *The Spanish Inquisition, 1478–1614: An Anthology of Sources* (Indianapolis: Hackett Publishing Company, 2006), 154.

2. Gustav Henningsen, ed., *The Salazar Documents: Inquisitor Alonso de Salazar y Frías and Others on the Basque Witch-Persecution (1609–1614)* (Leiden, The Netherlands and Boston: Brill, 2004), 340, Document 12.69.

3. Martín Del Rio, *Investigations into Magic*, trans. and ed. P. G. Maxwell-Stuart (Manchester and New York: Manchester University Press, 2000), 189.

4. Girolamo Menghi, *The Devil's Scourge: Exorcism During the Italian Renaissance*, ed. and trans. Gaetano Paxia (Boston: Weiser Books, 2002), 79.

5. Francesco Maria Guazzo, *Compendium Maleficarum*, trans. E. A. Ashwin; ed. Montague Summers (London: Jon Rodker, 1929; reprint ed., San Diego: The Book Tree, 2004), 15.

6. Ludovico Maria Sinistrari, *Demoniality; Or Incubi and Succubi, A Treatise*, ed. and trans. Isidore Liseaux and anon. (Paris: Isidore Liseaux, 1879), 219: available online from Google Book Search.

CHAPTER 7

Witch-Hunting in Northern and Eastern Europe

The regions of northern and eastern Europe also experienced witch hunts, although on a scale much lower than that in Western Europe. The northern European region of Scandinavia comprised the modern states Denmark, Norway, Iceland, Sweden, and Finland. All these realms were in flux from 1500 to 1800, as they sought to dominate each other and their neighbors. In the east, the Holy Roman Empire, the Russian Empire, and the Ottoman Empire battled over large territories that today have become Poland, Hungary, and several smaller states. Poland and Hungary, under influence from German ideas, did hunt some witches, but Eastern Orthodox Christians were in general never as concerned with diabolic activity as were the Roman Catholics and Protestants. Only Orthodox Russia experienced witch-hunting to a notable degree.

No real witch-hunting took place in the southeastern Europe ruled by the Muslim Turkish Ottomans. The Muslim sultans and their administration did not fear a satanic conspiracy. Islam did not have much of a witch concept and the Turkish authorities did not indulge their Christian subjects in allowing any hunts either. Whatever witch-hunting did take place in these areas can best be attributed to Western influence. As westernization, or the adoption of political, social, economic, and cultural ideas from England, France, Germany, etc., traveled to other parts of Europe, witch-hunting was included as part of the intellectual baggage.

HUNTS IN SCANDINAVIA AND AROUND THE BALTIC

Both British and German cultural influence spurred the hunting of witches in Scandinavia. Roman law and its inquisitorial and torture methodologies inspired by German legal reforms reached into northern Europe. The shared Lutheran faith also transported the danger of witches from the German heartland to the Lutheran bishops of the North. The restraining authority of royal regimes, though, helped to reduce the severity of Scandinavian hunting.

Denmark

Early modern Denmark inherited various legal precedents against witchcraft from its medieval past, but nonetheless entered hunting comparatively late. Indeed, many Danes resisted witch-hunting during the sixteenth century. The attempt by King Christian II (r. 1513–1523) to introduce witch-hunting based on torture contributed to a rebellion that cost him his throne. New laws in 1547 protected accused witches from unfair judicial procedures. They allowed neither testimony from disreputable persons, such as felons or witches, nor torture. Irregularities in the next few years prompted more reforms in 1576. These reforms required death sentences to be reviewed by the high court in the capital city of Copenhagen. They also allowed easy appeal of cases tried by jurors, who, as local neighbors, might be prejudiced against an accused witch because of *infamia*. These measures reduced the number and viciousness of Danish hunts.

Denmark saw its first serious witch-hunting under the influence of the Lutheran Bishop Peter Palladius of Sealand (r. 1537–1560). His trials uncovered swarms of witches, of which fifty-two were executed, probably by burning at the stake, as in Germany. A few decades later, King Christian IV (r. 1588–1648) became involved in a hunt at Køge in 1612–1613. The burning of eleven women had enflamed his fear of witches. The king approved laws of moral reform in 1617 that included a redefinition of witch-hunting. Witches who made diabolic pacts were to be burned, although cunning-folk guilty of superstition should merely suffer fines and exile to another province. The reform also required testimony in witchcraft cases from two solid citizens who were not witches, although in practice, courts did not always stick to these high standards.

Most of the Danish trials that occurred over the next few years only involved *maleficia*, not the diabolic pact and consequent conspiracy. Since the central government failed to set up an inquisitorial method to solicit charges against witches, most cases were brought by neighbors complaining of damages caused by witchcraft. Many courts actually followed the rules established by the law and upheld high standards of evidence. This resulted in numerous acquittals. The number of trials spiked between 1626 and 1656, perhaps reflecting the crises of the Thirty Years War. An economic recession during those years may also have sent peasants and burghers looking for scapegoats among the poor. In total, Denmark experienced about 2,000 trials, with about half the victims executed.

Norway

Danish kings ruled Norway after 1536. The same laws that moderated hunts in Denmark then also applied to the Norwegians. Local authorities, however, ignored the laws more often than the Danes did. Some Norwegian clergy wanted to punish any superstition, including the work of cunning-folk, with death. Submitting to clerical pressure, the Danish king between 1584 and 1593 established witch concepts that drew on harsh Lutheran theology and imposed the death penalty for any kind of magic, whether the Devil was involved or

not. Many of the subsequently accused were homeless or beggars, whom the prosperous classes viewed as a drain on society. Norway experienced about 1,400 trials,
but only a quarter of that number were executed. Given the frequent use of illegal
torture to extort accusations and evidence, that number is surprisingly low.

Norway's most famous witch, Anne Pedersdotter, burned in 1590. Her husband, Absalon Pedersøn Beyer, a learned Lutheran minister in Bergen, may have
pushed reforms too far for the liking of his parishioners, who went after him
through his wife. She survived her first trial in 1575 for bewitching her husband's uncle to death. Some years after her husband's death, her accusers struck
again. City officials arrested, imprisoned, and put her on trial, but they did not
torture her and she did not confess. Among the evidence against Anne was her
servant Elina's claim that Anne had turned Elina into a horse to ride to a sabbat.
There witches had tried to wreck ships at Bergen by raising a storm or burn the
city to ashes. When a storm appeared during the trial, authorities became more
convinced of Anne's guilt. This second trial led to Anne's conviction and execution on April 7. A royal law shortly afterwards in 1593 restricted further hunts.

In 1670, the quarrels of wife Lisbet and her husband Ole Nypen with their
neighbors in Trondheim culminated in a trial for witchcraft. The charges against
each other were ludicrous, including that Lisbet had cursed one woman's eyebrows
to grow so long that she could not see and had caused another woman's husband
to have female breasts. On a more rational level, the court did not like how Lisbet
had adapted Christian language in charms to cure illnesses and wounds. Even
though torture failed to get confessions to anything worse, the court executed the
Nypens for their poor reputation, curing people through removal of demons, having harmed neighbors, and taking the Lord's name in vain. The executioner cut
off Ole's head before he burned them both, Lisbet still being alive.

In far north, the Sami or Lapp people of Finnmark were drawn into a set of
trials from 1652 to 1663 in the town of Vardø that involved several dozen people. The Vardø trials reflected ethnic differences: the crime of folk magic was
applied to Sami cunning-men, but ethnic Scandinavian women faced more traditional charges of witchcraft and the diabolic pact and the sabbat. Magistrates
dunked some suspected witches in the frigid waters of the North Sea to gain
confessions. Officials used heated pincers on others or racked them, applying
sulfur to their breasts. Under such torture, many admitted to forming pacts
with the Devil and training more witches to harm people and property, drive
away fish, sink ships, and even transform into seals or whales. Magical abilities
were transmitted from teacher to student witch through drink or certain foods.
The judges declared that such witches, "due to their own committed evil deed
have forfeited their lives to fire and flames."[1]

Iceland

Iceland also lay under Danish authority, but only loosely because of the long
distance across the North Sea and the Atlantic. Danish kings alternately
exploited and ignored Iceland. Economic conditions worsened throughout the

witch-hunting period. Danish law both established and softened the hunts. Sheriffs appointed from Denmark were obligated to pursue witchcraft, but legal procedures offered some protections, especially after 1686, when executions had to be appealed to Copenhagen. Another moderating influence was the lack of belief in the sabbat ideology.

Although Icelanders took up witch-hunting, victims were few and overwhelmingly male. Of about 120 persons put on trial between 1604 and 1725, only ten were women. Of the twenty-two burned at the stake, only one was a woman. The Icelanders' focus on "High Magic" or sorcery, rather than "Low Magic" of the diabolic pact or even *maleficia*, offers one explanation for this ratio. Such sorcerers were believed to use poetry from forbidden books of magic (*galdrabœkur*) to achieve their spellbinding. Anything written in runes, a writing that had preceded the Latin alphabet adopted during the conversion to Christianity, provided damning evidence. Therefore, illiterate peasant women could not do this sorcery.

The first witch burned in 1625. The local sheriff, Mágnus Björnsson, blamed ghosts for a recent plague, but one dying boy fingered Jón Rögnvaldson as a witch. A search of Rögnvaldson's house revealed a sheet of writing in runes, which proved his sorcery. Sherriff Björnsson, who referenced the *Malleus Maleficarum*, quickly had Rögnvaldson tried and burned.

The number of trials increased after the 1630s, as more demonology seeped in from Denmark. Most hunts, though, remained limited to a few individuals, never breaking out into a panic. The residents living in isolated homesteads failed to embrace witch accusations as a means for dealing with social tension.

SWEDEN

Sweden had a reputation as a land of witches, gained from a popular history of the region, Olaus Magnus' *Historia de Gentibus Septentrionalibus* ("History of the Northern Peoples"), published in 1555. Magnus, somewhat skeptically, mentions the popular tradition of the Blåkulla (or Blocula, the Blue Mountain) as a meeting place of witches. Bodin cited the book for his belief in the many witches and wizards in the North. The publication of the *Historia* may have helped spark Sweden's first outburst of hunting in the mid-sixteenth century. Cases drew the royal attention of King Gustav I Vasa (r. 1523–1560), who exhorted his people to apprehend witches. Although torture was not usually a common part of the Swedish legal practice, magistrates often made an exception for charges of witchcraft, in accordance with the concept of either *crimen exceptum* or *lèse-majesté*, a crime against the king.

Legal reforms under enlightened kings Charles IX (r. 1604–1611) and Gustavus Adolphus (r. 1611–1632) ended hunts for a while. The reformed legal procedures required significant evidence (as many as six witnesses) and brought the cases under centralized courts, where they could be supervised. Also in an enlightened manner, Queen Christina (r. 1632–1654) reportedly outlawed all witch cases, except where murder was involved. As a result, fewer than 200 trials took place in Sweden, and about half of the accused were found innocent, despite the use of ordeals, pricking, and hearsay evidence. It appeared that witch-hunting would remain rare in Sweden because of the enlightened policies of these monarchs.

The Mora Hunt

Unfortunately for innocent children, a large and notorious witch hunt seized the imagination of the Swedes, beginning in 1664 in the province of Dalarna. In December of that year a poor boy accused his family of leading him off to the Blåkulla. There they had celebrated some odd feast. The court dismissed these stories, but the tales grew. In 1668, Elaus Skragge, a pastor in the village of Elfdale near Mora (or Mohra), began to hear of girls being kidnapped for use in devil worship. Several arrests and investigations followed. Local authorities nonetheless lacked sufficient evidence for proving any real crime, much less Satanic plots. The accused were freed.

The idea of a diabolic conspiracy, however, refused to disappear so easily. The young King Charles XI (r. 1660–1679), of a more fearful mind than his predecessor Queen Christina, heard of the incident. Intrigued, the king launched his own investigation. He sent a royal commission of judges, clergy, professors, and lawyers to investigate in August 1669. Many on the panel began to believe the fantastic stories. The more religious of them even tried to cure the diabolic influence in the region through sermons and prayer meetings. These events only drew more attention to the magical events.

The local children, who were threatened by the alleged kidnapping plots, shared stories with one another. Adults may also have bribed or coerced their children to give evidence, in a hope for leniency. Witch finders pointed to guilty parties. Elaborate fantasies were told of how strange women had drawn many children to a meadow under the Blåkulla. The Devil appeared to them in fancy clothing, usually a gray coat, red and blue stockings with long garters, and a tall hat with linen of diverse colors wrapped around it. He then led them into the mountain like a Pied Piper, as they rode on strange beasts or on enchanted people. Some children believed this trip to be real, whereas others thought it happened only in spirit while they slept. In either case, they passed through a gate into a great palace underneath the mountain, where devils and angels acted out a bizarre sabbat. The beasts grazed and the ridden people slept, while in many rooms the children feasted on bacon, oatmeal, bread, milk, and cheese. These tales represent typical peasant dreams of lands of plenty, just as Isabel Gowdie had in Scotland. According to a contemporary English version of events, after feasting, "the Devil used to play upon a Harp before them, and afterwards go with them that he loved best into a Chamber, where he committed venereous acts with them…. [A]nd that the Devil had Sons and Daughters by them, which he did marry together, and they did couple, and brought forth Toads and Serpents."[2] The Devil gave the witches tools to harm people with headaches and magical animals to steal food, but they were unsure whether they actually murdered anyone.

Large numbers of children and adults, with some testimony amplified by torture, established a vast smorgasbord of evidence for prosecutors. Credulous authorities accepted these odd tales as a basis for arrests and convictions, even though testimony of minors under fifteen years was officially forbidden by law. The penalties escalated according to age. Officials beat children under the age of nine for three Sundays in a row. They beat forty of the children aged between nine and sixteen years in a public place every Sunday for more than a year. Authorities beheaded and burned the corpses of seventeen adults. Pastor Skragge's version of the Devil's work appeared in both Dutch and German in 1670 and soon gained a wide readership, also being reprinted or referenced in works by Glanvil, Cotton Mather, Balthasar Bekker, and Francis Hutchinson.

The case did not end there, as witch kidnappings spread to children in coastal villages and even to Stockholm by 1675. Almost 200 women and dozens of men over the age of sixteen were beheaded and then burned, with at least one woman being burned alive. Views changed when new commissions led by Dr. Urban Hjärne took over the investigation. He questioned the children carefully and severely. He exposed their stories of temptations and sabbats as figments of imagination. The regime stopped the trials by 1676, subsequently prosecuting some witnesses for giving false testimony. This scandal largely ended the witch hunts in Sweden, and elsewhere in Europe. Indeed by the 1720s an attempt to start a hunt based on children's testimony was quickly halted, and the accusers themselves wound up prosecuted instead. The Swedish regime finally removed the crime of witchcraft from the law books in 1779.

Finland

Nearby Finland had been under Swedish control, which thus guided its witch-hunting. Witchcraft had been outlawed in 1554, and the charge reinforced in 1573 with religious excommunication. King John III of Sweden himself ordered a search for witches in Finland in 1575. Still, trials remained comparatively few, totaling about 1,000. The first witch execution, for vague *maleficia* caused by a cunning-woman, took place in 1595 in Pernaja. The courts found fewer than half of the accused to be guilty and only executed about 200 people. Other, milder punishments included fasting on bread and water, fining, flogging, or running the gauntlet. The person punished by running the gauntlet ran between two rows of men who would hit the person along the way. As in Iceland and Sweden, most accused witches were male, at least until the ideas of Carpzov and other strixologists brought a diabolical emphasis on women as witches after 1650. Before that, indictments mostly focused on issues of healing magic and *maleficia*.

Finland experienced most of its witch hunts from the 1650s to the 1680s. Several professors and students at Finland's university, the Turku Academy, were charged with practicing diabolic arts. More numerous were conflicts in villages provoked by begging or by neighbors' disputes. For example, a judge in Åland arrested the beggar Karin Persdotter in 1665 for divination. She freely confessed her special powers, came to accept that a diabolic pact had given them to her, and then denounced thirteen women she had seen at a sabbat at the Blåkulla. The judge obligingly arrested and tortured the other women with thumbscrews to gain confessions. The largest number of trials took place in the small village of Österbotten between 1665 and 1684. Members of wealthy families denounced each other because they believed business failures had been caused by the *maleficia* of diabolic witchcraft. A few trials drew on children's fantasies, similar to the incident in Mora in Sweden.

The Court of Appeal at Turku released the last accused witch in 1701, refusing to carry out her death sentence. Ninety-nine years later, a half-dozen men beat to death an old beggar woman they thought was a witch. This offense was deemed illegal mob violence, however, not official witch-hunting. Officials beheaded the ringleader and exiled others of the mob for taking the law into their own hands. The responsibility of the government for public order had replaced fears of diabolic witchcraft.

Estonia and Livonia

Witch-hunting in Estonia and Livonia (modern day Latvia) sprang from Swedish and German influence. The majority of the population was ethnically Baltic. At the end of the Middle Ages, the Teutonic Knights had culturally and politically dominated the region. These mostly German crusaders had shifted their efforts from Palestine to the Baltic region during the fourteenth century in order to conquer and convert the last remaining pagans in Europe. The Knights converted to Lutheranism because of the Reformation. Soon afterwards the region came under Swedish power.

Laws against witchcraft dated back to the fourteenth century, but witch-hunting began late, only in the sixteenth century and only with a few trials. Hunting intensified during the seventeenth century under the influence of Lutheran Sweden, in urban areas influenced by Western European traders. The *Neun ausserlessen und wohlbegründete Hexen-Predigten* ("Nine Selected and Well-founded Sermons against Witchcraft"), published in 1626 by the superintendent of the Livonian Church, Herman Samson or Samsonius (r. 1622–1643), conveyed German ideas of witchcraft to the local people. He acknowledged that some who claimed to be witches were mentally ill and should be healed, but others did have a pact with the Devil and caused harm. That kind were to be burned alive, although he offered no reliable method on how to tell the difference. The courts regularly used torture to examine accused witches.

In 1667–1668, Samson and other like-minded Protestant officials worried that the surviving remnants of paganism might lead the Livonians back to Roman Catholicism. Because of their late and forced conversion by Germans, the Baltic peoples probably had the most pronounced pagan tendencies in Europe. Meetings in sacred groves and on venerated hills had continued after Christianization. Church authorities therefore targeted the cunning-folk who practiced the Low Magic of healing and divining. The authorities likewise blamed witches for deaths brought on by poisoning, often by cursing beer. Some witches allegedly transformed into werewolves, as at Meremoisa in 1623, where several women confessed to concealing their magical wolf skins under stones when not wearing them to kill animals. At least the more extreme concepts of the sabbat and diabolic pact did not appear to have been spread into the Baltic regions.

The Lutheran authorities mostly hunted cunning-men along the Baltic, rather than cunning-women. In Estonia, as in Iceland and Finland, men comprised the majority of the accused witches. Only about 200 trials seem to have been held. Of these, slightly more than a quarter ended with executions, either by burning at the stake or decapitation by the sword. In the final case concerning witchcraft in Estonia, in 1816, the court reprimanded both accused and accusers for believing in superstitious nonsense.

HUNTS IN EASTERN EUROPE

Poland-Lithuania's unique government and religious structure allowed some dreadful witch hunts to take place, although they occurred relatively later than in the rest of Europe. The decline of the state's royal authority from the fifteenth to the eighteenth centuries contributed to this lag. Any moderating influence of central authority vanished, as aristocrats and nobles increasingly dominated their own territories and districts, electing and then ignoring the kings. Eventually the *Sejm*, or Polish parliament, gained an absolute right of veto over any law. After that, any single noble representative could frustrate reform. The power of the central government withered away. As a result, local authorities enjoyed too much discretion to hunt witches, as had happened in the Holy Roman Empire. The Devil (or sometimes Russian witches) proved easier to blame for the political situation than the nobles themselves. The nobles remained free of accusations of witchcraft, which, not surprisingly, fell on commoners and the poor, mostly women.

Religious divisions contributed to the problems. While Poland is famous for being one of the most Roman Catholic countries in Europe today, in the sixteenth century, as the Reformation began, the population was divided by many religious traditions. Remnants of Slavic paganism mingled with diverse Protestant reformers. The Roman Catholics slowly fought their way back to ascendance by 1648. Jesuits and other hard-liners equated any defiance of the strict Roman Catholic line with heresy, and hence, with witchcraft.

Nonetheless, secular courts dominated the witch trials, rather than ecclesiastical tribunals. Some clergy thought secular courts were not harsh enough, whereas others admonished them for excessive cruelty. For example, Bishop Casimir Czartoriski of Cujavia and Pomerania in 1699 tried to encourage the authorities to apply fair legal procedures. The common people lodged most of the accusations of witchcraft. Because the central government in Poland was so weak, common people often took the law into their own hands. Lynching of witches typified Polish hunting, a practice very rare in any other state. It claimed as many as half of the several thousand victims. Although Polish authorities burned a witch as early as 1511, the years between 1675 and 1720, saw the worst of the persecutions.

Two of the very last executions for witchcraft in Europe appear to have taken place in Polish territory, although some scholars question whether or not the executions really took place. During 1793, the Prussians in occupied Posen hanged two witches. The sentences seem to have been carried out by local officials on their own authority, in violation of centralized legal procedures. Official Prussian policy had already forbidden the death penalty for witchcraft. In any case, legally constituted authorities executed no more witches in any European land after this incident.

Hungary

South of Poland lay the Kingdom of Hungary, whose people, the Hungarians, or Magyars, descended from medieval Asiatic invaders and preserved their own distinct language and culture. The first Christian king, St. Stephan (r. 1000–1038), outlawed witchcraft, although only a handful of trials were held during the Middle Ages. The numbers began to rise after 1526, when the Habsburg dynasty of Austria, who were also commonly the Holy Roman Emperors, claimed rule of the land. At the same time, though, the Ottoman Turks conquered much of the kingdom. The Habsburgs drove the Turks out by the late seventeenth century, while crushing repeated Hungarian attempts at independence.

With Austro-German takeover, witch-hunting multiplied. The Hungarians lacked any significant demonological writings of their own, so they borrowed from German texts. They incorporated Carpzov's witch-hunting advice (see Chapter 3) into their laws after 1690, spreading his diabolical ideas and harsh judicial procedures. Friction between the occupying German-speaking soldiers and the natives with their strange customs incited some hunts. The continued use of the law of *lex talionis* (which allowed an accused to countersue if charges remained unproven) and ordeals, though, moderated some of the extremes of witch persecutions.

The diversity of the Hungarian kingdom complicated its integration into the Habsburg realm. The Reformation conflicts of Lutherans, Calvinists, Orthodox, and Roman Catholics may also have contributed to a heightened awareness of the problems of the Devil. The first hunts seem to have been launched by Lutherans, followed by some Roman Catholics, and finally, the Calvinists. Both of the latter drew inspiration from Alpine hunts in Austria and Switzerland. The Hungarian Kingdom also included varied ethnic groups and territories besides the Magyars. In the north were Slovaks; in the West lived Croatians; and in the East dwelled Rumanians in the "land beyond the woods," Transylvania. Transylvanians had begun the first witch hunts in the sixteenth century, executing more than a dozen witches, many of them mid-wives and cunning-folk between 1565 and 1593.

The name Transylvania is, of course, commonly associated with Dracula and vampires. Folk beliefs in vampirism are closely interwoven with those of witches. Like the *striges* and *lamiae* of ancient Rome, vampires were also monsters who killed babies and drank blood. Vampires differed from living witches because they were "undead," those whose corpses refused to rest in peace in their graves. Essentially, vampires were witches who had been improperly executed, which allowed them to come back from the grave and harm the living. By demonic power, vampires would rise at night and attack people by drinking their blood or bringing misfortune. They shared the witch's power to fly and could metamorphose into animals such as a wolf or a bat.

The most famous vampire, Dracula, was more than the invention of the nineteenth-century author Bram Stoker. Stoker created his fictional vampire Dracula by adapting folk tales and legends that had grown around the historical figure of Vlad III (r. 1456–1462, 1477–1479), a prince of Wallachia, which lay east of Transylvania. Vlad had various pseudonyms. One was "Tzepesch" (judge). Dracula means "son of the dragon," a reference either to Satan in the biblical Book of Revelation or Apocalypse or to his father, Vlad II. The historical Prince Vlad fought against the Ottoman Turks, who were invading Transylvania and Romania. In doing so, he imposed harsh rule on his own people, earning the nickname "the Impaler" from his favorite method of execution. First a long pole, perhaps twenty feet high, was set straight up from the ground. A bound victim was then carried up on a ladder and forcibly pushed down on the pole. Death came relatively quickly from damage to internal organs and loss of blood. But the body, as a deterrent to others, was left to slowly slide down the pole and rot. Vlad impaled victims by the dozens, or possibly even hundreds, for a wide range of crimes. The people, as his name Dracula indicates, in time associated him with demon worship and magic, as well as with the fear of vampires.

Elizabeth (or Erzsébeth) Báthory

Another famous reputed vampire, Elizabeth (or Erzsébeth) Báthory, lived in neighboring Hungary and Austria. Widowed in 1604, Elizabeth allegedly began to find comfort in murderous activities. She took young virgins, drained them of their blood for her to bathe in and then ate their flesh. Her trial from 1609 to 1611 ended with her loss of lands and authorities imprisoning her in a castle. Enemies in her family and the Habsburg regime may have exaggerated accusations in order to weaken her powerful family. Other Báthory relatives in Transylvania over the next few years also used witchcraft accusations against one another to consolidate power. Reacting to these cases, the Transylvanian Diet reinforced laws against witches in 1614.

Many Hungarian witch-vampires were not inspired by individuals, such as Dracula or Elizabeth Báthory, but rather by military-like groups. In addition to a typical sabbat, many Hungarian sorcerers (*táltosok*) allegedly marched under officers, accompanied by martial music and banners. The beliefs brought by ethnic German soldiers into Hungary may account for these views. Hunts of these groups culminated in the worst Hungarian hunts, taking place in Szeged between 1728 and 1744. The accused ranged from the lower classes to the government officials. Many witches were tested both by swimming and by being weighed. Authorities burned between thirteen and thirty-four people, although the Emperor Charles VI spared others. In 1730 a certain Arnold Paul gained notoriety through his claim to be haunted by a Turkish vampire. A few more mass trials sprang up in the 1750s that drew the attention of the ruler of the Habsburg territories, Maria Theresa.

Maria Theresa

"Empress" Maria Theresa (r. 1740–1780) and her enlightened despotism ended witch-hunting in her realm. The case of Rosina Polakin, whose corpse had been exhumed as a vampire, posthumously beheaded and burned in 1755, drew the monarch's attention. Maria Theresa sent her own court physicians, John Gasser and Christian Vabst, to investigate. They returned with many unbelievable tales of superstitious activities in the provinces. Meanwhile, her main court physician, Gerard van Swieten (b. 1700–d. 1772), had already begun reforming modern medicine in Austria, improving medical study at universities, care at hospitals, and treatment at asylums. As the head of the Commission for Censorship, van Swieten wanted to ban supernatural superstition. His own book, *Remarques sur le Vampyrisme* ("Remarks on Vampirism"), in 1755 addressed the issue in the manner of the Enlightenment and dismissed vampires as nonsense.

Encouraged by these advisors, Maria Theresa soon issued laws that definitively ended the hunts in all her realms. A law of 1755 first suspended any hunting involving vampires, necromancy, or divination. The next year, a commission investigating the matters drew up a law prohibiting any witch-hunting whatsoever. The latter was incorporated in Maria Theresa's law reform, the *Constitutio Criminalis Theresiana*. Although magic was still considered a crime, prosecution required substantial evidence. The enlightened rule of Maria Theresa's son Joseph II (r. 1780–1790) ensured that witch hunts became a mark of ignorance that was no longer supported by the Austrian regime. In 1787, he removed all criminality of witchcraft and magic from the legal codes and soon after abolished torture. By that time about 500 witches had been executed, and many others had been punished with lighter sentences.

Russia

To the East of Austria, the Russian Empire was just entering the sphere of European influence during the centuries of the witch hunts. Russia therefore shared in the ideology necessary to pursue witches, although hunts hardly existed in other areas under Eastern Orthodox Christianity. A serious fear of witches began at the royal court, not in the monasteries or cathedrals. Tsar Ivan III (r. 1462–1505) believed that his first wife had been killed by magic and that another wife was trying to kill him with magic. Tsar Ivan IV (r. 1533–1584), nicknamed "the Terrible," seems to have worried about witches, although it is probable that he used accusations to eliminate political rivals. In 1551, he convened a church council called the Stoglov (or Hundred Chapters of Regulations). The council recommended ecclesiastical trials for witches. The trials, in turn, would send excommunicated persons to the secular imperial government for execution. This system was in line with the Western European treatment of heresy. Although the tsar agreed to outlaw magical practices, he shifted jurisdiction from the church courts to secular, usually military, tribunals. This began a more intense period of hunting, although the secular courts may have helped to moderate the intensity. All of this typified Ivan the Terrible's efforts at centralization of the government by using cruelty. Ivan's torture and executions of many thousands of his people, whom he suspected of treason, make the witch hunts seem a minor incident in comparison.

The death penalty for sorcery was codified in 1652, but Russian hunts remained small and limited. Other tsars lacked the same concern as Ivan III or Ivan IV. Unique Russian torture techniques included using hot wedges pushed between bound hands and feet or icy water poured over the victim's head. Russians also preferred to punish witches with penance, fines, or pillorying, rather than with burning.

As elsewhere, a widespread fear of *maleficia* existed in Russia, especially because many Russians believed that incantations (*zogovor*) could cause illnesses. Some historians suggest that the Orthodox Church's inability to convert the Russians fully from paganism to Christianity played a role in this fear, as was the case in neighboring Estonia. Disasters such as famines and plagues could also spark small persecutions. For example, authorities burned a dozen women at Pskov in 1411, for allegedly causing a plague.

Shriekers

One unusual kind of Russian witches were the "shriekers" (*klikushi*). These were (mostly) women who claimed to be possessed, a condition which they demonstrated through wailing, barking, and writhing during worship services. Russians believed that sorcerers' spells or poisonings enabled demons to take possession of shriekers, and they could only be freed through exorcisms. Shriekers seem to have been a manifestation of simple peasant beliefs and religious zealotry. The *klikushi* began to appear in the eleventh century and continued to occur in Orthodox churches long after the hunts ended, even into the twentieth century. Witch trials concerning *klikushi* tended to focus on individual accusations, though, and rarely broadened into a mass hunt.

At Lukh, a village northeast of Moscow, however, complaints against *klikushi* did expand into a panic in 1657. Several women were hiccupping, writhing in pain, and screaming out the names of local residents. An investigator from Moscow, Ivan Romanchiukov, at first found no one willing to accuse others of witchcraft. By applying torture with red-hot pincers to crush people's private parts, however, he gained several confessions. One suspect, Ianka Salautin, admitted that he "set spells loose in the wind and in smoke. Whomever he looks in the face, even if from afar, will be struck by that bewitchment."[3] Romanchiukov had three men decapitated and a woman buried alive as punishment for inflicting harm on others.

Shortly thereafter, Tsar Peter I "the Great" (r. 1682–1725) tried to bring rationalism and order to his state. He increased the imperial government's controls over the Orthodox Church. He also set out to discourage belief in superstitious behavior, including possessions. He made it a crime to fake a possession, a ruling that diminished assertions of *klikushi*. One law punished fraudulent possession by condemning the defrauders to the galleys, after having their nostrils slit open.

A major series of hunts in the late seventeenth century by a military tribunal tortured and tried almost 100 people in Moscow. The hunts were partly concerned with charges of political plots and factions. The majority of the accused were consequently men who had access to political office. These hunts resembled late-medieval hunts in England or France, or earlier Russian hunts, where accusations of witchcraft were used to weaken political rivals.

More progress toward ending hunting came from Tsar Anna (r. 1730–1740). In the second year of her reign, she called all witchcraft a fraud. The law of May 20, 1731, condemned sorcerers as deceivers who, if they admitted their swindling without being tortured, were not punished. Nevertheless, superstitious belief persisted. An epidemic of hiccupping near Archangel (Arkhangelsk) afflicted hundreds and led to witchcraft accusations by peasants against one another. A long government investigation, though, failed to decide whether the outbreak had been caused by natural, divine, or demonic causes. Additionally, dozens of accusations against men for sorcery also ran through the courts in the mid-eighteenth century, encouraged by some Orthodox clergy.

All witch-hunting ended under Tsar Catherine II "the Great" (r. 1762–1796). Catherine was a German princess who had been brought to Russia to marry the heir to the throne. When her husband became tsar, however, Catherine engineered a plot to remove him from power and take the throne for herself. Afterward she tried to rule in the manner of enlightened despotism. She reformed the laws of the realm, including the laws for hunts, which she ended in 1770.

Although the governments in Eastern Europe stopped supporting witch hunts, belief in witches continued among the common people well into the twentieth century. Neighbors would, at times, attack accused witches, occasionally resulting in murder. Even today, folk beliefs in creatures of darkness lead to disturbances of the peace. Nearly always, though, the government discourages people from taking justice into their own hands and from blaming evil on supernatural forces. As long as governments refuse to accept a witch ideology, assaults on people accused as witches remain limited.

NOTES

1. Quoted in Liv Helene Willumsen. "Witches of the High North: the Finnmark Witchcraft Trials in the Seventeenth Century," *Scandinavian Journal of History* 22 (1973): 210.

2. George Sinclair, *Satan's Invisible World Discovered (1685)*, A facsimile reproduction with intro by Coleman O. Parsons (Gainesville, FL: Scholars' Facsimiles & Reprints, 1969), 180–81.

3. Brian P. Levack, ed. *The Witchcraft Sourcebook* (New York and London: Routledge, 2004), 218.

CHAPTER 8

Beyond the Witch Hunts

The history of the witch hunts reveals how a powerful fantasy took root within Europe, cultivated by religious, intellectual, and political leaders and nourished by popular beliefs and fears about magic. Between 1400 and 1800, many had believed that witches immediately threatened Christian society, because of their magical abilities to do *maleficia* through diabolic pacts with the Devil. The trials of witches then unfolded in particular times and places according to the decisions of individual ruling authorities to act upon this prevailing fear.

In some ways, the witch hunts, as constructed and carried out, seem a detour from the main course of European history. First of all, the supernatural nature of the crimes of witchcraft and sorcery makes them almost unique in Western jurisprudence. All other crimes, such as murder, assault, theft, or burglary, demand the physicality of criminal activity in bodies and property. Even crimes about religious matters, such as blasphemy, idolatry, or heresy, did not require a supernatural event: the actual cursing, worshipping, or rejecting could be witnessed and provided as evidence. In contrast, the fantastic aspects of witchcraft never permitted a sensible approach. Accusing, arresting, trying, convicting, and punishing people for magical crimes presented unique complications about proof. Unfounded suspicion turned into guilt only through exaggerating poor reputations, reinterpreting physical blemishes, extorting confessions, and ignoring common sense. With witchcraft, the incredible became possible.

Even the notion of a conspiracy lacked any solid proof. Strixologists mainly relied on the belief of the supernatural ability of the Devil to bind many people together. Theologians concocted a fear of Satan's organizing witches, bringing them together at sabbats, or writing their names in his book. Unlike heretics who were caught in secret meetings, no witches were ever apprehended at a sabbat, and no copy of Satan's little black book ever turned up. All that magistrates had to go on were confessions and accusations by neighbors and

strangers against one another, often delivered under torture. No good arguments or physical evidence supported the idea that groups of witches worked
together to threaten European society.

In addition, witches were not, and are not, an inevitable part of Christian
doctrine. The magical thinking that permeated Christianity did not require killing witches. Christianity did discourage magic, including that of numerous
cunning-folk. Contrary to expectation, hunters rarely focused their hostility
and justice on these cunning-acts. Wise-women coexisted with the dominant
Christian ideology both before and after the age of the hunts. Their "Low Magic"
of petty charms and spells hardly threatened society with collapse. Similarly,
Christian authorities could disapprove of pretentious Renaissance wizards and
sorcerers who played with the "High Magic" of grimoires and spell books, trying to raise demons and control nature. Yet again, these higher classed intellectuals rarely drew ire and retribution for their fruitless tinkering with the
metaphysical. When either of these two groups did come under scrutiny, religious leaders often treated these sinners with preaching, prayer, and penance,
showing Christian grace and mercy. Witchcraft could have likewise been treated
with similar leniency or benign neglect.

Instead, the persecutors' beliefs in witches turned disapproval of magic into
hunting of witches. There is a difference between either believing in or disliking
witches and hunting them. Hunting was an intellectual fashion. The political
and religious elites of Europe thought witches not only inverted proper social
values, but actually caused harm in the physical world and could destroy society. To defend witch hunters by saying that they were caught up in mentality
of their time neither clarifies nor excuses the hunts. Such a relativist defense
might see hunters' actions as sincere and necessary, given the premises of their
culture. Their worry about eternal salvation, the possibility of sinners suffering
forever in hell rather than enjoying bliss in the presence of God, made hunters
take matters seriously enough to crush alleged witches with the wheels of
justice.

This interpretation notwithstanding, equally sincere and confident contemporary theologians and ideologists disputed witch-hunting. Many strixologists
repeatedly tried to define the danger that witches posed as leaving no other
option to the conscientious Christian. Always, however, alternatives existed
within the mindset and abilities of early modern Europe. At no point did
everyone believe in the reality of witches and their danger. Those alternate
views explain why hunting remained confined to limited times and scattered
localities. No government neglected to prosecute murder or theft, while
many, even most, refused to hunt witches. Skeptics of witch-hunting always
remained throughout the Burning Times, even if their voices went unheeded
too often by those who set the fires at the pyres. By 1800, the skeptics
had won.

Meanwhile, those unfortunate decisions to hunt witches yielded tens of
thousands of executions and much suffering. The death toll has been especially

difficult to measure, given the fragmentary nature of the records. Reasonable calculations range from a minimum of 35,000 to a maximum of 1,000,000 dead. Recent historians have tended to reduce their estimates of the numbers of victims executed. Many more people at the time, though, were affected by the hunts than those who endured the ultimate penalty. The total of victims includes anyone put on trial and found innocent, all the political and court personnel, witnesses, friends, and relatives. Such numbers reach into the millions. Although these numbers hardly attain the level of a holocaust or a genocide, they nonetheless show how too many people suffered for a crime that did not exist.

WITCHES AFTER THE WITCH HUNTS

As the witch hunts faded into history, witches slowly became characters of fiction and imagination in Western Civilization. The Romantics of the nineteenth century were drawn to witchcraft, but hardly believed in it. The Brothers Grimm collection of fairy tales relegated witches to childish fantasies. Magic has even become a weapon for heroes, not just a tool of evil. Today, the fans of Harry Potter stories, first made popular in England, see witchcraft and wizardry as a morally neutral tool. In Potter's fictional world, evil comes not from the Devil, but from selfish characters. In this imaginary United Kingdom, evil is opposed by upright action, not by fearful arrests, torture, and executions that ensnare the innocent, as the witch hunts did in Great Britain for so many centuries. Many television shows, from *Bewitched* to *Charmed*, portray witches as misunderstood heroines, whether in preserving the modern family or saving all society from attack by evil supernatural beings.

A similar positive view of witches has also been promoted by religious systems that arose in the twentieth century. In particular, Aleister Crowley and Gerald Brosseau Gardner from Great Britain cobbled together fragments of pagan ritual and witchcraft tradition to create the foundations of modern Wicca and Neo-Paganism, as well as various New Age sects. At the same time, Anton Szandor Le Vey founded modern Satanism, which promotes a counter-cultural Nietzschean will-to-power, in addition to using ideas and rituals drawn from the age of the witch hunts. These new belief structures often use supernatural understandings of nature to satisfy the human need for spiritual meaning. Even some Christians still believe in demons with dangerous powers of possession. The idea persists among many that some individuals can cause supernatural forces to harm our natural reality. Very few people in the West today, however, call for hunting down these new witches.

Despite these approaches to magic embraced by many, negative perceptions and even attacks on purported witches have continued. Sporadically, over the past 200 years, mobs and individuals have assaulted alleged witches in Europe. When mobs or neighbors tried to provoke attacks on witches, however, local magistrates usually upheld the law by arresting disturbers of the peace, not by burning the alleged witches. In contrast, violence against witches still regularly takes place in sub-Saharan Africa, parts of Asia, and the Pacific. In the nineteenth century, European colonial powers ended witch persecutions in these areas, by force of law. Nevertheless, revived and mutated traditional beliefs now blame witches for misfortune, illness, and death, and especially for AIDS. Although few governments have sanctioned witch persecutions, they often ignore the cruel actions of their citizens against alleged witches and offer few protections or compensations.

People in the West today, though, should not claim any moral superiority over either contemporary witch persecutors or forebears who believed in the impossible. We still have "witch hunts" against imaginary enemies. Not so long ago, in the 1980s and 1990s, the media and courts suddenly became obsessed with daycare molestation rings and Satanic murder cults. The witch hunts returned, as prosecutors charged people with horrible, fantastic crimes, including the classic human sacrifice, cannibalism, and unnatural, incestuous sex orgies. Evidence came from the pressured testimony of children, "recovered memories," or medical examinations detecting signs of abuse. Since then, cooler heads of the FBI have found no evidence of any organized Satanic cult that killed babies. The medical evidence noting odd scars or bumps—reminiscent of the search for Witch's and Devil's Marks—has also been dismissed as invalid. There do exist pedophiles and murderers who commit horrific acts, but zealotry and fear exaggerated fantasy into false convictions.

Those who supported witch-hunting committed grave errors within the intellectual context of their age. Voices spoke out against the natural reality of magic and the actual existence of witches throughout the age of the witch hunts. The Christian churches never dogmatically and unequivocally took a position to destroy witches. The entire culture was not wholly bamboozled by dreams of demons. Indeed, if witches had been real, one could justify hunting them, just as today's societies do hunt terrorists. That no witches existed who made pacts with demons and worked harmful magic makes their sufferings and deaths even more sincerely tragic.

HISTORIANS' THEORIES ABOUT THE WITCH HUNTS

Since the witch hunts began, people have grasped for explanations. Historians only use the scientifically based empiricism and rationalism of the historical method to develop theories as comprehensive explanations for historical events and trends. A review of some of theories explaining witch hunts offers useful frameworks for making sense of these tragedies.

Certain historians start by avoiding judgment on supernatural attitudes, instead taking a position similar to certain anthropologists studying primitive tribes who suggest that we respect the point of view that witches actually worked spells. These relativist scholars maintain that historians need not bother about whether or not magic was real, only whether people acted as if it were real. Certainly, some historians feel they should not insult the intelligence of people in other cultures, since many issues of the supernatural still have no conclusive answer that would satisfy everyone.

Nevertheless, some world views are more empirically valid than others. For example, when studying cosmologies of ancient peoples, or most famously the astronomy of Copernicus or Galileo, it does, in fact, ultimately matter whether the earth revolves around the sun or not, not just what people at the time thought about it. Copernicus's and Galileo's being mostly correct in their views of nature and their contemporary opponents being mostly wrong does affect our evaluation of who did what was right and what was wrong in the controversy. To be neutral toward every strongly held belief constrains our ability to learn from mistakes in the past.

A few modern historians, actually, have believed that witches and their powers were real. In the nineteenth- and early twentieth-century, historians like Jules Michelet or Montague Summers took the tortured confessions of witches at their word. Witches did, these historians believed, worship the Devil and practice dark magic. In the 1920s, Margaret Murray claimed witches were persecuted pagans who worshiped a horned god Janus or "Dianus." This "Murrayite Theory" is still often cited by today's defenders of witchcraft and paganism. Historians doubt that paganism survived in western Europe after the ninth century. Folk traditions and fertility celebrations were absorbed into the Christian framework and did not offer a rival religious system. Both these kinds of theories, real witches or living pagans, envision the lower, oppressed people seizing an alternative worldview against the ruling elites. While a very small possibility exists that such opposition or relevant magical activities may have happened, historians can find little empirical evidence in support of the proposition.

Other historical theories focus on the persecutors of the witches. Some of the first generation of scholars to apply careful methodology in examining witches, like George Lincoln Burr or Henry Charles Lea, suggested that greed for money or desire for power motivated the hunts. The Church invented witches to crush opponents and grow rich in a fraud that hurt humanity. The majority of scholars have noted, though, that many witches were among the poorest of society, and hunts rarely paid for themselves. Usually once a hunt did begin convicting members of the wealthy elites, other untouched rich and powerful persons feared for their own lives and livelihoods and shut the hunt down. Other early historians thought the conflict between Protestants and Roman Catholics fueled the hunts. Because the Devil was at work tearing the Church apart, he may have used witches as well as theologians. Such hostility killed very few witches, however. Protestants and Roman Catholics usually killed witches who belonged to their own faith systems.

"SCIENTIFIC" THEORIES

A very popular set of "scientific" theories involves some sort of illness as the causal agent. This interpretation satisfies an understandable desire for removing human responsibility for the hunts. Instead it blames biological infections, poisons, or hallucinogenic drugs. A widespread panic, especially among government officials who had to accept the crazed reports as fact, could hardly originate from a few people's hallucinations from mushrooms, toad's skin, henbane, ravings of syphilis, or psychoses from ergotism, triggered by mold sometimes found in grain.

Psychologists have offered several explanatory models, although they have reached no general consensus on a mechanism for how weird beliefs actually begin, spread, or decline. Some propose notions like collective delusions or "culture-bound syndromes" that describe neurotic conditions that permeate a social mental fabric in wide population. Mass hysteria, sometimes refined as "mass sociogenic hysteria," also describes strange and untrue ideas that suddenly take hold in groups of people. Some Freudian psychological views suggest projections of ego and superego onto demons and sexual dreams and the Devil. Possession cases might be explained by dissociation, or splitting one's personality into the good self and the misbehaving bad side, all blamed on the Devil. The guilt of those unable to attain perfect moral behavior they perceived that Christianity demanded may have led to psychological conflict. Confessions from children of interaction with demons might be a coping mechanism for sexual abuse. Even at the time, many skeptics attributed "melancholy," depression, and senility to women who confessed to witchcraft. All these medical causations, however, remain impossible to prove with patients long dead.

Some early historians of the hunts suggested that particular regions of Europe were more prone to social crises that found an outlet in fear of witches. Mountain areas, either because of thin air or economic difficulties, were the first candidates. Another possibility was that economic competition during the Commercial Revolution disrupted the long-established social bonds of guilds in towns or family networks in rural villages. Further research, however, has indicated a wide variety of locations and economic circumstances, even for the early hunts, thus disproving those narrow causes.

Certainly theories that draw on natural, social, or economic disasters have much to recommend them. There are clear correlations between outbreaks of plague and famine and hunts that blame witches for these misfortunes. Nevertheless, the same district or town might experience a hunt, while its neighbor, suffering the same conditions, did not. Disease and hunger have been regular throughout history, so the question of why witches were blamed at a certain time and place often remains insufficiently explained.

SOCIOLOGICAL THEORIES

Since the early modern period experienced a sudden rise in the power and authority of national governments, some historians have linked the witch hunts to that development. In this view, early modern governments were able to apply newly efficient legal procedures, the prestige of universities and intellectuals, and a responsive system of collecting revenues toward the hunting of witches. However, these explanations do not account for the hunts driven by local commoners or again the question of why witches were chosen as targets rather than other real or imagined threats.

Authorities of both central and local governments were interested in increasing their control, and they saw witchcraft as one more threat to the proper hierarchical order. Regimes systematized criminality, including infanticide and prostitution, to ensure that people, especially women, would conform to proper social roles and behaviors. Some interest groups may also have used the hunts to increase their influence, such as an abbey against a bishop or a town council against a mayor. Legal jurisdictions were often fluid, and the assertion of the right to carry out justice in a particular place or over a certain group of people established enduring political power. The social disruption that could arise from widespread arrests and panic, though, makes witch-hunting a rather poor tool to promote stable centralized government. The uncertainty of accusation and evidence might only promote intimidation, rather than respect for authority.

Convincing theories of social functionalism or social accusation have satisfied some historians looking to explain the hunts. These theories draw on ideas of anthropology, psychology, and postmodernism, describing how societies define themselves by including some and excluding "others." Witch accusations functioned as "boundary maintenance" to reinforce and define the limits of socially acceptable behavior. A village community having too many old folk and beggars to care for could eliminate them with a clear conscience by recasting them as evil enemies of society. Through projective identification, a person attributes his own unconscious impulses to another person. Thus a male judge with confused sexual desires might label a young woman a seductress or even a witch using love magic. The arrest and conviction of the woman would satisfy the judge's own psychological need to be normal. Blaming witches provided an outlet for anger about and fear of natural calamity, dreams, and nightmares. It was easier to blame someone you knew than to blame God or arbitrary events.

These theories, though, do not take into account motives of individual accusations (such as local feuds and grudges) and contemporary explanations of those involved (the religious and political context). And why should the hunts be so vicious? And again, why should witchcraft be the specific target in these years? The answers lie in the ideas of those who believed enough to hunt.

WITCH HUNTS AND WOMEN

Perhaps the most proclaimed recent theory sees witch-hunting as women hunting, an expression of misogyny or hatred toward women. Overall, over several centuries, the majority of victims were women, perhaps as many as three-quarters of the accused. In individual hunts, the numbers varied widely. Some hunts focused almost entirely on women, whereas others, especially many before 1400 or some in Normandy, Estonia, or Iceland, only included men. From the variety of motives for fearing the witch, there was no one stereotype that fit all witches. Many accused individuals were people on the margins, but the rich and powerful might be charged also. The witch hunts should not be generalized as an attack against poor, old women.

Nevertheless, the numbers of female victims, the sexualized methods of persecution, and many misogynist foundational ideas all signify a notable female dimension to the witch hunts. The specifics of the hunts grew out of Western society's long tradition of female subordination. Laws and customs showed how women were valued less than men. In practical terms, this devaluation included paying women less, restricting their control of wealth and property, and forbidding access to many professions.

Connected to this subordination was a common male view of women as both sexually less restrained and intellectually less developed. Many of the crimes associated with witchcraft mirrored cultural activities in which women predominated. Killing babies and using their corpses could be associated with childbirth; giving suck to demons, with nursing infants; poisoning, with cooking; and spoiling milk and butter, with milking cows and churning. Women had a reputation for gossiping, which was actually against the law in early modern times. Many a nag was punished with the scold's bridle, a metal mask, often with an animal shape, which the guilty wife was forced to wear in the street or at the pillory, in public acknowledgment of her poor behavior. Men also often blamed sexual problems such as impotency and infertility on women. Their sexual fantasies and fears dominate the pages of inquisition testimony. Women were also seen as more connected to folk magic of herbs, whereas men were more connected to scholarly magic of books—women's magic was associated with country culture and men's with cities and universities.

A common image of the witch, both during the hunts and today at Halloween, is an old hag. This stereotype is valid in that older women, often widows with children, were the most vulnerable members of society. Economic explanations suggest that the changing family under early capitalism left women at a disadvantage. Many widows were vulnerable to accusations of witchcraft because they had no one to defend them, no family or resources. Other reasons include the disassociation the young have with "old folk," who, with their strange, out-of-fashion clothing, seem so different. Unusual physical characteristics such as moles, red hair, or bent posture could also be associated with witchcraft. Older people, male or female, tend to be crankier, senile, and sickly.

Most important, though, was reputation. Older women had a long time to make enemies and damage relationships, especially if identified as connected to witches at a young age. Suspicions increased if a relative had been a witch. People saw witches as deviant, quarrelsome, uppity, dirty, and unkempt. They avoided church-going or misbehaved while there. Sociologists often term this disreputable fame *infamia*. The female witch became one focal point for society's worries.

Women also cooperated with the witch-hunting system. Men controlled the justice system used to hunt witches, since the roles of judge, lawyer, magistrate, professor, and clergyman were legally prohibited to women. Within the system, though, women did act as strip searchers, as well as jailers, cooks, and cleaners. Even more important was women's maintenance of social expectations. Neighbors gossiped about, formally accused, testified against, and attended the executions of fellow women. Using the Devil and harmful spells replaced hostile gossip and insult. Some historians say that in doing so, women helped construct and maintain the social and moral roles expected of each other. The modern idea of joining together in liberation from male superiority hardly existed during the hunts. Instead, women eagerly struck at those of their gender who subverted accepted female social roles. Women accusing women internalized the value system that placed women in an inferior position relative to men. Women may have grasped the power of accusation first and used it against another, because the male-dominated society denied them power elsewhere. Accusations, however, could always boomerang back and draw everyone into the net of mutual suspicion.

THE WITCH HUNTS, PAST AND FUTURE

Probably no ultimate explanation for the witch hunts will ever completely satisfy either historians or victims. The assortment of scholarly theories accounting for the hunts offers only partial explanations. Variations in time, place, motivations, and results make comprehensive explanations nearly impossible and multiple causations essential. The growing stacks of scholarship and popular writing may overwhelm anyone interested in the subject, while so much remains unanswered. Scholars will undoubtedly propose additional theories to explain other aspects of witch-hunting.

The diversity of the witch hunts makes it nearly impossible to draw common threads. Some hunts were limited and nonlethal. Others were widespread and uncontrollably murderous. Some regions saw hardly any hunting, ever. Others experienced periodic revivals of witch persecutions. Sometimes the common folk of the locality pushed for hunts. Other times, the elites from centralizing regimes imposed them. Some of those elites were religious leaders, preachers, and professors, whereas others were secular princes, lawyers, and magistrates. Some hunters targeted women as witches. Other inquisitors charged mostly men. Most explanations must remain hunt specific.

This book only offers the briefest of review of the witch hunts. Before 1400 witches did not concern most educated people in Europe. In 1600 most educated people saw witches as a danger to society. By 1800 almost no educated people believed that witches existed at all. Ideas developed and spread among the Christian clergy convinced elites of the dangerous witch conspiracy. Secular courts then carried out the majority of hunting and torture. Some witch hunts took place because their originators had selfish, cruel, or destructive motives.

Disease, both physical and mental, afflicted perpetrators and participants. Eco-
logical, social, and economic developments destabilized traditional values,
allowing witches to be blamed for change. Governments trying to broaden
their powers and the institutions that supported them fashioned a framework
for policing new forms of criminality. Some members of society found in
witchcraft a release valve for built-up social pressures. Too many hunters hated
women.

In conclusion, the biggest question remains as to why anyone focused on
witches. Other real and undeniable scapegoats existed: Jews, homosexuals, for-
eigners, beggars and the poor, the elderly, widows, and orphans, many of
whom did repeatedly suffer neglect, discrimination, and persecution. Blame
could also be placed on the people who actually have the real power and influence to alleviate the difficulties that any society faces. Witch-hunting fulfilled a
need for those who took part in it while it lasted. After a certain time, that
need no longer was fulfilled by witch-hunting. No good explanation exists for
the targeting of witches, except perhaps that an imaginary enemy was easier for
diverse people to agree upon than the real agents of destruction.

People are always looking for someone to blame when misfortunes happen.
It is easy to grab onto something simple rather than confront the real and
intractable problems that trouble societies all through the ages: economic difficulties, social inequality, domestic violence, poverty, disease, crime, war, or the
inability to alleviate disasters quickly. If the witch hunts can help people better
to comprehend reality and themselves at all, it is probably in realizing their
own readiness to fear and use violence against other people.

REBEKKA LEMP

It is appropriate to close this brief history with the story of one more accused
witch, yet one who could speak, however briefly, in her own voice. History
remembers Rebekka Lemp because she sent several letters to her family from her
prison, which were then confiscated and preserved in the court records of
Nördlingen, a city in the south of the Holy Roman Empire. In 1589, forty-year-
old Rebekka was a mother of six living children and the respectable wife of the
well-regarded and prosperous Peter Lemp, who held office in Nördlingen's government. Late that year, the mayor, John Pferinger, and his council launched a
witch hunt that lasted until 1598 and took the lives of one man and thirty-four
women, including Rebekka. A witch who had burned at the stake in May 1590
had earlier denounced Rebekka for witchcraft, but town officials waited until
June 1, while Peter Lemp was away from town, to arrest his wife.

In one letter from her prison, she wrote to her husband, Peter, of her first
experiences with torture:

> O you, my most chosen treasure, should I be torn from you so innocent? May
> such be ever and always held against God. They force one, that one must confess.

They have martyred me. I am as innocent as God in heaven. If I only knew the least bit of such matters, then I would deserve that God refuse me entrance into heaven. O you, beloved treasure, what is happening to my heart? Alas, alas, my poor orphans. Father, send me something so that I may die. I must otherwise despair as a martyr. If you cannot do it today, do it tomorrow. Write to me within the hour.[1]

To gain evidence, the council applied torture as many times as necessary. One woman, Maria Hollin, actually held out during fifty-six sessions of torture, which included thumbscrews, legscrews, and the strappado. Because she refused to confess, they released her. Rebekka and many others were not so strong-willed. They confessed to having sex with the Devil, flying to meet with him, and dancing with him at sabbats. He gave them gray powders with which they killed men and livestock. They admitted to murdering their own babies, digging them out of graves, cooking, and eating them at feasts and banquets in prominent town buildings. That Nördlingen's officials had never noticed these banquets, or that the cemetery remained undisturbed, did not bother them, knowing as they did how the Devil deceived.

Pleading letters from her children and from her husband failed to convince the judges of her innocence. Instead, Rebekka's request for a means of dying led to a further charge against her of attempted suicide. On September 9, 1590, they burned Rebekka on the hill outside of town. As the flames reached her, she screamed, while many people, including her family, looked on. Her voice and those of her fellow executed witches went silent before their time. Their history, nevertheless, deserves remembering.

NOTE

1. "Letters from the Witch Trial of Rebekka Lemp," trans. Brian A. Pavlac, *The Witch Hunts (A.D. 1400–1800)* (2008) available at http://departments.kings.edu/womens_history/witch/lemp.html (accessed 4 December 2008).

GLOSSARY

alchemy: the occult practice of trying to master physical elements, especially to create gold.

allotriophagy: the illness of swallowing unusual objects such as pins and nails. Spitting up of strange objects was associated with demonic possession.

amulets: small objects worn on the body or attached to clothing that were believed to create or protect against magic. Religious amulets, such as holy medals or sacred relics could also be included in this category, although their effects were considered miracles.

Anabaptists: small sects of Christianity that developed during the Reformation. The adherents of the larger Christian groups of Roman Catholicism, Lutheranism, and Calvinism persecuted the Anabaptists. Today's denominations of Mennonites and Hutterites descend from the original Anabaptists.

Anglicanism: the English form of Christianity that developed during the Reformation. The Church of England combines elements of other Christian sects, especially Roman Catholicism and Calvinism (called Puritanism in England).

astrology: the occult practice of studying stars and planets in order to reveal their influence on humans. See DIVINATION.

augury: the study of birds, usually by cutting them open for their digestive organs, in order to predict the future. See also DIVINATION.

auto-da-fe: the public religious ritual of executing heretics carried out by the Spanish Inquisition.

belief: an idea held by a particular person or a society with which others may disagree because of lack of evidence or suitability of competing beliefs or knowledge. Some beliefs, though, better reflect the preponderance of evidence than others.

benandanti: a group of peasants in northern Italy who adapted a fertility cult into Christianity, believing they magically fought against witches and demons on behalf of their neighbors.

Black Mass: a perverted form of the Christian Eucharist or Mass used in demonic worship. It differs from the versions at sabbats, in that a human priest or presider merely invoked Satan, who was not physically present. It appeared fairly late in witch-hunting.

blasphemy: insulting the Christian faith, through words or misuse of sacred objects.

Calvinism: the branch of Christianity founded during the Reformation by John Calvin (1509–1564), called reformed churches in general. Its followers were known as Huguenots in France, Presbyterians in Scotland, and Puritans in England and America. The practice of its religion emphasizes strict moral behavior.

Canon Episcopi: a law of Western Christianity from the ninth century that determined that the night ride, and by extension witchcraft, was a mere illusion. Later strixologists and demonologists felt compelled to argue against or around it.

capitalism: an economic system of economic practice based on the practice of reinvesting profits from businesses into commercial enterprises. Its use after the fourteenth century came to make Europe the wealthiest and most powerful region in the world by 1800.

Catharism: a heresy that arose in western Europe especially in southern France and Northern Italy during the twelfth century. Its superficial belief derived from Christianity, but became more of a dualism. Christian leaders exterminated the heresy through crusade and inquisition. In doing so they began to attach ideas of diabolism to the Cathars. The term Cathar, corrupted as *gazar*, became a synonym for witch. Not to be confused with Waldensians.

Christian Humanism: a version of humanism begun at the end of the Middle Ages that tries to adapt both the emphasis on proper human living and the study of the wisdom of ancient Greece and Rome to Christianity.

Christianity: the belief that the God of Judaism became incarnate as a person in Jesus Christ, whose death during crucifixion and subsequent resurrection allows Christians to attain eternal life in Heaven. From its origins in the ancient Roman Empire, it has since broken apart in schisms into many branches, large and small, each claiming orthodoxy. See ANABAPTISTS; ANGLICANISM; CALVINISM; LUTHERANISM; THE ORTHODOX CHURCH; ROMAN CATHOLICISM; WALDENSIANISM.

conjuration: (1) specifically, to summon and dispel demons, either with the intent of gaining knowledge or forcing the spirits to carry out some command. The method is similar to or a perversion of exorcism. (2) Generally, to carry out magic by using rituals and spells.

countermagic: using magic to fight magic. Because it was in self-defense, many of its users did not consider themselves to be practicing witchcraft, although Christian authorities generally disagreed.

coven: a group of witches, often thirteen in number, who met together to organize and practice their craft. The concept appeared very late in witch-hunting.

crimen exceptum: the legal principle that a crime was so serious that normal methods and rules that protected civil rights could be suspended. Authorities often invoked this concept during the witch hunts, because people believed the diabolic conspiracy of witches created imminent danger.

cunning-folk: wise-men and -women who practiced simple magic, such as divination, healing, casting love spells, finding objects, or defending with countermagic in local communities throughout Europe. Authorities sometimes hunted cunning-women and -men as witches, although they usually claimed to derive their abilities from good spirits and angels rather than demons.

demon: an imaginary supernatural being believed to be able to influence human affairs.

demonolatry: the worship of demons, which Christians considered to be blasphemy and heresy.

demonology: the study of demons, their organization, their powers, and how to control them. Sometimes called diabology.

Devil, the: the belief of Christianity that a fallen angel ruled over a place of eternal punishment for sinners called Hell and that he also tried to tempt and harm people in the natural world. His name derives from the Greek word for demon (*diabolos*). Christian theology often referred to the Devil by the personal names Satan (adversary, opponent) or Lucifer (the Light-bearer).

Devil's Mark: a spot on the body left by the Devil as a sign of his pact with a witch. Witch hunters might identify any unusual lump, scar, or blemish as a Devil's Mark, claiming it did not transmit pain or bleed when pricked. The Devil's Mark should not to be confused with the Witch's Mark, but the terms often become interchangeable both in early modern and contemporary literature.

diabolism: the belief that demons and the Devil have the power to harm human beings.

divination: the practice of trying to predict the future through magic or occult means.

dualism: a religion, such as Catharism, that claimed two great opposing forces of good and evil were trying to control the universe.

Early Modern Europe: the period in European history from the end of the Middle Ages to the French Revolution (1789–1815). The witch hunts took place mostly during this time.

empiricism: the belief that our senses correctly perceive reality and the natural world.

Enlightened Despotism: the political theory adopted by many kings and queens during the Enlightenment that combined absolute rule with the idea of government promoting human progress.

Enlightenment, the: the period in early modern Europe from about 1650 to 1800 that saw the rise of skepticism toward the supernatural by many elites, encouragement of humanitarianism, and promotion of good government.

Eucharist, the: a liturgical ceremony in many branches of Christianity, during which the faithful believe that bread and wine are transformed into or take on the presence of the body and blood of Jesus Christ. Jews, heretics, and witches were often alleged to have stolen sacred wafers of bread from this ceremony for use at either the sabbat or a Black Mass.

"evil eye": the superstition that a look from one person to another can cause harm. Also called fascination.

excommunication: a penalty by the Church for stubborn sinners, which forbade them access to the Sacraments. This act threatened their salvation and also usually set a person outside the civil law as well.

exorcism: the ritual used to end a possession, namely to cast demons out of people.

familiars: supernatural creatures associated with the witch as representatives of the Devil and other demons. Familiars or imps might be fantastic spirit creatures or take the form of animals such as toads or cats. They may help or hinder the witch's practice of witchcraft. Especially in England, they were believed to use the Witch's Mark on the person of a witch to feed and suckle milk or blood.

heresy: a system of religion that differs enough from an official orthodoxy that authorities consider it dangerous and try to suppress it. Rather than creating a new religion from scratch, heresies often overemphasize some aspects of the complex collection of doctrines, dogmas, rituals, and practices originating in a parent religion. Should a heresy survive long enough, it may become its own religion or a recognized branch of the originating faith system. Christian authorities often defined witchcraft as heresy. See CATHARISM, WALDENSIANISM.

historical method: the practice of modern historians to question evidence and produce opinions and theories about the facts of the past, modeled on the scientific method.

history: the study of the past based on rationalism and empiricism.

Holy Office of the Inquisition: a bureaucratic arm of Roman Catholicism intended to fight Protestantism, but also involved in the witch hunts. Founded in Rome in 1542, it operated under that name until 1965.

humanism: a belief, first promoted by the Greeks and Romans, that living properly in the world of human experience is of more importance than acting on a belief in a supernatural afterlife. It is often connected to secularism and humanitarianism.

humanitarianism: the attitude that human beings ought to treat one another with care and respect.

idolatry: the worship of idols or statues, usually believed to contain the essence of divine beings. Christianity condemned idolatry as demonolatry.

incubus: a demon in male form that uses seduction and sex to harm people. See SUCCUBUS.

infamia: the Latin word used to describe the bad or antisocial reputation attached to a person. Being known as an outsider, troublemaker, or criminal made an accusation of witchcraft more likely.

inquisition: the legal method of investigating crimes adapted by the Church in the Middle Ages to combat heresy. The medieval Church in the Latin West and its successor, the Roman Catholic Church, encouraged this method to hunt first heretics and then witches.

interdict: the Church's ceasing to perform sacraments within a region until its rulers had carried out reforms or gained forgiveness for transgressions.

Islam: the religion founded in Arabia during the seventh century AD by Mohammed, based on submission to God (Allah). Its doctrines drew on Judaism, Christianity, and paganism, although Islamic practices strongly rejected most elements of the latter. Islam's success in converting people from Spain to India threatened Christians, who sometimes identified Mohammed (or Mahomet) as a demon.

Judaism: the religion of the ancient Hebrews and their descendents the modern Jews, who believe that they are the chosen people of the one God who created the universe. A Jewish form of sorcery was the Kabbalah or Cabala.

lamia (plural: *lamiae*): an ancient Latin word for witch, especially one that sucks the blood of children at night.

latria: the worship owed to God only. Perversions of proper worship included idolatry and demonolatry, which might lead to witchcraft.

lex talionis: "law of retribution" allowing someone to sue an accuser of false charges. When the law was in force, it restricted witch hunts.

ligature: tying knots in strings or ropes in order to render a man impotent by magic.

Lucifer: See THE DEVIL.

Lutheranism: the branch of Christianity founded by Martin Luther (1483–1546) that denied the authority of the Roman Catholic Church and emphasized individual reliance on faith in God.

magic: (1) using supernatural knowledge and powers to affect the physical world. Scholars often make a distinction between "High Magic", gained through learning the occult (often called sorcery) and "Low Magic" derived from one's nature or supernatural spirits or demons (often called witchcraft). The purpose or goal also distinguishes between evil "black magic" intended for harm and good "white magic" aiming to help. Authorities in Christianity nearly always condemn any kind of magic, preferring faith in miracles. Modern science considers any such magic or miracles to be impossible. Many modern believers in magic often spell it with a final *k* (magick) to distinguish it from the second definition, next. (2) In modern culture, the tricks used by a magician to entertain with feats that only seem impossible, but are accomplished with sleight of hand, distraction, and technology. See MAGICIAN.

magician: (1) In medieval and modern Europe, an alternate word for a male witch or sorcerer. (2) In modern culture, an entertainer who uses technology, distraction, and sleight of hand to create tricks that have the illusion of magic.

maleficia: the Latin word for the kinds of evil deeds for which witches were feared. Against people, these acts ranged from minor assaults of inflicting pains, compelling love, or inducing impotence to major crimes such as theft, demonic possession, and murder. Against nature, *maleficia* involved anything from stopping a cow's milk or preventing butter being churned, through igniting arson, to raising storms.

Mass, the: See THE EUCHARIST.

metamorphosis: the belief in magical transformation, namely that people can change into animals and back again. See WEREWOLF.

Middle Ages, the: the roughly 1,000 years of history in Western Europe between the fall of the western half of the Roman Empire (the fourth century) and the Renaissance (the fifteenth and sixteenth centuries). Witch-hunts only began at the end of the period.

miracles: the belief in Judaism and Christianity that God, often in response to prayer, can break through the natural order to either help or harm humans and the world.

natural philosophy: the application of philosophy to understanding the natural world perceived by the senses. It developed into science during the sixteenth and seventeenth centuries.

necromancy: (1) the occult practice of using dead bodies for divination or magic. A necromancer technically uses only dead bodies, but the term may be a synonym for a magician (1) or sorcerer. (2) any form of "black magic" (nigromancy or goety).

Neo-Platonism: the philosophical beliefs adapted from the ancient Greek philosopher Plato. This philosophy emphasized the greater importance and truth of the supernatural over the natural world.

night ride: the belief that supernatural beings rode through the countryside and forest, especially during the full moon, and attracted humans to go along with them. The *Canon Episcopi* declared the night ride to be mere illusion and belief in it a sin.

occult: the belief that secret knowledge exists and can be learned both better to understand and to affect the natural world. This knowledge differs from science in that it often involves supernatural methods such as sorcery and witchcraft. Although occultists during the Renaissance often recognized early science as one way to comprehend the universe, modern scientists maintain that occult knowledge does not empirically exist.

Orthodox churches, the: In the eleventh century, Christianity suffered a schism or division into two branches, although each claimed to maintain proper Christian orthodoxy and aspired for a universal, or catholic, church of all Christians. Orthodox churches began to organize around ethnicity (Greek, Serbian, Bulgarian, Ukrainian, etc.). The Orthodox Christians did not much hunt witches, except somewhat in Russia. The Western Christians would themselves split again during the Reformation.

orthodoxy: the official version of a belief or religion enforced by authorities.

paganism: any of the religions of polytheism (belief in many gods) practiced in ancient Europe or the Middle East. They usually involve fertility rites and ceremonies of ritual sacrifice. The stories that explain the activities of the gods of pagan religions are usually called legends or mythology by modern scholars.

philosophy: a system of thought that tries reasonably to explain the human place in the universe. The application of the supernatural and religion often plays a significant role, as in scholasticism.

pillory: either a pillar to which a guilty person was chained or wooden devices (sometimes called the stocks) that imprisoned the legs, arms, and/or neck. Either version exposed the guilty person to public humiliation.

possession: the belief that a demon could take over the consciousness, partially or completely, of a person. In Christianity, an exorcism could cast the demon out.

pricking: using pins to find a Witch's Mark or a Devil's Mark. The witch was not supposed to feel pain or bleed at the pin being stuck into flesh.

Puritanism: See CALVINISM.

"putting to the question": an alternate phrase or euphemism for torture.

rationalism: the belief that the human mind can make sense of the universe.

Reformation, the: the division, or schism, of Western Christianity during the sixteenth century into the various branches of Roman Catholicism, Lutheranism, Calvinism, Anglicanism, and Anabaptists.

religion: a complex social organization which uses stories, doctrines, and rituals to explain the interaction of the supernatural and the natural as well as the place of humanity therein. See PAGANISM, DUALISM, JUDAISM, CHRISTIANITY, ISLAM.

Renaissance, the: the revival of the culture of ancient Greece and Rome beginning after the Middle Ages, during the fifteenth and sixteenth centuries.

Roman Catholicism: the branch of Christianity which after the Reformation continued the medieval Church in western and southern Europe under the authority of the popes in Rome.

sabbat: the ceremonial gathering of witches and the Devil. The use of this particular word probably reflects antisemitism, aligning it with the Jewish holy day of rest, spelled "sabbath," or after the building, the synagogue, where Jews gather to worship.

Satan: See THE DEVIL.

Scholasticism: the medieval system of philosophy based on the logic by the ancient Greek philosopher Aristotle.

science: the study and explanation of how nature works. Modern science considers its own operations, the scientific method, as objectively true and verifiable, based on empiricism and rationalism, while other belief systems are subjective, being dependent on emotional, personal, or irrational interpretations.

scientific method: the step-by-step process of solving a problem about how nature works as used in science. The method begins with a hypothesis (a reasonable guess at the solution) and then draws conclusions after experimentation and observation. Scientists share their conclusions with the scientific community and the public for further verification, modification, or rejection.

scratching: the belief that drawing blood from a witch could relieve the witch's spell from a victim of witchcraft. Victims would attack the witch using fingernails, pins, or even knives.

skepticism: the attitude of doubting information that has not been tested through rationalism and empiricism. Increasing skepticism about the supernatural since the Enlightenment has led to non-Christian deism, agnosticism, and atheism. Skepticism is also a key component of modern science.

spell: an incantation used for magic.

sooth-saying: See DIVINATION.

sorcery: best considered a form of "High Magic", which requires literacy and learning. It often involved rituals of conjuration and divination. In English, a man who practices sorcery is called a sorcerer and a woman a sorceress. Many use the term sorcery, though, as a synonym for witchcraft.

Spanish Inquisition (1481–1834): the unique version of the inquisition used in Spain to make sure that Jewish and Muslim converts to Christianity stayed orthodox. Its involvement in the witch hunts soon became very limited.

stocks: wooden devices that imprisoned the legs, arms, and/or neck and exposed the guilty person to public humiliation. They were also sometimes called the pillory, although those might also be pillars to which a guilty person was chained.

strappado: a torture device based on a simple pulley. The examiners tied the victim's arms behind the back, and then they hoisted the victim up into the air. This usually dislocated the shoulders, which was not considered to be permanent damage. Weights might be added to the feet, or the rope repeatedly jerked (squassation) to add to the intensity of torture. See Illustration 12.

strix (plural: *striges*): the Latin term from ancient Rome for a witch, especially in the form of a monstrous screech owl.

strixology: the genre of writing about the reality and dangers of witches. Strixologists might be either opposed to or in favor of witch-hunting. They often wrote in the context of theology and demonology.

succubus: a demon in female form that uses seduction and sex to harm people. See INCUBUS.

supernatural: the belief that mysterious forces and significant realities exist outside empirical, observable nature.

superstition: an exaggerated belief that supernatural forces could affect human health or fortune through either unintentional actions or simple rituals. Although the belief may fit into a religious system, the term superstition could be applied to practices disapproved of by orthodoxy.

swimming: the test derived from the early medieval trial by ordeal, that sacred water would reject a witch. Hunters then tested accused witches by throwing them in vats or bodies of water. If the blessed water "embraced" the person, meaning he or she sank, that person was innocent. If the person floated, the holy water had "rejected" the person as evil. Sometimes called an "ordeal by cold water" or "ducking," although that was also a form of torture that pushed a person under water.

synagogue: See SABBAT.

torture: the infliction of mental or physical pain by government authorities in order to gain information or exact punishment.

transvection: flying by magical means.

trial by ordeal: the attempt to decide guilt or innocence of a crime by having the accused undergo a test of physical pain. It was believed that the divine would guide the outcome so justice would be served. A common ordeal used in the witch hunts was swimming.

vampire: "undead" corpses that are believed to come back and haunt the living, especially by sucking blood.

Waldensianism: a heresy that arose in Western Europe especially in southern France and northern Italy during the twelfth century. The religion emphasized the asceticism of Christianity. Christian leaders nearly exterminated the heresy through crusade and inquisition, but Waldensian churches survive today and are acknowledged by most as a branch of Christianity. The term "Waldensian," especially in French, became a synonym for witch. Not to be confused with Catharism.

warlock: the word often used for a male witch in modern popular culture, but not much seen in the historical evidence.

weighing: a means to test whether a person was a witch. Evidence of weighing less than expected became proof or being a witch, based on the assumption that heavy people could not fly. The scales in Oudewater provided certificates that people were not witches, because they weighed an appropriate amount.

werewolf: a human who through metamorphosis can take on the lupine form and return to human shape.

witch: a person who uses control over the supernatural to affect the natural world, often intending harm to people and property. Strixologists and demonologists often consider the "Low Magic" of witches different from the high magic of sorcerers in that their abilities are innate or done without much scholarship or expertise. The witch hunts often attached the witch's power to a pact with the Devil. The medieval and early modern cunning-folk as well as modern witches of Wicca and paganism usually claim to do no harm.

witchcraft, **witchery**: the specific kind of magic practice by a witch. It might be considered different from sorcery.

witch-doctor: the person in tribal societies who can contact the supernatural, often in the form of a trance. The "doctor" often specializes in curing people from spells cast by witches, attacks by demons, and possession.

witch hunt: (1) the efforts of government authorities to investigate, arrest, prosecute, and punish people considered to be witches. These took place in the nations of Europe and their colonies mostly between 1400 and 1800. (2) In modern culture, the persecution of any person or group targeted as dangerous by authorities, even though the target constitutes no serious threat to society.

Witch's Mark: The belief that familiars would suckle or nurse blood or milk from a spot on the body, most frequently used in the British hunts. Witch hunters might identify any unusual lump, scar, blemish as a Witch's Mark, claiming it did not transmit pain or bleed during pricking. The Witch's Mark should not to be confused with the Devil's Mark, but the terms often become interchangeable both in early modern and contemporary strixology.

wizard: (1) an alternate name for a male witch or sorcerer. (2) In modern popular culture, a fictional person with magic powers.

SELECTED BIBLIOGRAPHY

GENERAL STUDIES OF THE WITCH HUNTS

Ankarloo, Bengt, and Gustav Henningsen, eds. *Early Modern European Witchcraft: Centres and Peripheries.* 1990. Reprinted by Oxford: Oxford University Press, 2001.

Ankarloo, Bengt, and Stuart Clark, eds. *Witchcraft and Magic in Europe.* 6 vols. Philadelphia, University of Pennsylvania Press, 1999 through 2002.

Bailey, Michael D. *Magic and Superstition in Europe: A Concise History from Antiquity to the Present.* Critical Issues in History. Lanham, MD: Rowman & Littlefield, 2007.

Barry, Jonathan, and Owen Davies, eds. *Palgrave Advances in Witchcraft Historiography.* Basingstoke, UK: Palgrave Macmillan, 2007.

Behringer, Wolfgang. *Witches and Witch Hunts.* Themes in History. Cambridge, UK: Polity Press, 2004.

Briggs, Robin. "'Many Reasons Why': Witchcraft and the Problem of Multiple Explanation." In *Witchcraft in Early Modern Europe,* edited by Jonathan Barry, Marianne Hester, and Gareth Roberts, 46–63. Cambridge, UK: Cambridge University Press, 1996.

Clark, Stuart. *Thinking with Demons: the Idea of Witchcraft in Early Modern Europe.* Oxford: Oxford University Press, 1997.

Cohn, Norman. *Europe's Inner Demons: An Enquiry Inspired by the Great Witch-Hunt.* New York: Basic Books, 1975.

Golden, Robert, ed. *ABC-CLIO Encyclopedia of Witchcraft: The Western Tradition.* New York: ABC-Clio, 2006.

Klaits, Joseph. *Servants of Satan: The Age of the Witch Hunts.* Bloomington, IN: Indiana University Press, 1985.

Levack, Brian P. *The Witch Hunt in Early Modern Europe.* 3rd ed. White Plains, NY: Longman, 2006.

Maxwell-Stuart, P. G. *Witchcraft in Europe and the New World, 1400–1800.* Basingstoke, UK: Palgrave, 2001.

Oldridge, Darren, ed. *The Witchcraft Reader*. 2nd ed. London and New York: Routledge, 2008.

Pickering, David. *Cassell's Dictionary of Witchcraft*. London: Cassel, 1996.

Russell, Jeffrey B., and Brooks Alexander. *A History of Witchcraft: Sorcerers, Heretics, and Pagans*. 2nd rev. ed. London: Thames and Hudson, 2007.

Scarre, Geoffrey. *Witchcraft and Magic in 16th and 17th Century Europe*. Studies in European History. London: Macmillan Press, 1987.

Trevor-Roper, Hugh. "Religion, the Reformation, and Social Change." In *European Witchcraft*, edited by E. William Monter, 27–34. New York: John Wiley & Sons, Inc., 1969.

Waite, Gary K. *Heresy, Magic, and Witchcraft in Early Modern Europe*. European Culture and Society. New York: Palgrave Macmillan, 2003.

Whitney, Elspeth. "The Witch 'She'/The Historian 'He': Gender and the Historiography of the European Witch Hunts." *Journal of Women's History* 7 (1995): 77–101.

Wiesner, Merry E., ed. *Witchcraft in Early Modern Europe. Problems in European Civilization*. Boston: Houghton Mifflin Company, 2007.

Zika, Charles. *The Appearance of Witchcraft: Print and Visual Culture in Sixteenth-Century Europe*. New York and London: Routledge, 2007.

WITCHES IN ANCIENT AND MEDIEVAL EUROPE

Flint, Valerie. "The Demonisation of Magic and Sorcery in Late Antiquity: Christian Redefinitions of Pagan Religions." In *Witchcraft and Magic in Europe: Ancient Greece and Rome*, edited by Bengt Ankarloo and Stuart Clark, 277–348. Philadelphia: University of Pennsylvania Press, 1999.

Graf, Fritz. *Magic in the Ancient World*. Translated by Franklin Philip; edited by G. W. Bowersock. Revealing Antiquity 10. Cambridge, MA: Harvard University Press, 1997.

Kieckhefer, Richard. *Magic in the Middle Ages*. Cambridge Medieval Textbooks. Cambridge, UK: Cambridge University Press, 1989.

Lambert, Malcolm. *Medieval Heresy: Popular Movements from the Gregorian Reform to the Reformation*, 2nd ed. 1992. Reprint, New York: Barnes & Noble, 1998.

Moore, R. I. *The Formation of a Persecuting Society: Power and Deviance in Western Europe, 950–1250*. 1987. Paperback reprint, Oxford: Blackwell, 1990.

Russell, Jeffrey Burton. *Witchcraft in the Middle Ages*. Ithaca, NY: Cornell University Press, 1972.

WITCHES IN THE HOLY ROMAN EMPIRE

Behringer, Wolfgang. *Witchcraft Persecutions in Bavaria: Popular Magic, Religious Zealotry and Reason of State in Early Modern Europe*. Cambridge, UK: Past and Present Publications, 1997.

Kunze, Michael. *Highroad to the Stake: A Tale of Witchcraft*. Translated by William E. Yuill. Chicago: The University of Chicago Press, 1987.

Midelfort, H. C. Erik. *Witch Hunting in Southwestern Germany, 1562–1684: The Social and Intellectual Foundations*. Stanford: Stanford University Press, 1972.

Monter, William. "Witch Trials in Continental Europe 1560–1660." In *Witchcraft and Magic in Europe: The Period of the Witch Trials*, edited by Bengt Ankarloo and Stuart Clark, 1–52. Philadelphia: University of Pennsylvania Press, 2002.

Roper, Lyndal. *Witch Craze: Terror and Fantasy in Baroque Germany.* New Haven, CT: Yale University Press, 2004.

Waite, Gary K. *Eradicating the Devil's Minions: Anabaptists and Witches in Reformation Europe, 1525–1600.* Toronto: University of Toronto Press, 2007.

WITCHES IN FRANCE

Briggs, Robin. *Witches & Neighbors: The Social and Cultural Context of European Witchcraft.* New York: Viking, 1996.

Ferber, Sarah. *Demonic Possession and Exorcism in Early Modern France.* London: Routledge, 2004.

Mandrou, Robert. "Magistrates and Witches in Seventeenth-Century France." In *European Witchcraft*, edited by E. William Monter, 127–143. New York: John Wiley & Sons, Inc., 1969.

Maxwell-Stuart, P. G., "Pierre de Lancre: Who Will Guard the Guards?" In *Witch Hunters: Professional Prickers, Unwitchers, & Witch Finders of the Renaissance*, 32–57. Stroud, UK: Tempus, 2003.

Monter, E. William. *Witchcraft in France and Switzerland: The Borderlands during the Reformation.* Ithaca, 1976.

Mollenauer, Lynn Wood. *Strange Revelations: Magic, Poison, and Sacrilege in Louis XIV's France.* University Park, PA: Penn State University Press, 2007.

Rapley, R. *A Case of Witchcraft: The Trial of Urbain Grandier.* New York and Manchester: Manchester University Press, 1998.

WITCHES IN THE BRITISH ISLES

Almond, Philip C. *The Witches of Warboys: An Extraordinary Story of Sorcery, Sadism, and Satanic Possession.* London and New York: I. B. Tauris, 2008.

Gaskill, Malcolm. *Witchfinders: A Seventeenth-Century English Tragedy.* Cambridge, MA: Harvard University Press, 2005.

Larner, Christina. *Enemies of God: The Witch Hunt in Scotland.* Baltimore: The Johns Hopkins University Press, 1981.

Levack, Brian P. *Witch-Hunting in Scotland: Law, Politics and Religion.* New York & London: Routledge, 2008.

Macfarlane, Alan. *Witchcraft in Tudor and Stuart England: A Regional and Comparative Study.* New York: Harper & Row Publishers, 1970.

Maxwell-Stuart, P. G. *An Abundance of Witches: The Great Scottish Witch Hunt.* Stroud, UK: Tempus, 2005.

Norton, Mary Beth. *In the Devil's Snare: The Salem Witchcraft Crisis of 1692.* New York: Knopf, 2002.

Poole, Robert, ed. *The Lancashire Witches: Histories and Stories.* Manchester: Manchester University Press, 2002.

Thomas, Keith. *Religion and the Decline of Magic.* New York: Charles Scribner's Sons, 1971.

Willis, Deborah. *Malevolent Nurture: Witch-Hunting and Maternal Power in Early Modern England.* Ithaca, NY: Cornell University Press, 1995.

WITCHES IN SOUTHERN EUROPE

Cervantes, Fernando. *The Devil in the New World: The Impact of Diabolism in New Spain.* New Haven and London: Yale University Press, 1994.

Duni, Matteo. *Under the Devil's Spell: Witches, Sorcerers, and the Inquisition in Renaissance Italy.* The Villa Rossa Series: Intercultural Perspectives on Italy and Europe, 2. Syracuse, NY: Syracuse University Press, 2007.

Ebright, Malcolm, and Rick Hendricks. *The Witches of Abiquiu: The Governor, the Priest, the Genízaro Indians, and the Devil.* Albuquerque: University of New Mexico Press, 2006.

Ginzburg, Carlo. *The Night Battles: Witchcraft and Agrarian Cults in the Sixteenth and Seventeenth Centuries.* Translated by Nee Tedeschi. Baltimore: Johns Hopkins University Press, 1983.

Henningsen, Gustav. *The Witches' Advocate: Basque Witchcraft and the Spanish Inquisition (1609–1614).* Reno: University of Nevada Press, 1980.

Martin, Ruth. *Witchcraft and the Inquisition in Venice 1550–1650.* Oxford and New York: Basil Blackwell, 1989.

Maxwell-Stuart, P. G., "Martín Del Rio: Laying Down the Rules," in *Witch Hunters: Professional Prickers, Unwitchers & Witch Finders of the Renaissance.* Stroud, UK: Tempus, 2003.

Perry, Mary Elizabeth, and Anne J. Cruz, eds. *Cultural Encounters: The Impact of the Inquisition in Spain and the New World.* Berkeley, Los Angeles, Oxford: University of California Press, 1991.

WITCHES IN NORTHERN AND EASTERN EUROPE

Ankarloo, Bengt. "Witch Trials in Northern Europe 1450–1700." In *Witchcraft and Magic in Europe: The Period of the Witch Trials,* ed. Bengt Ankarloo and Stuart Clark, 53–95. Philadelphia: University of Pennsylvania Press, 2002.

Klaniczay, Gábor, "Witch Hunting in Hungary: Social or Cultural Tensions?" In *Witchcraft in Early Modern Europe,* edited by Merry E. Wiesner, 74–86. Problems in European Civilization. Boston: Houghton Mifflin Company, 2007

Worobec, Christine D. *Possessed: Women, Witches, and Demons in Imperial Russia.* DeKalb, IL: Northern Illinois University, 2001.

Zguta, Russell. "Witchcraft Trials in Seventeenth-Century Russia." *American Historical Review* 82 (1977): 1187–1207.

INDEX

Illustrations referenced in the index are indicated by italic F and number. All illustrations follow page 108.

ABOUT THE AUTHOR

BRIAN A. PAVLAC is Chair of the History Department at King's College in Wilkes-Barre, PA, where he teaches European History. Professor Pavlac is the author/translator of the book *A Warrior Bishop of the Twelfth Century: The Deeds of Albero of Trier*, by Balderich.